The Fall of Hong Kong

'The excitement of the narrative never flags . . . vivid authenticity . . . a stirring, often heart-breaking book'
EVENING STANDARD

'Courage, cowardice, humour and horror all have their place in a quite remarkably detailed but graphic story'
YORKSHIRE EVENING NEWS

'Written in a white-heat of indignation' TRIBUNE

'A vividly written story of heroism in defeat . . . Mr Carew pulls no punches' BIRMINGHAM MAIL

'Grim . . . stark . . . controversial' NEW BOOKS

THE FALL
OF HONG KONG

Tim Carew

Pan Books London and Sydney

First published 1960 by Anthony Blond Ltd
This edition published 1963 by Pan Books Ltd,
Cavaye Place, London SW10 9PG
3rd printing 1976
© Tim Carew 1960
ISBN 0 330 24893 6
Printed and bound in Great Britain by
Hunt Barnard Printing Ltd, Aylesbury, Bucks

ILLUSTRATIONS
IN PHOTOGRAVURE

(between pages 120 *and* 121*)*

ACKNOWLEDGEMENTS

My thanks are due to the authors of the following publications, all of which were of incalculable value to me in the writing of this book:

Supplement to the *London Gazette*—despatch by Major-General C. M. Maltby, CB, MC, late GOC, British Troops in China.

The War Against Japan (Volume One), by Major-General S. Woodburn Kirby, CB, CMG, CIE, OBE, MC (Her Majesty's Stationery Office.)

A Record of the Actions of the Hong Kong Volunteer Defence Corps, by the late Major Evan Stewart, DSO (Ye Olde Printerie, Ltd, Hong Kong.)

Grey Touched with Scarlet, By Jean Bowden.

Prisoner Of The Japs, by Gwen Dew (Heinemann).

Short story '*The Brigadier's Two-Gun Christmas*', by Jack Pearson—*Combat Magazine*, November, 1956.

The Story of Wake Island, by Colonel J. P. S. Devereux (Panther) for permission to quote the axiom of the United States Marine Corps which applied so forcibly to the defenders of Hong Kong.

The Thistle (Journal of the Royal Scots).

The Middlesex Regiment, by Lieutenant-Commander P. K. Kemp.

I am also indebted to Mr Derrick King of the War Office library who made all official records so freely available to me and to Major Dick Smith of the Depot of the Middlesex Regiment for his unfailing help.

Finally I thank all the people who drew on memories that can only have been painful: officers of all three services, civilians and other ranks. One and all rallied to a cause which, I trust, has not been a lost one.

TIM CAREW

INTRODUCTION

On December 8th, 1941, Japan launched an all out offensive against Hong Kong. On Christmas Day—just seventeen days later—the Colony was surrendered.

This is the story of those seventeen days. It is the long, true and terrible story of a battle and of the men who fought it: British, Indian and Canadian soldiers; sailors and airmen; civilians of many different nationalities. These are the people who, with sudden and violent unexpectedness, were jolted from sybaritic security into a maelstrom of savagery.

This is not a pretty story; stories about defeat never are. But it is an indictment against unpreparedness and complacency and therefore a story that must be told.

Christmas, 1963, will find Hong Kong prosperous and secure; serene and everlasting. That is how it was when the Japs came.

For nothing like this must ever happen again. . . .

AUTHOR'S NOTE

THE writing of this book has, for me, been a humbling experience. Perhaps I should explain this, for I like the look of myself and the sound of my own voice as much as the next man. I am not, by nature, a particularly humble person.

I am not averse to letting people know that I was wounded by a grenade in Burma, although to this day I have no idea where it came from. I also quite fail to see why I should add that several of the fragments which hit me were, in fact, stones.

Now my coyly modest war reminiscences die in my throat. All the people who appear in this book have shared a common experience: they all fought a desperate losing battle against a numerically vastly superior enemy with no hope of relief; they all endured nearly four years of hideous privation as prisoners of the Japanese, most bestial of captors.

I too fought the Japanese, but in 1944 the tide was turning against them; it was, so to speak, our turn to go in to bat. After being wounded I snuggled between crisp white sheets and was interminably fussed over by delicious nurses. I then spent a halcyon month's sick leave in Kashmir where the most serious crisis was lack of ice in the drinks. For the Hong Kong wounded there were no white sheets and no sick leave. There was only pain and misery and, in many cases, death as the ultimate release.

That is why I am now more humble than I was. And about time too.

TIM CAREW

DEDICATION

I AM of the opinion that every book, whatever its claims to literary posterity, merits a dedication. In search of inspiration for something with which to embellish Page Nine, I took eight books at random from my own bookshelf.

Two were dedicated to 'My Mother'; another two to 'My Wife'. Yet another two were written for ladies who may or may not have been the wives of the authors. Two more, war stories both, were dedicated to former comrades who had inspired the author to write of the catastrophic deeds recorded between their covers.

I was clearly getting nowhere. I toyed with 'To The British Soldier', but that seemed too banal and hardly fair; men and women of some seventeen different nationalities were involved in the battle for Hong Kong: British, Scottish, Indian, American, Canadian, Scandinavian, Chinese, Portuguese and many others. Not all were soldiers, but all suffered with varying degrees of bravery.

No, 'To the British Soldier' would not do. But from a long list of probables (as the racing journalists say) I narrowed the field down to three men: Sergeant Marable (known to a privileged few in the Sergeants' Mess as 'Horrible'), Corporal Goddard and Private Milroy. All served in the First Battalion (Duke of Cambridge's Own) The Middlesex Regiment.

In four years of captivity—years of appalling humiliation, malnutrition, misery, cruelty and privation—this indefatigable trio were ever present thorns in the sides of their captors. They reduced the Japanese to exasperation and, eventually, unwilling admiration. They indulged in insubordination and what the British Army euphemistically termed 'dumb insolence'. They flagrantly sabotaged every Japanese working project with the most explicit trade union efficiency. They greeted beatings and deprivation of Red Cross parcels with loud and defiant raspberries and the ribald utterances that only instinctively spring to the lips of the indestructible East End Londoner. They devised an illicit still and drank to ultimate victory in a concoction which would have made Red Biddy taste like still lemonade.

The selection of these three men may cause an outcry from other military quarters. But they were representative of the type of man which the Japanese tried to humble—and so signally failed to do so.

They were, in fact, British Soldiers.

CHAPTER ONE

But the word of the Lord came to me, saying, thou hast
shed blood abundantly, and has made great wars: thou
shalt not build an house unto my name, because thou
hast shed much blood upon the earth in my sight.
First Book of Chronicles, Chapter 22, verse 8.

INCOMPETENCE in high places; unpreparedness; complacency.
This distressing trinity of human weaknesses has accompanied the initial stages of every British military endeavour
in the twentieth century. A distinguished historian has written
that the British Army loses every battle except the last one;
with certain reservations this is very near to being the literal
truth.

The British Lion, unlike its cousin which is in steady
employment with Metro-Goldwyn Mayer, is a somnolent
beast with an inordinate capacity for sleep after a heavy and
indigestible lunch: only when subjected to some grievous
insult will it roar and go into destructive action.

It would be idle to pretend that the national defects quoted
above did not contribute towards the surrender of Hong
Kong to the Japanese on Christmas Day, 1941. To those
ingredients were added old and atrophied civil servants,
corrupt Government administration, an inefficient police
force and a supine and ostrich-like conception of modern war
and what it entailed. Indeed, it would not be too much to say
that Hong Kong was doomed from the start.

In Hong Kong was to be found the old and the rare (at
duty-free prices); the exciting and the exotic; the breathtaking and the colourful—everything, in fact, that typifies the
Wondrous East, hand in hand with the comfort of an up-to-
date British Colony.

In this flowery sentence, a travel brochure has caught the
full flavour of Hong Kong between the wars. For it had always
been like this, ever since this lush island of thirty-two square

miles was formally ceded to Great Britain by the treaty of Nanking, in 1842. For the next ninety-nine years, ruled with benevolent despotism by a succession of British Governors, Hong Kong was a centre of world trade and a naval and military base *par excellence*. With characteristic national perversity, Japan deprived the island of a century of uninterrupted and benign British rule.

Soon another rich prize was to come Great Britain's way. The Convention of Peking in 1860 gave the Kowloon Peninsula to Britain and in 1898 she leased the New Territories from China for ninety-nine years. By the turn of the century the pattern of Hong Kong was unshakably established: an international trading centre; an *entrepôt*; a *parvenu* port. Every country in the world did business in Hong Kong. Soon the island came to resemble a débutante, dressed in a cheongsam slit to mid-thigh, who had more eligible escorts than she could cope with.

Like a reactionary squire in bucolic surroundings, Hong Kong looked eastwards with tolerant condescension: the vastness of China approximated to a large and uncouth neighbour of dubious upbringing who had never really learned to behave properly. Japan was scarcely mentioned in polite society at all—apparently she suffered from some genus of international halitosis which put her irrevocably beyond the pale. About the only thing that could be said in their favour was that they had fought a war against the Russians in 1904.

If the Japanese were mentioned at all it was in complimentary terms: if your Martini was quickly and deftly shaken and served cold, strong and dry, as like as not the barman responsible was a Jap; if your shoes shone so that you could shave in the toe-caps, then the shoe-shine boy was probably a Jap; the barber, who bowed you from the chair looking and feeling like a million dollars, was usually a Jap (a Chinese hairdresser would pocket the tip and flick a towel over you as if he were disposing of a mosquito); the masseur, who smilingly soothed away aches and all but tore your limbs from their sockets, was inevitably a Jap. In the field of espionage they were no less successful and never, in the history of spying, had enemy agents had it so easy.

Security, prosperity and uninhibited gaiety characterised the British way of life in pre-war Hong Kong. The sea bathing was as good as anywhere in the world; the weekly race meeting, even though it would not have stood up to a Jockey Club enquiry, drew vast crowds (the last peacetime meeting was, in fact, held two days before the Japanese attack and voted one of the best ever); the fabulous hotels and the ten-page menus in the restaurants went to make up a sybaritic near paradise.

The wealth and technical resources of Britain, coupled with the integrity and industry of the Hong Kong Chinese, had combined together to transform a barren rock into one of the world's finest cities.

The teeming city of Victoria with its busy streets, well-stocked shops, opulent restaurants, suicidal rickshaw drivers; the sampan town of Aberdeen, where the people are born, live and die afloat; the grandeur of the great granite rock known as the Peak, which to Hong Kong is as Mayfair is to London or the East Side to New York: indeed, an Englishman with his home on the Peak could truly be said to have 'arrived' in Hong Kong and to have attained the highest state of social elevation that the island had to offer.

Shek-O, Big Wave Bay, and Repulse Bay: glorious beaches where the best sea bathing in the world can be enjoyed all the year round. Across Victoria Harbour by ferry to the Ritzy and cosmopolitan Peninsula Hotel. Then to the quiet calm of the hills in the New Territories where the farmers, endlessly battling against nature, grow rice, maize and vegetables. The ancient walled villages of Old China, the Buddhist monasteries, the duck farms where millions of Peking ducks are reared to provide some of the most succulent Chinese dishes... in 1939 all this was tranquil and everlasting. Everywhere there were unusual and fascinating smells: a mixture of cooking odours plus a strange blending of flowery fragrance. Nothing could change all that. . . .

The European in Hong Kong, whether he was a merchant, a banker or a civil servant, lived at worst spaciously, at best fabulously. No one had less than three servants which represented the barest minimum of gracious living. A bachelor junior official lived in a style to which his home-based counterpart could never aspire: he occupied a palatial flat or bungalow and his comfort was in the hands of a houseboy, a cookboy and a wash-*amah*—any Chinese woman servant, whether her province be the kitchen, the ironing board, the nursery or the scullery, is an *amah*. He could be sick all over the living-room, demand bacon and eggs, alcoholic refreshment or a woman at 4 am, throw his clothes out of the window, invite twenty friends in for drinks or hold an impromptu strip poker party, secure in the knowledge that a smiling and cat-footed Chinese would do his bidding and decently remove all traces of debauch and send him off to work the next morning, bathed, shaved and immaculately clad. If he wanted an overdraft at the bank, he encountered no cold smile from the manager but a cold drink instead.

'Boy!' . . . the shout echoed in every European house in the Colony. If you wanted a dose of fruit salts at 3 am you shouted 'boy!'; if you shied a cigarette packet at the waste paper basket and missed it, you shouted 'boy!'; if a toddler had an 'accident' on the carpet, you shouted 'boy!'; if you wanted a window opened, you shouted 'boy!' It made life so much simpler when you knew that somewhere within earshot was a Chinese boy, aged from sixteen to seventy, who would make you forget that life at home could be a practical and unpleasant thing.

The Ladies, of course, were on the best thing of all. To the Ladies of Hong Kong domesticity and housework had become dirty words. A hostess who wanted to throw a dinner party told 'Number One Boy' (who passed on the news to 'Cookie') and then promptly forgot about it until the first guests arrived. Their children, if they had any, were the responsibility of the *amahs*, who loved them fiercely and possessively and spoiled them atrociously.

Marketing, as opposed to shopping, was another dirty word. Shopping, of course, had nothing to do with searching and queueing for a nice bit of steak, a fresh herring, a cauliflower, a tin of mushroom soup, or a packet of soap flakes. Shopping was browsing through the emporiums with their silks, satins and brocades; *objets d'art* of ivory, jade, agate and rose-quartz; lacquer work and camphorwood; porcelain and pewter.

Nor was it necessary or even particularly desirable to eat at home too often. In the restaurants, at ludicrously low prices, toothsome delicacies from Peking, Canton, Swatow and Tientsin figured on the menus: chop suey, shark's fin soup, sweet and sour pork, noodles. . . .

Alcohol, ever essential fuel to the white man in the tropics, flowed across hotel and club bars and in private houses in a continuous spate: beer, so cold that you could hardly taste it;

Martinis, so dry that it seemed that the Vermouth jigger must have been waved over the shaker like a magic wand; side-cars, bronxes, Manhattan's, angels' kisses; Scotch on the rocks, Scotch and soda, Scotch straight; brandy and dry ginger ale for the morning after.

It was, as anyone who was there will nostalgically tell you, a lovely life. . . .

British unpreparedness, complacency and political idiocy always rebound at the beginning of a war on one man: Thomas Atkins. It is the Regular Army, the pathetically ill-equipped professional soldiers who, to use their own phrase, 'carry the can back'.

But generally the soldiers were not popular with the civilian population whose feelings for them ranged from good humoured tolerance to active dislike. Rudyard Kipling had it thus:

> For it's Tommy this, an' Tommy that, an'
> 'Chuck him out, the brute!'
> But it's 'Saviour of 'is country' when
> the guns begin to shoot. . . .

The regular soldier of the 1930s, that mean-spirited period in British history when the country floundered in torpid apathy against a background of mass unemployment and hunger marches, joined the Army for economic, alcoholic, amatory but rarely patriotic reasons.

He joined at a time when there was no Welfare State and no overtime (indeed, there was frequently little 'time', in the strictly trade union sense, of any sort)—he enlisted, in fact, because he was out of work and the problem of the next square meal was becoming increasingly pressing.

A few youthful romantics enlisted because they were attracted by a recruiting poster depicting a laughing warrior incongruously attired in khaki from the waist up and football kit from the waist down against a background of biblical palm trees. Others, again, used the British Army as a fortuitous refuge from determined young women armed with real or imagined paternity orders. The peacetime British Army demanded few references and if a recruit was eighteen years old and fit he was in for seven years, like it or do the other thing. . . .

Their fathers, of course, had regaled them with stories about the 1914–18 war to which they had listened with tolerant amusement. The youngsters of 1930 were lucky, even if they were hungry and out of work. *They* would not be the dupes of power-hungry politicians; *they* would not be called upon to choke out their lives in the putrefying mud of Flanders, while the gilded staff swilled claret in well-appointed *chateaux* miles behind the front line. *They* would travel the world at the tax-payer's expense, play football, drink astronomical quantities of beer and light-heartedly co-habit with girls of every race, creed and colour. It was an intriguing prospect for a young man who earned fifteen shillings a week if he was lucky. . . .

Ask a British soldier what he fights for and he will glare at you suspiciously, scenting a trap. Having satisfied himself that you are neither a pressman nor a politician, he will spit (literally or metaphorically), fumble for the right word with his tongue along the inside of his upper lip, shrug his shoulders, grin ironically, scratch the back of his neck and either say nothing or that he doesn't know. The fact finders sigh sympathetically and then proclaim that the British soldier fights for his home in England.

It hardly seems credible that love of home—in most cases a mean house in a damp and overcrowded slum, long overdue for demolition—prompted men to fight uncomplainingly for seventeen days without rest, only to swear horribly and break down in tears over the guns that the High Command decreed could be fired no more on Christmas Day, 1941. But they were not tears of misery, remorse or self-pity; they were untrustworthy tears of fierce and bitter rage.

In the 1930s British infantry battalions enjoyed an extrovert and well ordered existence. Occasionally, to placate the tax-payer (who, God knew, had little enough to worry about then), they were called upon to be shot at by wily tribesmen on the North West Frontier of India and truculent Arabs in Palestine. But for the most part, undeterred by the rumblings of Hitler and Mussolini, they marched and countermarched; sloped arms and presented arms; went to camp once a year; expended blank ammunition on Salisbury Plain, when the Treasury permitted; enjoyed paid holidays on an unprecedented scale and delighted the public at tattoos at Aldershot and Tidworth. Between the two world wars the British soldiers in Hong

Kong had never had it so good. A weekly wage of fourteen shillings a week would appear to preclude the possibility of sustained enjoyment for a private soldier ten thousand miles from home. But the food was free and plentiful; beer in the wet canteen was twopence per pint and only 5½d in the downtown hotels. One shilling and threepence per week purchased the services of a servant, and such essential military chores as blancoing, polishing, sweeping out the rooms, washing clothes and even shaving became an amusing recollection of life in barracks in England. Nor were marital comforts the prerogative of the married men: ten shillings per month provided an accommodating young woman who furnished all the comforts of home. These ladies became known as 'dahnhomers' because if a soldier was asked where he was going for the evening he as often as not replied 'dahn 'ome', implying an evening of uninhibited domesticity with his Chinese girl friend. A soldier who tired of his 'dahnhomer' need never worry because supply invariably far exceeded demand in a commodity that has always been an essential adjunct to the well-being of the British soldier.

The soldier is a normal man who is constantly called upon to rise superior to an abnormal environment. He constantly falls in and out of love and his preoccupations with tender passion frequently get him into trouble. With the exercise of a modicum of prophylactic care, the soldier in Hong Kong found that the 'dahnhomer' solved nearly all his emotional troubles; discipline, beer and the mail from England looked after the rest.

A vintage soldier with tattoo marks commemorating half a dozen sojourns overseas will unhesitatingly point to the clasped hands, serpent, ship in full sail or headstone on some portion of his anatomy and proclaim that Hong Kong has all the other overseas stations licked to a frazzle. Army life in Hong Kong was good indeed, with afternoons given over to sleep and swimming, and evenings to sport. It was also the worst possible preparation for the serious and bloody business of war.

The outbreak of war in September, 1939, did little or nothing to affect life in Hong Kong: indeed, if anything, the tempo of the cocktail parties increased. Although the Island was put on a war footing, there was little sense of urgency about the process. It was realised, of course (although not by everyone), that Japan was in sympathy with the Axis powers, but by some inexplicable process of reasoning it was argued that Japan could best further her interests by remaining neutral. In Whitehall the situation was airily disposed of on October 26th, 1941, with the following reassuring appraisal: 'The consensus of opinion is that war in the Far East is unlikely at present.'

In the light of the catastrophic events to come, the forces for the defence of Hong Kong seemed almost laughable. Naval power was limited to two antique destroyers and a few motor torpedo boats. Supremacy in the air depended on three obsolete Wildebeeste torpedo bombers with a maximum speed of 100 m.p.h. and two Walrus amphibians.

There were four infantry battalions in the Colony, two British and two Indian: they were the 2nd Royal Scots, 1st Middlesex (Machine Gun Battalion), 5/7 Rajputs and 2/14 Punjabis.

The 1st Middlesex were composed of regular soldiers: professionals who had been trained to a fine peak of discipline and efficiency—a remarkable feat on the part of their commanding officer, having regard for the civilian sloth and complacency that surrounded them. But their CO, Lt-Col 'Monkey' Stewart, was no stranger to war and had won the Military Cross in Flanders. He was also imbued with the cynical tolerance with which the professional soldier regards the Government. Consequently, turning a deaf ear to the complacent utterances of clubroom strategists, he maintained his men in a state of constant readiness—for anything.

The Middlesex Regiment had been in many tight corners before—as many, certainly, as any other British infantry regiment of the Line.

In 1811 they won undying fame at the battle of Albuhera, the fiercest and bloodiest battle of the Peninsular War. They stood unflinching against a murderous fire of shell and grapeshot, and held the hill which they had captured in a counter-attack against a column which outnumbered them by more than four to one. Their Commanding Officer, lying mortally wounded, exhorted his troops: "Die hard, my men, die hard!" From that day onwards the Middlesex Regiment became universally known as 'The Diehards'. At Albuhera 430 men out of 570 were killed or wounded; the dead were found with their faces to the enemy and all their wounds in front. The French

18

General Soult described them thus: "There is no beating these troops, in spite of their generals. I turned their right and pierced their centre: they were everywhere broken and the day was mine. Yet they did not know it and would not run."

The Middlesex are a run-of-the-mill infantry regiment. Many other regiments won more Victoria Crosses; there are other regiments who have won more fame in the field of sport and musketry; there are smarter regiments and there are more exclusive regiments; there are regiments who can boast less sickness and crime; there are regiments who have done more sojourns overseas.

For all that, wherever the mud was deepest, the shelling fiercest, the rations and water shortest, the weather vilest, the odds most desperate, it was safe to assume that a platoon or a company of the Middlesex was somewhere near and many a commander has had reason to be thankful for this fact. The men who bawled a raucous 'NO!' to the ageless and rhetorical query 'Are we downhearted?' were very probably from the Middlesex.

The men of the Middlesex were predominantly Londoners: men short of stature but large of heart. They hailed from parts of London which rarely figure in the itinerary of an American tourist: Stepney, Shoreditch, Bow, Hackney, Poplar, Lewisham, Peckham and Bethnal Green. They were representative of the permanent Londoner—virile, cunning, cheerful, cocky, brave. Most of them had a background of poverty and malnutrition. Their fathers frequently beat their mothers and their mothers frequently beat them. They were unscrupulously dishonest in their dealings with the rich; recklessly generous with anyone poorer than themselves. They were and are entirely indestructible. Many of them swore that they would starve rather than have a steady job with a regular wage—and then unaccountably enlisted in the Regular Army for seven years.

Their voices were staccato and they prefixed every noun with the same untuneful and copulative adjective. Every sentence contained rhyming slang: the wife was the trouble an' strife; the kids the Gawd forbids; if they had no money (as was frequent) they were hearts of oak (broke) or boracic lint (skint). Beer was pig's ear, boots daisy roots, a suit a whistle and flute, a road a frog and toad, the stairs the apples and pears.

They had their own financial phraseology: a pound was a 'oncer', ten shillings 'arf a bar', five shillings a 'dollar' or 'Oxford scholar', half-a-crown a 'tosheroon'.

At first sight they looked calculated to break any drill sergeant's heart; there is, however, no record of this in the annals of the regiment. . . .

It was appropriate enough that the Royal Scots, the First of Foot, should have been in the battle for Hong Kong. Charter to form the regiment was given by King Charles I in 1633 and, as senior infantry regiment of the Line, they had the distinction of taking their place on the right of all other infantry of the line on parades and ceremonies. There was a total absence of ceremony in the fighting for Hong Kong, but throughout most of the battle the Royal Scots maintained the position that had been their privilege and pride for over three hundred years.

In the 17th century the Regiment had fought under several Kings of France and Louis XIV gave it precedence over all French units.

From its earliest days the soldiers of the Royal Scots have been recruited from Edinburgh and the Lothians. The Lowland Scot is not the easiest man to get to know: he is apt to be dour, not over-articulate and suspicious. He is less volatile and quick-tempered than his cousin from the Highlands; slower to take offence, less prone to get involved in a fight before he knows what the fight is about (the Highlander tends to hit first and ask questions afterwards). But his dogged tenacity in attack and defence have been a byword for three centuries.

He looks you straight in the eye and is not very interested in you unless he knows you well. He is loyal to the core and faithful unto death, when once loyalty and fidelity have been won and given.

But in 1941 all was far from being well with the 2nd Royal Scots. First and foremost, they had been abroad far too long. Although they had been warned to stand by for return to England, nothing had ever come of it. To make matters worse, many of the best senior NCOs were sent back to England on the outbreak of war and their replacements were of dubious quality.

Their numbers were seriously depleted by malaria. No one

would wish malaria, with its attendant shivering, blazing fever and crippling weakness, on his worst enemy. But the fact remains that malaria, like venereal disease, was regarded as a self-inflicted injury and to contract it was a punishable offence. Mosquito-repellent cream and quinine tablets were issued to all soldiers and provided a reasonable degree of immunity. Unhappily, many of the Royal Scots appeared to think that they were under some kind of divine protection and scorned to use these elementary precautions. The mosquito, however, is no respecter of persons and will bite a Scot as cheerfully as an Englishman: the melancholy figures of Royal Scots' admissions to hospital spoke for themselves.

Other battalions had survived worse vicissitudes than those visited on the Royal Scots; others again had stagnated as only a bad battalion can. Similar misfortunes overtook battalions in India, but Army life in India was more austere and there were frequent reminders in the shape of riots that soldiering could be a hard and dangerous trade. There were also tours of duty on the turbulent North West Frontier where every rifle was loaded with live ammunition and there was the ever-present threat of a hail of bullets or a gory hand-to-hand struggle against the savage Pathan; the Royal Scots were to get this all too soon, but nothing in their training in Hong Kong had prepared them for such an eventuality. A tour of duty on the North West Frontier would, in all probability, have done the 2nd Royal Scots a power of good.

The Commanding Officer sets the tone of any battalion, and the responsibility for the mediocrity of the Royal Scots must belong to Lieutenant-Colonel D. McDougall, MC. Colonel McDougall had fought with gallantry and distinction in the First World War, but 1940 found him, in cricketing parlance, playing out time. He sailed for England early in 1941 and handed over to the second-in-command.

To put new ginger into them the Royal Scots needed John Wayne (in one of his more militant roles), Colonel Nicholson (of River Kwai fame), George Armstrong Custer, General 'Blood and Guts' Patton, Attila the Hun or a synthesis of the five. Instead they got Lieutenant-Colonel Simon White, MC.

Simon White was brave, honourable, kind and just. He could never have been anything but a singularly gallant gentleman. A Military Cross was but just recognition of continuous and selfless bravery in France. This same selfless bravery was continually in evidence during the fighting in Hong Kong, and his subsequent courage and determination as a prisoner-of-war earned the unstinted praise of everyone who met him. He died of cancer after the war and bore this dread disease with the same fortitude that he displayed in two wars and nearly four years of privation in Jap hands.

The 2nd Royal Scots did not need Simon White, though the British Army and the country is so much poorer for his absence. They needed the type of Commanding Officer for whom the British soldier has only one word.

God grant that brave and gentle Simon White has found the rest that he so justly earned. . . .

The Indians were a mixture of reservists—time-expired men recalled for duty at the outbreak of war—and raw youngsters. The Rajputs and Punjabis, martial races both, have produced some of India's finest fighting men. But a reservist of any nationality, his service behind him and civilian life in front of him, must inevitably be something of an unwilling warrior: he has lost some of his cutting edge as a fighting man. For all that, both Indian battalions acquitted themselves with splendid valour in the vicious fighting that followed.

It was not until November, 1941 (and even then the threat of Japanese invasion had not reached serious proportions), that this slender force was reinforced by two Canadian battalions, the Winnipeg Grenadiers and the Royal Rifles of Canada. It must be said here and now that, through no fault of their own, these regiments added little to the lustre of Canada. They were despatched to Hong Kong at a week's notice after a lengthy period of stagnation as garrison troops in the West Indies and Newfoundland respectively; they were largely untrained in anything but the most perfunctory internal security duties and the security of Newfoundland and the West Indies had been refreshingly constant for many decades. Indeed, in the West Indies, the gravest military crisis likely to be encountered was a defective refrigerator or a mild hurricane; many of them had less than six months' service. Their appearance on the island prompted a senior staff officer, among whose many virtues tolerance was not the most prominent, to say that they were 'straight off the trees'. Nevertheless, in fairness to the Cana-

22

dians, it must be said that individual acts of extraordinary gallantry were many and frequent.

To these four battalions, together with a sprinkling of inadequate artillery and the usual heterogeneous collection of ancillary troops, were added the Hong Kong Volunteer Defence Corps. Conscription for British residents had been introduced in the Colony in 1940 when it was realised that the war was developing into something more than a minor irritation. Their training was conducted on the same casual and lighthearted lines as that of Britain's pre-war Territorial Army.

Businessmen, bankers, engineers, pressmen, customs officers, PWD officials, dockyard officials; men on their way up in their jobs and men on their way out; rich men, poor men, alcoholic men and abstemious men: men from no fewer than seventeen different nationalities became front line soldiers almost overnight. Their ages ranged from nineteen to sixty-five and many of them were called upon to produce reserves of strength and courage that they did not know they possessed. Men who, in the preceding ten years, had lifted nothing heavier than a glass found themselves manhandling machine guns across mountainous country; men who had encountered nothing more frightening than the prick of a doctor's needle were to know the sickening and sadistic pleasure of driving a bayonet into human flesh.

These, then, were the men who were to face 60,000 battle-hardened and ruthless Japanese. . . .

It seemed, however, that towards the end of November, 1941, there was nothing to upset the even tenor of life in Hong Kong. A military spokesman in Singapore—clearly a man with an illustrious future—came out with the following reassuring statement: '. . . the danger is rather that Japan may drift into war by continuing her present foreign policy; it seems possible that this may lead to a conflict with the Democratic Powers sooner or later.' Air Chief Marshal Sir Robert Brooke-Popham, Commander-in-Chief Far East, is credited with saying that 'Tojo was scratching his head', but forbore to make any mention of the presumably less purposeful scratching that was going on in Whitehall.

British understatement is a staple ingredient of a hundred

23

war novels and a score of indifferent war films; it is invariably good for a laugh. But these communiqués on Japanese intentions must surely take pride of place.

For the civilian population of Hong Kong it was business as usual. The Ladies shopped, swam, gossiped, exchanged scandal and made lists of people they ought to invite to dinner some time; their husbands bought, sold, insured, exported, imported and had one for the road. Over their drinks they said: "Couldn't possibly happen, old boy."

Meanwhile Japan, like a predatory landowner in a bad old-fashioned melodrama, looked towards Hong Kong and made covetous hissing noises. . . .

CHAPTER TWO

For junior officers and other ranks, the fortunes of war are clear cut: if your name's on it you get it; if you survive there are possible decorations, campaign stars and eventual prospects of promotion to Field-Marshal (Private Bill Slim of the Royal Warwicks became Field-Marshal Sir William Slim, GCB, GBE, DSO, MC, Governor-General of Australia).

Gallantry in action is not inevitably a stepping stone to promotion: in the recent war young officers found wanting in battle, who might well have faced a firing squad a quarter of a century earlier, have found security, comfort and promotion in well appointed headquarters far from, if not madding crowds, ignoble strife. Their most critical military crises became a missing bren gun barrel or a Methodist, who by some unexplained ecclesiastical error, had joined the ranks of the Sacred Heart.

Going up the scale one found unsuccessful company commanders who were kicked upstairs to the command of reinforcement camps with the rank of lieutenant-colonel; lieutenant-colonels, who led their battalions to nothing but disaster, got pumped up into brigadiers and indulged in Plazatorovian inductivity:

> In enterprise of martial kind
> When there was any fighting,
> He led his regiment from behind—
> He found it less exciting.
> But when away his regiment ran
> His face was at the fore-oh!
> That celebrated, cultivated,
> Underrated nobleman,
> The Duke of Plaza Toro . . .!

But for generals, the dividing line between success and failure is a very narrow one and luck plays a big part in any outstandingly successful campaign. If the luck falls one way, it can mean a field-marshal's baton or the governorship of a colony; if the other, retirement to the gentle breezes of Bournemouth, the impoverished tillage of unreceptive soil or the secretaryship (unpaid) of territorial associations or other military novelties.

A general is supposed to win battles, and if he wins them with the minimum loss of life he gets the adulation of the civilian population. If he loses them, complaints about bad luck, the weather, the terrain and inefficient subordinates will fall on deaf and unsympathetic ears: he either gets a bowler hat or a big hand.

The general who rallies a seemingly beaten army and presses on regardless to victory may find himself, on retirement, an active director of numerous companies and a sleeping director of many more; he will administer such diverse concerns as breweries, insurance companies, the Jockey Club, the Betting Board, railways, the National Coal Board and independent television companies. He will be knighted (possibly twice) and even be awarded a peerage. If he is an American, a Frenchman, an Egyptian or a Cuban he may end up ruling the country.

It goes without saying that he will write his memoirs and commit searing remarks about other generals to thirsty print, reasonably certain that no libel action will result (probably other generals will be writing even more vitriolic prose about him). These memoirs will be serialised, translated and even filmed—indeed, his memoirs may earn him three years' Army pay and allowances overnight. He will fight battles again to a bemused audience of millions on television: war veterans will grunt guarded approval, while a less tolerant generation will sit it out politely because 'Wagon Train' is due on the other channel.

This digressionary preamble is by way of leading up to the fortunes of two generals, neither of whom have written their memoirs or appeared on television. One, a snarling brute beast, met a richly deserved end on the scaffold as a war criminal. The other cultivates dahlias in Somerset and spoils his grandchildren atrociously. . . .

Possibly no general in history initially had it so good as Major-General Ito Takeo of the Imperial Japanese Army. For six years he had been fighting the Chinese and had reluctantly come to the conclusion that they were not so very different from his own soldiers: they fought with the same dogged and resentful fury and the same disregard for human life as the Japanese. Like the Japs, they went into the attack in hordes and the amount of their casualties was a matter of supreme indifference to the High Command.

From earliest childhood they had been brought up to war and in their youth had been beset by one burning problem: how to get enough to eat to keep themselves alive for one day longer. They saw sudden, horrible and obscene death every day of their lives. They had seen their wives, mothers, sisters, daughters, aunts and grandmothers raped by the marauding Japanese. Life was cheap enough in an army which had no pensions, War Graves Commissions, toasts to fallen comrades or cafeteria-type meals. To them a single day of survival equalled in relative importance a decade of Western existence.

After these years of desperately fought carnage, Ito Takeo wanted to have a crack at a less resilient race. The British and Americans, as every right-thinking Japanese knew, were soft, effete, reactionary and stupid. They reduced the yellow, brown and black races under their heel to a humiliating level of degrading subjugation—a favourite Japanese propaganda leaflet depicted a huge and bloated John Bull consuming a gargantuan porterhouse steak while the natives grovelled on the ground at his feet, begging for a few grains of rice.

Some Jap generals, Ito Takeo well knew, had been forced to commit *hari-kari* as a result of failures against the Chinese. There would be little prospect of that for him if all he had to defeat was a handful of wine-swilling, oversexed and sybaritic Europeans. It would be the keenest pleasure to humble and degrade them; to rape their womenfolk; to take over their restaurants, clubs and bars.

It was hardly surprising, therefore, that Major-General Ito Takeo viewed his next assignment—the capture of Hong Kong —with enormous confidence and pleasurable anticipation. . . .

Japanese intelligence agents in Hong Kong made sure that Ito Takeo got away to a flying start. The consular staff blandly looked out of their office windows, noted every minute detail of the defences and gave the predetermined number of diplomatic cocktail parties. The waiters, barmen, hairdressers and masseurs watched, listened and reported assiduously. The Japanese drinking halls in Wanchai were voted by the British troops to offer more in entertainment value than anything the

Chinese could produce. The Japs smilingly offered them cold beer, exotic food, accommodating women, generous credit facilities—and listened.

The finest men's hairdresser in Hong Kong was a Jap who had been in the Colony for seven years. He cut the hair of two successive governors, generals, brigadiers, the Colonial Secretary, the Commissioner of Police, the officer in charge of the Special Branch and the Chairman of the Hong Kong and Shanghai Bank. After the capitulation on Christmas Day, 1941, he smilingly presented himself to his former employers in the uniform of a Commander of the Imperial Japanese Navy.

But the star turn was unquestionably Colonel Suzuki, seconded from the Japanese Army for duty in Hong Kong for the purpose of learning English. An astute British Intelligence officer made the alarming discovery that, after nearly twelve months in the Colony, the Colonel had not so much as mastered a single English phrase except 'By Gad, sir!'. On being questioned, Suzuki smiled blandly and explained through an interpreter that he was, in fact, an intelligence officer. He regretted exceedingly that he had learned no English, but his intelligence duties took up all his available time.

Here was red-faced British authority with a vengeance. The Intelligence officer told the General Staff Officer 1st Grade who told the General who told the Colonial Secretary who told the Governor. Colonel Suzuki continued to smile seraphically and amass more detailed information about our military dispositions and defences. In the evenings he dined at the Parisian Grill and attended cocktail parties.

After a million spoken words, five thousand written words and more indecisive pauses than a man could count, the Government stormed into action. Colonel Suzuki, thundered a Government spokesman in Hong Kong, three months later, must be expelled from the Colony forthwith, if not sooner. His presence there was an insult, a disgrace, a blunder of the first magnitude. The Foreign Office, like a hostess who is too polite to drop a hint to a guest who will not leave, demurred: Britain and Japan were not at war, therefore Colonel Suzuki could not be expelled—such an action would be a grave affront to Japan. Colonel Suzuki's smile grew broader and he continued his one-man espionage campaign unfettered in any way.

Eventually Colonel Suzuki departed of his own accord. At the end of November, 1941, a bare fortnight before the Japanese struck, he shook hands with everyone, bowed politely, wrote the Japanese for '*p.p.c.*' (*pour prendre congé*) in all the right books and departed for Japan. He still knew no English, but he did know details of the British defence plan down to the last strand of barbed wire.

The Japanese Intelligence agents in Hong Kong were invariably polite. A prominent citizen, who was also the secretary of the Japanese golf club, obtained a permit to build a new clubhouse in the New Territories. Directly behind the new clubhouse was a machine gun emplacement. With disarming courtesy, the Jap explained to the British building contractor that the clubhouse would in no way obstruct the field of fire.

"But who could possibly want to attack us from that direction?" inquired the builder.

The club secretary smiled, a secret and beatific smile. "Who indeed?" he said.

(The initial Japanese attack subsequently came across the Japanese golf course and heavy casualties were inflicted from this very emplacement.)

Other Japanese spies were less ambitious, and contented themselves with taking jobs as coolies in the dockyard. This, of course, simplified the assessment of our meagre naval forces considerably.

As a result of all this uninterrupted espionage, almost every dead Japanese officer, after the fighting was over, was found to have on his person a map—a lithograph reproduction of our own battle maps—which gave exact details of our defences. Thanks to the barbers, the barmen, the waiters, the taxi drivers, the masseurs, the consular staff and the indefatigable Colonel Suzuki, they were in possession of a complete Order of Battle and knew the names of all the senior officers. In the variegated history of war, no army ever attacked with such explicit information about their enemy.

Thirty years in the Indian Army, which included World War One, continuous active service in the Persian Gulf, Mesopotamia, Egypt, Salonica and a score of skirmishes on the North West Frontier, had convinced Major-General (Temporary) Christopher Maltby, MC, that things are very rarely what they seem. Hong Kong in September, 1941, when he arrived to take over as General Officer Commanding British Troops in China, was no exception to this hypothesis.

His predecessor, Major-General Edward Grasett, CB, DSO, MC, a Canadian, had served his country faithfully and gallantly in the First World War in the Royal Engineers. Since 1923, however, he had occupied a succession of comfortable staff appointments, and the command of British troops in China, remotely removed from the war with Germany, was the most comfortable one yet. Three years in Hong Kong had induced in him a feeling of light-hearted facile optimism, which was the least promising basis for the mounting of a defence against a ruthless and fanatical enemy.

The Japanese, declared General Grasett to a captive audience of officers, were bluffing and would continue to bluff to the last. War with them was out of the question because Japan could best serve her interests by remaining neutral.

General Maltby, fresh from the more astringent atmosphere of India's turbulent North West Frontier, did not agree. General Grasett resembled a nanny who, on handing over her charge with assurances of perfect cleanliness, lands her successor with a baby that wets its bed three times nightly and steadfastly refuses to mount the pot.

The Governor, Sir Geoffrey Northcote, KCMG, was old and ill and ineffectual: perhaps it was unfair to expect him to be anything else. Thirty-seven dedicated and devoted years in the Colonial Service in murderous heat had left him a sick man. Much of his service had been spent on the stultifying Gold Coast, and by early 1941 he was mentally and physically exhausted. The blame, if blame there be, lies with theForeign Office who should have retired him three years earlier. Instead of wrestling with Chinese affairs (for which thirty-seven years in Africa scarcely fitted him) he should have been adding tone to rural England.

Very early in his tenure of command, Maltby smelt a large and unmistakably Japanese rat. It was clear to him that war with Japan was imminent, in spite of the lukewarm embassy despatches from Tokyo (these in themselves should have spelled danger to anyone who knew anything of the Japanese character). However, any representations he made to the Government or to Whitehall were met with so much evasion and expert obstructionism that he was forcibly reminded of the hoary chestnut about the private soldier who, on being asked by a passer-by in Whitehall which side the War Office was on replied: "Ours—I 'ope!"

In September, 1941, General Grasett departed to Canada on the road which was to lead him, via the command of a corps and a division, to the post of Lieutenant-Governor and Commander-in-Chief of the Channel Islands. In November, Sir Geoffrey Northcote was invalided home and succeeded by Sir Mark Young, shrewd and energetic old Etonian and ex-Rifle Brigade officer, with a fine record of achievement in such varied outposts of Empire as Ceylon, Sierra Leone, Palestine, Barbados, Trinidad and Tanganyika. Two new brooms had arrived, but far too late to sweep clean. . . .

On the night of December 4th, 1941, Major-General Maltby dined with the officers of the 1st Middlesex. A general, like a schoolmaster, is apt to have favourites: in Maltby's variegated command, the Middlesex were something of a favourite of his.

This was understandable. Thanks to their Commanding Officer, Lieutenant-Colonel H. W. M. Stewart, OBE, MC—universally known as 'Monkey Paul'—their morale, discipline, smartness on parade, good humour and efficiency would have gladdened any commander's heart.

'Monkey' Stewart was and is something of a legend in the Middlesex Regiment. Second World War Middlesex men of the 1st Battalion will talk endlessly of Shamshuipo, Kobe, The 'Lisbon Maru', Repulse Bay, Red Hill, Devil's Peak, Stanley Peninsula and the Wong Nei Chang Gap, but the conversation will inevitably wander back to 'Monkey' Stewart. They will recall with affection, albeit tinged with awe, the man whose kindly eyes belied his ultra-military appearance; the long nose and fierce moustache that appeared round the corner of cookhouses, demanding to sample the men's dinner; his unheralded inspections of anything from toenails to spare gun barrels; his sudden raids on unauthorised and clandestine games of billiards in the recreation room (in particular they will remember how, on one occasion, he concealed himself behind a chair before pouncing on three men who should have been attending education classes. On emerging from his hiding place, he first reprimanded a man for potting his opponent's ball before double-marching the offenders to the guardroom). Then there was the time . . . but a complete book could be written about 'Monkey' Stewart alone.

'Monkey' will still be a legend when lesser men are dust. In battle he was everywhere at once: wherever the fighting was thickest, his immaculate figure was to be seen encouraging, joking, cajoling. Later, in Japanese captivity, he was untiring in his efforts to improve the lot of his fellow prisoners-of-war and died in a prison camp, physically and mentally exhausted. 'Greater Love Hath No Man Than This . . .'

From the officers' standpoint the Middlesex are not, and never have been, an expensive regiment. To the layman this statement may require some qualification. Before the First World War practically every infantry regiment of the Line required that its officers possessed some private means (the Brigade of Guards and the Cavalry were, of course, a law unto themselves in these matters and regarded the infantry of the Line with tolerant condescension).

With the virtual annihilation of the old Regular Army at Mons, the Great War became something of a social leveller: stockbrokers commanded battalions; insurance salesmen companies; shipping clerks platoons. Formidable bank balances were of little use in the mud of the Somme.

Between the wars the British Army concentrated fiercely on the intricate business of getting back to peacetime and, so to speak, audited its books. Every regiment had its share of traditional glories which they carried with casual grandeur, but sometimes with an overtone of snobbery. In some regiments private means of a thousand pounds a year were considered to be desirable; others could barely manage on six hundred and fifty; some young officers, endowed with a mere four hundred, found themselves perpetually and painfully in debt.

Many officers, finding themselves at a financial disadvantage from which there seemed to be no escape, sought social banishment but monetary security with the King's African Rifles, the West African Frontier Force or the Sudan Defence Force. Secondments of this nature promised little in the way of social advancement but considerable financial independence when the time for long leave came round. (In 1912 my father, finding life insupportable on five shillings and threepence per day—his mess bill was seven shillings per day and his private means twenty pounds per year—betook himself to East Africa

32

for seven years and found some measure of opulence for the first time in his life.)

There were other regiments again, exclusive in their own right, whose officers had no private means at all. Some of these were regarded by their better endowed comrades with scarcely concealed disdain, as if they ate peas with a knife or displayed their braces in the Royal Enclosure at Ascot. Some Commanding Officers, indeed, told financially embarrassed subalterns that "that sort of thing may be all right for the —— Regiment but it certainly won't do with *us*." One of the poorer regiments was the Middlesex Regiment (Duke of Cambridge's Own).

It was early impressed on a junior officer of the Middlesex that his professional efficiency and the welfare of his men came before his bank balance, the name of his tailor or his prowess on the polo field.

In spite of the fact that they were not an 'expensive' regiment, a Middlesex Officers' Mess guest night in Hong Kong was a sumptuous affair. The officers wore peacetime mess dress: short, scarlet 'bum-freezing' jackets, tight, dark blue overalls with a single narrow scarlet stripe, patent leather Wellington boots. Here and there, on the left lapels of the more senior officers, could be seen the miniature medals which denoted service in almost forgotten campaigns.

There were cocktails in the ante room: strong, iced and deftly served by soft-treading waiters. Smoke thickened; talk buzzed: talk of home leave, polo, last Saturday's race meeting, swimming, the battalion's chances in the Army boxing championship. There was, of course, no mention of women or 'shop'—the Regular Army's two taboos in the Mess. Excursion into either of these two conversational traps could mean an expensive round of drinks, which the guilty officer in all probability could not afford.

Maltby chatted with a group of subalterns in the bluff and avuncular way that characterises General officers on guest nights, but his heart was heavy with foreboding. He remembered other young men, a quarter of a century earlier, who chatted inconsequently over their cocktails with, on average, life expectancy of another fortnight. The General sternly relegated such gloomy thoughts to the back of his mind, took another cocktail from a mess waiter and resolved to enjoy himself. . . .

The band, perspiring gently under the stern stare of the

bandmaster, played discreet selections from Gilbert and Sullivan, 'The Belle of New York' and 'Rose Marie'. Then, at a given signal, they broke into 'The Roast Beef of Old England' as the officers filed into the dining room. They settled themselves up and down the long table, banked with flowers and candles. The mess silver, stood bravely on the table. The scene was secure, serene, and everlasting.

It was the last time for nearly four years that the officers of the 1st Battalion the Middlesex Regiment were to dine together.

Plague, fever, lawlessness, impecuniosity and incompetence figured large in Hong Kong's early days as a British Colony: by 1941 all these defects had disappeared for ever, except for the incompetence which flourished like a malignant weed in a well-kept garden. The sad fact is that the Far Eastern Intelligence Service (a misnomer, if there ever was one) seemed to have more than their fair share of the incompetence.

Intelligence sources before the outbreak of war with Japan pointed to exceptional military activity in Canton and Bocca Tigris. This was airily explained away as being either a concentration for an advance north-west from Canton on to Kunming, or the development of a base of supply and staging depot for an all-out attack on Thailand. The appearance of forty troop transports in the neighbourhood of the Indo-Chinese coastline was assumed to be reinforcements to combat a new thrust by Chiang Kai-Shek's armies in the North.

Highly trained specialist Intelligence officers in the Far East Combined Bureau at Singapore probed, examined, collated, wrote minutes to one another, theorised, temporised, scratched their heads, put flags in maps, took them out again, pursed their lips, drank cups of coffee, chain-smoked, argued, sent signals to Whitehall, got promoted, got sacked, got returned to regimental duty and had nervous breakdowns in their efforts to assess Japanese intentions. It was left to a Japanese deserter, a private (fourth class) to state them in a single sentence—and then no one believed them.

Private (Fourth Class) Yashinoa was fed up with the Imperial Japanese Army and didn't care who knew it. He had joined the Army because a friend of his in Tokyo had told him that it was a life of glory, honour and unbridled rape. None of these things had come Yashinoa's way; instead he had been

34

abused by officers and slapped around by brutal noncoms. His leaves had been cancelled, he seemed to have walked the length and breadth of China and he hadn't raped a woman yet. There seemed little future in such an existence, so, in search of co-prosperity, he slipped across the frontier by night and presented himself with a courtly bow to the nearest British unit.

He was greeted with considerable fervour. After a huge meal (which was the equivalent of three days rations for a Japanese soldier) he was given a packet of American cigarettes and delivered to an interpreter. He then stated simply that the Japanese were massing large numbers of troops and heavy calibre artillery north of the frontier.

The Far East Combined Bureau, in their earnest quest for information, amassed further facts about the Japanese, all of which were subsequently proved to be totally wrong:

(1) That Japanese night work was poor.
(2) That Japanese light automatics were not as numerous as ours or so up-to-date.
(3) That the cream of Japanese manhood had been dissipated in the war with China.
(4) That the Japanese Air Force was of a low standard and that their bombing was poor.

Many prominent civilians continued to regard the threat of Japanese aggression with stony disbelief. On December 5th General Maltby met a high-ranking executive of the Hong Kong and Shanghai Bank and warned him that he proposed mobilising the volunteers, which included all the Bank's European staff.

The banker regarded Maltby like a schoolmaster confronted by a small boy who had made an uncouth noise in class.

"But my dear General," he expostulated, "that will mean closing the bank. It's absolutely unthinkable." Like the Windmill, it was the proud boast of the Hong Kong and Shanghai Bank that it never closed.

"If my guess is right," retorted Maltby, "it will be a long time before any bank in Hong Kong opens again. I'm afraid the time has come to take the war seriously."

"I assure you that in the bank we take the war very seriously indeed," said the banker, as if the prosecution of it was his own personal responsibility. He went on with massive con-

35

descension: "It is perhaps difficult for you, as a soldier, to realise it, but I have my finger"—he brandished it fiercely—"on the pulse of the Far East's finances. I tell you, that to close the Bank will invite disaster, if not economic ruin."

Nevertheless, the Hong Kong and Shanghai Bank—that bastion of Far Eastern prosperity, known to the irreverent as the 'Honkers and Shankers'—*did* stay open until midday on December 8th, manned by the thinnest of skeleton staffs. During the Japanese occupation it housed the Japanese Government, but the Japs never destroyed the ledgers in the vaults. Consequently, every account was in meticulous order in August, 1945, when the Allies reoccupied the Colony: a neat line had been drawn under each account and Japanese civil servants unwittingly lived and worked over swollen balances and interest-free overdrafts, while the Bank's customers endured the misery of captivity—a situation of supreme irony.

To put Hong Kong on an immediate war footing would have involved drastic and far reaching changes, if not economic chaos (the businessmen of the colony were very quick to point this out to Maltby when he tried to get a word in edgeways about the imminence of Japanese attack).

Fuel stores, power houses, docks and wharves would have to be demolished; shipping and lighters would have to be sunk; thousands of junks and sampans would have to be cleared from the harbour; vast quantities of food stocks and other vital necessities would have to be moved from the mainland to the island. In his despatch General Maltby states: 'It will be appreciated that to take such irrevocable and expensive steps . . . was impossible until it was definitely known that war with Japan was inevitable. The civil authorities felt that they were not in a position to put into full force all the numerous measures required during the preliminary or the precautionary period of the Civil Defence plan.' He might have added that he was convinced that war was inevitable, but was unable to convince anyone else of the fact. Whatever recriminations Maltby may have had afterwards, he was proved right.

The War Office were sympathetic but powerless to help. Maltby had to resign himself to the fact that no reinforcements would be forthcoming, owing to the demands of other theatres of war. Everything possible, said the War Office primly, must

36

be done to combat a *concrete* German enemy as opposed to a *hypothetical* Japanese one. Hong Kong, therefore, was out on a limb—a hostage to fortune.

The pre-war defences of Hong Kong, like the preparations for war, were on a limited scale and designed to deny the harbour to an enemy and not to retain the harbour for the use of our fleet—two antique destroyers and a few motor torpedo boats. This object, combined with the forces available, necessitated a plan to defend the Island of Hong Kong only. Such was the inertia and complacency of Hong Kong between the wars, that this plan was considered eminently satisfactory and no one ever got around to thinking up another one.

In any case, who was ever going to attack Hong Kong?

The arrival of the two Canadian battalions caused Maltby to make a swift change of plan (in the light of subsequent events, it may not have been an entirely wise plan but at least it represented positive action—something entirely new in the Colony).

Prior to the arrival of the Canadians, the 2/14 Punjabis had been given the task of operating on the mainland with the specific role of fighting delaying actions. The other three battalions—2nd Royal Scots, 5/7 Rajputs and 1st Middlesex—were to form the island defence, together with the Hong Kong Volunteer Defence Corps.

With the arrival of the Canadians, a hasty new plan was formed: 2nd Royal Scots, 2/14 Punjabis and 5/7 Rajputs were to be on the mainland; The Royal Rifles of Canada, the Winnipeg Grenadiers and 1st Middlesex were to be on the island. Thus, when the Japanese attack came, only two battalions—the Punjabis and the Middlesex—knew their roles. The Canadians did not have time to get to know anything, but they opined to a man that Hong Kong was one hell of a good assignment. . . .

Maltby found himself on the threshold of a full scale war with a list of material deficiencies that would have daunted Genghiz Khan.

The weaknesses of the air and naval forces precluded the possibility of any effective reconnaissance seawards or landwards: the land forces in Hong Kong were, so to speak, without eyes or ears. Maltby wrote without bitterness: 'Study of the past history of Japanese operations had led me to believe that they were past masters in combined operations . . . lack of distant seaward reconnaissance was a distinct handicap.' Unfortunately study of Japanese operations made by the majority of pre-war officers had been limited to the Russo-Japan war of 1904: the Japs had come on quite a bit since then. . . .

There was a grave paucity of anti-aircraft guns, both light and heavy: indeed, the existing anti-aircraft defences were so weak that they would be barely capable of resisting an imaginary attack by Hong Kong's own air forces.

There was no radar equipment. Admittedly a survey had been made in 1938 but 1938 was a year of peace and good will. Radar in 1938 was an amusing toy, like television in the same year: the light-hearted experts who embarked on this survey resembled suburban householders trying to keep up with the Jones's. . . .

There was so little transport that only one company from a battalion could be carried at once. There was a shortage of British drivers, but they were later reinforced by Chinese civilians. The latter were described by Maltby with admirable restraint as 'largely of unknown quantity': this classic piece of euphemistic understatement was sombrely confirmed when locally enlisted Chinese drivers not only deserted in large numbers, but took the additional precaution of immobilising their vehicles prior to departure.

The mortar—that devastating killing weapon which has contributed so much to victories on land—was in a particular category of misfortune. Every battalion had 3-inch mortars but there was no ammunition. Maltby, presumably in an effort to be kind, wrote: 'It was unfortunate that the equipment situation in other theatres of war had not permitted earlier despatch of the garrison's mortar ammunition.' It was unfortunate indeed: mortar ammunition did not arrive until November and then only seventy rounds per battalion, both for war and practice—approximately enough for five minutes' intensive bombardment. There was no time for practice and these precious bombs were fired for the first time in battle. They didn't last long.

The 2-inch mortar, the 3-inch mortar's equally vicious baby brother, fared worse: ammunition was not delivered until the battle was over a week old. It looked as if the infantryman would have to defend Hong Kong with machine guns, rifles, bayonets—and guts.

On December 5th three Japanese divisions, approximately 60,000 men, concentrated at To Kat, just eight miles from the frontier.

The Far East Combined Intelligence Bureau, who always had an answer to anything except a direct question, had the matter in hand and immediately burst into explanatory print. 'Visible Japanese preparations,' they declared severely, 'are more likely part of a general tightening up to concert pitch, rather than the final touches before plunging off the deep end.'

On December 6th the usual Saturday race meeting was held at Happy Valley racecourse. . . .

Saturday night in Hong Kong had followed the same pattern for so many years that it was unlikely that the threat of war would interfere with social life to any appreciable extent. As Major-General Ito Takeo briefed the commanders of his infantry regiments—Colonels Doi, Tanaka Ryosabura and Shoji Toshishige: three ruthless and determined men, all seasoned fighters against the Chinese—the British population briefed one another for the gargantuan parties that inevitably followed the race meeting.

Many lingered in the bars and private boxes on the race-course after the last race had been run: the same scene is enacted on racecourses the length and breadth of Great Britain.

"Old Moneyfeather's got a new jockey—swears he's going to take his trousers off to see if he's got a tail."

"Bloody animal never tried a yard."

"Well, what d'you expect? It's owned by that old robber San Yeh."

"Saw old Pin Yong going to the five hundred dollar window at the tote so I had to back the one he did."

"Boy! Same again!"

"That thing which won the third was chock full of dope."

"So was the jockey, if you ask me——"

"I didn't ask you, old boy. . . ."

"Well, there's no need to get shirty about it, old man. . . ."

"Oh, isn't there? You happen to be talking about my horse. If you're accusing me of doping my animals——"

"Put a sock in it, old man. Drink up and have another. . . ."

"BOY!"

The crowds thinned out at the racecourse bars until only a hard core of determined alcoholics remained to revile owners, horses, jockeys and the calculators of tote dividends.

Soon they were swarming into one another's houses and the cocktails circulated with desperate abandon. Tables were booked at the Parisian Grill, the 'Grips' (the universal name for the Hong Kong Hotel), the Repulse Bay and the Peninsula. Men made assignations with other men's wives; women made assignations with other women's husbands; men and women found out about these assignations and threatened immediate divorce proceedings; flying dhobis galloped in and out of flats and bungalows with newly starched and snowy white dinner jackets; young women lowered the necklines of their evening dresses and older women fought a cosmetic battle against the ravages of time; men drank too much, excused themselves, insulted each other, found they had no evening socks, mixed cocktails wearing nothing but bath towels, removed the bath towels and continued to drink in their underpants; ordered taxis, forgot they'd ordered them as another round of drinks materialised, cursed their servants and wondered who was going to pay for the dinner.

It was Saturday night in Hong Kong. . . .

In the Nathan Hotel, in Kowloon, the Other Ranks were, as a new generation would phrase it, having themselves a ball. Perspiring Chinese waiters struggled between the tables with trays of beer; hip-rolling tarts with no bust to speak of and dresses slit to mid-thigh roamed the bar in search of custom; a Scotsman insulted a Welshman and was invited to come outside; two sailors off a Swedish freighter danced with one another, thus annoying the hostesses who felt themselves slighted; a sergeant of the Royal Engineers fell out of a rickshaw; a private of the Royal Army Ordnance Corps threatened to punch a military policeman on the nose—and did.

It was, after all, Saturday night in Hong Kong. . . .

Sunday, December 7th, 1941, was like any other Sunday in the Far East: that is to say, it was given over to relaxation and pleasure. There was cricket, golf, yachting and swimming for the energetic; for the clubroom athletes there were dinners, cocktail parties and dancing. Sunday in Hong Kong had always been like that as, indeed, it was for every English man

40

and woman in the tropics. There seemed to be no particular reason why this Sunday should be any different.

In England on a Sunday morning, a private soldier, who had not been quick enough to think up an unorthodox religion, went on a Church of England parade. Men with Presbyterian, Roman Catholic, Moslem, Congregationalist, Agnostic or Jew on Page One of their paybooks smiled in a superior fashion and got out of camp before they could be caught for fatigue duty. As an alternative to Divine Service, he peeled mountains of potatoes or scrubbed the Sergeants' Mess, the cookhouse or the recreation room. After dinner he either went to bed or played pontoon. It was, of course, advisable to get well clear of the barracks on Sunday afternoons because predatory orderly corporals lay in wait for the unwary and conjured up mysterious chores, such as picking up match sticks, by some strange system of magic that was known only to ambitious NCOs.

In Hong Kong, however, Atkins either went on Church Parade or else had the whole day off. If his name did not appear on the church parade list, the whole sunlit and sybaritic Sabbath was his to do what he liked with. The whole of Hong Kong and Kowloon was his too, except for certain forbidden areas where dubious houses of entertainment were under constant surveillance by lynx-eyed military policemen.

This Sunday's church parade—the last to be held in Hong Kong for nearly four years—was a brave sight, with contingents from every unit in the Colony present. The Royal Scots were piped on their way; the brass band of the Middlesex played a stirring march. As the compulsory Christians in their heavy boots trooped into the Cathedral, their closely-cropped heads bared, everything seemed traditional and tranquil.

General Maltby read the first lesson, taken from the Book of Matthew, Chapter Eight. . . . 'For I am a man under authority, having soldiers under me: and I say to this man, Go, and he goeth; and to another, Come, and he cometh; and to my servant, Do this, and he doeth it. . . .'

Tell a British soldier to sing and he will do so, without bothering to reason why. As the first verse of 'Praise My Soul, The King of Heaven' blared forth from five hundred throats, a tense-faced staff officer called General Maltby outside.

The news he brought was disquieting enough. Forward observation posts of the 2/14 Punjabis reported the massing of

Japanese troops north of Fanling. Private (Fourth Class) Yashinoa, late of the Japanese Imperial Army and currently probationary dishwasher in the Nathan Hotel, had been proved an accurate prophet.

During the service, in twos and threes, senior officers left the Cathedral in response to urgent whispers from orderlies and despatch riders. Before the last contingent had formed up to march from the Cathedral, General Maltby had called an emergency conference of all unit commanders. The terms of reference of the conference were simple and categorical: every soldier, sailor, airman and member of the Hong Kong Volunteer Defence Corps would be in his battle station by five o'clock that evening.

The European civilian population spent that last Sunday morning in traditional fashion. The mid-morning drinking sessions were in full spate—indeed, many of them continued far into the afternoon because Sunday lunch in Hong Kong rarely put in an appearance before half-past two. In clubs, hotel bars and private houses the conversation was brisk and manly:

"They say there's a bit of a flap on."

"Well, what's new about that? We've been having flaps since 1932."

"Wonder if they'll call out the volunteers?"

"Your crowd's a bit late, isn't it, old boy? I've got my orders to report already."

"I'm only the Company Commander, old boy; no one ever tells me anything."

"The Japs'll never chance their arm."

"If there's one thing I can't stand, it's a Jap."

"Oh, I don't know, old boy; that hairdresser in the Grips is a damn' nice chap."

"And the barman in the Parisian Grill. Mixes a Martini better than François in the Dorchester."

"Boy! Same again. . . .!"

But every able-bodied European of the Hong Kong Volunteer Defence Corps was in his battle station by cocktail time that evening and felt a better man for it.

That evening Maltby toured his positions. He strolled among his men, talking cheerfully to anyone who caught his eye. They were full of confidence and knew nothing of his fears:

fears that his men were woefully ill-equipped and exposed.

Maltby was satisfied with what he saw: the Royal Scots were dour and unperturbed; the Middlesex were cheerful and ribald—unit bookmakers were laying odds against a Jap attack; the Punjabis and Rajputs were fatalistic and expressionless, confident in their British officers whom they would follow to hell and back if need be; the Canadians were brash and optimistic and declared forcibly that they could lick the pants off any goddam sonofabitch of a Jap who dared to set foot on the island; the Volunteers thought the whole performance was a damned nuisance but if any Jap had nerve enough to come and attack them they'd get a bloody nose: what beat them was how they would *dare*. . . .

Some generals, able strategists and staff officers, have no idea how to talk to soldiers. They talk bluffly and avuncularly to privates but only for the look of the thing and never listen to their replies. One famous general always said: 'Good, good, splendid!' in answer to any private soldier's remark. To a man who informed him that he was six months overdue for home leave, that his wife had left him for a soft drinks traveller and that his new boots were too tight, he intoned 'Good, good, splendid!' Another, finding that he had Gurkhas and Africans under his command, mugged up a few stock phrases in Gurkhali and Swahili but spoke Swahili to the Gurkhas and Gurkhali to the Africans.

Maltby had spent twenty-five of his twenty-nine years' service as a regimental officer and soldiers in all their moods were no mystery to him. The men of the Punjabis and Rajputs were not so very different from the Stalwart Jats of his own regiment—the 9th Jats—and he spoke Hindustani as effortlessly as English.

But once he has committed his forces, a commanding general is, of necessity, a lonely man with absolutely nothing to do. He carries an enormous burden and carries it alone. Maltby could only return to Flagstaff House that evening and wait: if the Japs were ready, then so was he. He could do no more for the present and at least there could be no outcry from amateur strategists in England that the Army in Hong Kong had been caught with its trousers down. . . .

General Maltby ate a first-class dinner, drank a rather larger whisky and soda than usual and went to bed.

43

CHAPTER THREE

A T A quarter to five on the morning of Monday, December 8th, 1941, Major Charles Boxer of the Lincolnshire Regiment, Senior Intelligence Staff Officer at Fortress Headquarters, twiddled the knob of the wireless set and tuned in to Radio Tokyo. At first he heard nothing but an untranslatable crackling noise.

Boxer was very far from being the conventional Regular Army officer. The unreflective and routine-ridden life of a peacetime infantry officer bored him inexpressibly; the ceremonial parades, the kit inspections, the half-hearted manoeuvres on Salisbury Plain that comprised the training for war of the minute professional army of the thirties; the obsolescent weapons, the imaginary attacking force, the theoretical anti-tank guns represented by green flags, the horsed cavalry charging in line, the clicking of rifle bolts by bored infantrymen whose blank ammunition had run out. To Boxer it all added up to a monstrous waste of time.

But Boxer had found another outlet for his restless brain. From a very early age he had been fascinated by all things Oriental. When he had applied for a course of studies in Oriental languages his Commanding Officer had regarded him with a mixture of amusement and distaste; in the CO's experience young officers applied for language courses for only two reasons: they were either a little mad or else wanted to land themselves a cushy billet as military attaché in one of the more exotic countries.

Boxer made his point, not without difficulty. But when he arrived in Hong Kong he had qualified as a first-class interpreter in Japanese. It was as well for the garrison that he did.

He twiddled the knob again and listened intently. The Japanese announcer gabbled inconsequently about the programmes for that evening: there would be dance music, political commentaries and cookery hints.

Suddenly a new voice made itself heard—a harsh and metallic voice, in crude contrast to the lisping intimacy of the announcer's. Boxer wiped the sweat from his face, although

44

the night was chilly. The second voice informed Japanese nationals throughout the world and Major Charles Boxer that Japan was at war with Great Britain and the United States of America. . . .

There were two camp beds in the office. The other one was occupied by Boxer's opposite number, Major 'Monkey' Giles of the Royal Marines, Senior Naval Intelligence Staff Officer. Giles, more phlegmatic than Boxer, had obeyed the order to sleep in the office with the habitual stoicism of his corps: a Royal Marine obeys orders and does what he's told.

A Marine also masters the art of making himself comfortable in any circumstances, and by 10.30 pm on Sunday night, Giles was cosily installed in his camp bed, reading a 'whodunit' novel by Agatha Christie.

Giles and Boxer were old friends, but Giles quickly noticed that Boxer was worried. When he had come to a point in his novel where all Miss Christie's ingenuity would be needed to extricate the hero from a morass of circumstantial evidence, he closed the book, lay back and composed himself for slumber. Just before he did so he looked across the room and saw Boxer, headphones at ears, crouching over the wireless set.

"Anything good on, Charles?" inquired Giles.

"Nothing that you'd want to hear," was the discouraging reply.

Giles yawned prodigiously and went to sleep.

At twelve minutes to five he was awakened by shaking. He sat up, Marine moustache distinctly out of true, and said: "What's up?"

Boxer stood over his bed. "Up, Marines, and at 'em!" quoth he, with a jocularity that he was far from feeling. "We're at war!"

"I know," said Giles sleepily. "With a chap called Hitler. Shocking type." He opened one baleful eye. "Have you woken me up just to tell me that?"

"We're at war with Japan," said Boxer. It was a phrase he was to repeat many times before breakfast.

Giles sat bolt upright and then subsided weakly on his pillow. "It's out of the question," he said petulantly. "I'm playing golf this afternoon. Anyhow, I haven't got a tin hat." But he went to war just the same. . . .

"We're at war with Japan. . . ." "We're at war with Japan. . . ." The news was received by sleepy duty officers the length and breadth of the island and on the mainland: by infantry, artillery, engineers, service corps, sailors, marines, volunteers. This was no practice scare—*this was it*. . . .

Second-Lieutenant Iain MacGregor's sleep was rudely interrupted by the clamorous ringing of the telephone at his bedside in Flagstaff House. As ADC to General Maltby, he was the first to receive the news from Boxer.

An ADC, of necessity, eats, drinks and sleeps in close proximity to his general. Wherever a general goes, an earnest and worried young officer is inevitably six paces in rear. He cloaks his worry with a look of almost permanent disdain. The general may want his map case, his shooting-stick, his hip flask, his sandwiches, a cigarette, an evening paper, a razor blade, a pencil, an aspirin, a motor car or an indigestion tablet: the ADC is there to provide it. An ADC, is a master of all the social graces. He has, inevitably, been to a good public school and nearly always hails from one of the more fashionable regiments.

Only the fortunes of war had turned Iain MacGregor, junior partner in the ancient wine and spirit firm MacGregor, Caldbeck and Co. Ltd., into an *aide de camp*. He had seen ADC's before—in Shanghai, Singapore and Hong Kong—and had felt nothing but sympathy for them. He had not, in fact, ever cherished any ambition to be a soldier at all. In common with other young businessmen in the Far East, he had regarded the Regular Army with a certain amused tolerance. He had, it is true, served an unexacting military apprenticeship in the Shanghai Light Horse before the war, but any resemblance between the SLH and the Regular Army was purely coincidental: indeed, the *irregularities* of the SLH were frequently the talk of the town.

On the strength of Certificate 'A' at Marlborough and his service in the Shanghai Light Horse, MacGregor was commissioned Second-Lieutenant in the 2nd Royal Scots at the outbreak of war. But the Chief Staff Officer at Fortress Headquarters, Brigadier Peffers, had other plans for him. The Brigadier knew, as did everyone in the Far East, about Mac-Gregor, Caldbeck Ltd. He knew that every rubber planter in Malaya, every tea planter in Assam and Ceylon, every merchant in Borneo, China, Java, India and the Philippines, relied on this ancient firm of 'wine shippers' for their alcohol—the staff of life of the Englishman in the East. MacGregor knew all about the right drink at the right time; he was no stranger to gargantuan dinner parties; he had social and business contacts with all the prominent businessmen on the island. Obviously, he was tailor-made for the job.

An ADC must know about all these things. The cocktails at Flagstaff House must always be just so; the wine must be of exactly the right temperature; the seating plan at dinner must be a masterpiece of social manipulation. He must know, for instance, that the wife of Air Vice-Marshal Hector Sopwith-Halifax is at loggerheads with the wife of the Chief Justice and must therefore be placed at opposite ends of the table; he must know that Brigadier Redvers-Gough must on no account sit next to anyone but an Englishwoman; he must know that Admiral Sir Denys Frobisher-Ramillies must have plain Plymouth gin and water instead of cocktails. He must make disarming conversation but never monopolise it. He must have a lighter that always works. He must invariably be beautifully dressed. He must exercise a formidable charm with the daughters of the hierarchy and will probably marry one of them if he's not careful (but he'll lose the job if he does).

MacGregor had been with his platoon of Scotsmen a bare fortnight when the blow struck: he would report to Flagstaff House immediately for duty as ADC to the General Officer Commanding. Protests were useless and MacGregor moved in.

It turned out better than MacGregor had expected: General Maltby was a soldier first and a socialite last; his wife was not with him (many a young ADC has had his military career permanently soured by a general's lady);[1] his personal tastes were frugal and undemanding. Maltby, indeed, was sympathetic from the start. "Someone's got to do the damned job," he said, "so we might as well put up with each other."

General Maltby, in expectation of swift and sudden Japanese aggression, had ordered that both brigade commanders should sleep at Flagstaff House.

Soon MacGregor was hammering on doors and rousing brigadiers, colonels and majors from their beds. To each he said: "We're at war with Japan."

By 6.30 am they were all assembled: Brigadier Cedric Wallis,

[1] This in no way applies to Mrs Maltby, who is a lady of infinite grace and kindness.

Commanding the Mainland Brigade; Brigadier John Lawson, Commanding the Canadian contingent; Brigadier Peffers, Chief Staff Officer; all the senior staff officers of Fortress Headquarters. None of them were either feeling or looking their best.

Maltby said: "Well, gentlemen, we can now safely assume that we are at war with Japan." He was not the type of man who enjoyed saying 'I told you so', but at that moment he almost wished that Air Chief Marshal Brooke-Popham and Lieutenant-General Grasett had been present. . . .

Another businessman, turned soldier, was rudely awakened by the telephone that morning. Lieutenant Ewan Graham, duty officer of the 1st Middlesex, had passed a peaceful and uneventful night—so far. At a quarter past five the telephone jangled persistently at his elbow. It was Fortress Headquarters and the message was brief and to the point: 'We're at war with Japan."

Graham was considerably older than the average subaltern in his battalion; indeed, he was older than most of the captains. The outbreak of war had found him, at the age of thirty-six, a director of a grain exporting firm in the City. He had felt vaguely annoyed that he had been too young to fight in the First World War; now it seemed that he was too old to fight in the second. He had surmounted that problem because a friend of his in the City had a girl friend whose uncle was at the War Office. He was speedily commissioned—almost too speedily, it seemed—second lieutenant in the Middlesex Regiment and sent to Hong Kong where the prospect of war could scarcely have been more remote. Graham, in common with many other officers and men of the Middlesex, had requested a home posting in order to get into the war before it finished.

As a businessman, Graham had always made a point of double-checking improbable telephone calls and their source. This, he considered, must be a leg-pull initiated by a staff officer suffering from insomnia.

Major Boxer had had no sleep at all; furthermore he had heard a Jap announce that Japan was at war with Great Britain and the United States.

"You heard what I said," he said irascibly. "We're at war with Japan. That's all."

Captain Christopher Man of the 1st Middlesex was just getting used to the idea that he was married. Just six months earlier, he had met Topsy Marr, a physiotherapist newly arrived from England, and they had fallen inextricably in love. He had proposed and to his delight and surprise had been accepted. There were, of course, a number of problems to be surmounted before they could marry. Not the least of these was the Commanding Officer, Lieutenant-Colonel 'Monkey' Stewart.

Man went to the Colonel and asked permission to marry, a request that was refused in the most uncompromising terms. In any case, continued Colonel Stewart, warming to his theme, Man was too young to get married (he was 26). In his (Stewart's) day no officer was permitted to marry until he was thirty and was regarded with considerable suspicion even then. It was absolutely out of the question and damned impertinence into the bargain. Be damned if he knew what some of these young officers were coming to. . . .

Man stuck soldierly to his guns. Just because there were no service wives in Hong Kong did not mean that a soldier could not marry if he found a girl willing to marry him. Also, he reminded his colonel, the unwritten rule that an officer may not marry under the age of thirty did not apply in time of war. In England marriage was in the air. Didn't the Colonel ever read the marriage column in *The Times*?

The Colonel, scenting insubordination, declared forcibly that he didn't give a hoot in hell about the marriage column in *The Times*, or any other blasted newspaper, and that this wasn't England. Man was not getting married and he might as well get used to the fact.

"You can't stop us, sir," said Man simply.

The Colonel's face assumed a purplish hue, but he knew he was beaten. Then his face relaxed into its rare and extraordinarily charming smile.

"Blast your bloody impertinence," he said. "Go and marry the girl and see that I'm asked to the wedding."

At 6 am Captain and Mrs Man were aroused, not by their Chinese houseboy with tea and thin slices of bread and butter, but by Corporal Jim Hughes of 'Z' Company, which Man commanded. 'Z' Company was not, technically, a combat command and had been formed as an emergency measure.

49

It comprised the less brilliant machine gunners from 'A', 'B', 'C' and 'D' Companies and what the British Army irreverently terms 'odds and sods': cooks, bandsmen, buglers, drummers, storemen, drivers, mess waiters and what the RSM, Sergeant-Major Challis, charitably described as 'deadbeats'. This polyglot force were later to find themselves engaged in some of the heaviest fighting of the campaign and acquitted themselves superbly.

Corporal Hughes contemplated the sleeping Captain and Mrs Man gravely for a moment and then saluted with a loud and positive stamp of his iron-clad heels. Hughes must be one of the very few soldiers in this or any other war who has been privileged to see his company commander in bed with his wife.

Man awoke with a start, sat up, blinked and said: "What the hell are you doing here, Corporal Hughes?"

In peacetime, during the battle and in subsequent captivity, Hughes had worn a peculiarly deadpan expression which had earned him the nickname of Buster Keaton. It did not slip, even on this bizarre occasion. "We're at war with Japan, sir," he announced, still stiffly at attention.

Man jumped out of bed and struggled into his clothes. He tried to think of something to say to his wife, but the presence of Corporal Hughes put an effective brake on any romantic exchange. Finally he said: "Put your tin hat on", and went to his company. He was not to see his wife again for three years and eight months. . . .

The war started badly for Wing-Commander 'Ginger' Sullivan, RAF. Sullivan was no stranger to war: he had joined the Royal Navy Air Service in 1917 and had been actively engaged on the Dover Patrol, on the North West Frontier of India and in Iraq.

In August, 1941 he was posted to the Far East, and before sailing for Singapore was granted an audience by the Air Ministry Far East Planning Staff, an organisation which seemed to be exceptionally well versed in the art of planning but knew nothing about the Far East. War in the Far East, they informed Sullivan with crushing *sang-froid*, was extremely unlikely, but of course one must be prepared for it. The present set-up in Hong Kong was a bit ropey, but all that would soon be changed: new and better machines would soon be on the way. It was soon apparent to Sullivan that Hong Kong stood low on the priority list for air power, as, indeed, it did for everything else. If someone had invented a new brand of corned beef, the men in Hong Kong would undoubtedly have been the last to get it.

Sullivan walked into a cold and cheerless Whitehall with a heavy heart. 'I did not,' he declares, 'sail for Hong Kong with high hopes but rather with the conviction that I was about to jump into the mire with both feet.'

In Singapore Sullivan met Air Chief Marshal Brooke-Popham—an interview, he says, which afforded him little comfort. Brooke-Popham told him the same as the Air Ministry Far East Planning Staff, backing this information with impressive statistics about strong representations made to Home Government for more and better aircraft. All heads in Singapore, records Sullivan with pardonable bitterness, were well and truly in the sand about the imminence of Japanese attack. However, the swimming pool at the Tanglin Club was as cool and inviting as ever, and the food at Raffles Hotel as superb and delectably served.

When he arrived in Hong Kong on December 1st to take command of the RAF Station at Kai Tak, Sullivan quickly understood the carefree references to more and better aircraft. The present outlook was scarcely encouraging, as the establishment of aircraft consisted of four Vickers Wildebeeste torpedo bombers and three Supermarine Walrus amphibians, all with a maximum speed of 100 mph—with, as Sullivan's predecessor, Group-Captain Horrey, was at pains to point out, a strong wind behind.

This did not amount to even a token defence force. A torpedo bomber sounds like a formidable weapon of war, but those in Hong Kong lacked one particularly essential item of equipment—torpedoes. . . .

It was possibly as well that no modern types of aircraft did arrive, because the airfield was not suited for the operation of modern machines; it was, however, just good enough for the three civilian aircraft used to evacuate those people lucky enough to obtain a seat.

The defence of the airfield against low-flying aircraft was practically non-existent, consisting of four obsolete machine-guns. 'Had I known this,' observes Sullivan without rancour, 'I would have made a point of taking my catapult with me.'

Everyone in Hong Kong at that time, from Sir Mark Young to the junior storeman in the dockyard, was making despairing representations for something (with scant hope of getting it) and Sullivan quickly got into the act. He was promised new aircraft, but he knew that the best he could hope for was a delay in the outbreak of the Pacific war until this happy state of affairs had materialised—'a hope,' he says, 'to which I did not wholeheartedly subscribe'; he was promised the services of a river gunboat to lie off the seawall, but it never appeared; he was promised more anti-aircraft guns, but never saw them; plans for the building of aircraft shelters in the hills behind the airfield were on paper (and no doubt still are).

Gradually the realisation dawned on Sullivan that his was a forgotten unit. By five minutes past eight on the morning of December 8th, 1941, it had ceased to be a unit at all.

William Lampard, a junior civilian armament supply officer in the Royal Navy's Dockyard, lived in a pleasant bachelor flat in Kowloon. At 7.20 am on the morning of December 8th he crossed to Hong Kong on the ferry and scanned the morning paper: the only reference to Japan was a small paragraph about Jap transports off Thailand.

On arrival at the Dockyard, Lampard was confronted by a sergeant of police wearing a steel helmet.

"Why are you wearing that?" he asked.

The policeman eyed him with tolerant condescension. "There's a war on," he explained.

"I know," said Lampard, "it's been running for a couple of years now."

"We are at war," repeated the police sergeant with an italicised effort of patience, "with Japan—as from this morning at a quarter to five."

Lampard's first reaction was one of frank disbelief. Like everyone else in Hong Kong, he had become used to 'flaps': false alarms which invariably fizzled out to nothing. As a second-lieutenant in the Dockyard Defence Corps he had received two hours' military instruction per week from a bored and condescending sergeant of Royal Marines. 'When you've lived on a smoking volcano for a few years,' records Lampard, 'you're not particularly impressed when someone observes that there are flames coming out of the top.'

Another dockyard official pointed skywards, in the direction

52

of Kai Tak aerodrome. "Look!" he exclaimed, "there are the fighters we've been waiting for all this time!"

They were fighters, but they weren't ours. Seconds later the first bombs fell on Kai Tak. . . .

There are few more delicious sensations than waking early in the morning with the full knowledge that you do not have to get up. If it happens to be Monday morning, the situation takes on an added piquancy.

Sister Sybil Spencer of the Colonial Nursing Service, attached to Kowloon Hospital, experienced this sensation on the morning of Monday, December 8th, 1941. Monday was her day off and the whole glorious, idle, sun-drenched day stretched pleasurably before her.

Her bed was on the verandah of the nurses' home and the sun shone full in her face. It was just three minutes to eight o'clock and between sleeping and waking she began to plan her day. First and foremost, at least another hour in bed was indicated. Then she would ring the bell and Ah Fong would bring her a cup of tea. A bath and a spun-out, leisurely breakfast would follow. She would sit over her second cup of coffee and smoke a cigarette. At about eleven——

The Japanese bombs rained down on Kai Tak aerodrome and Kowloon city. Before nine o'clock had struck Sybil Spencer was in her ward, receiving the first casualties. . . .

Private Christopher Hanshaw—twenty-two years old, five feet three inches tall, formerly butcher's errand boy, springer of mattresses and sprayer of bed posts in Cricklewood—went to war with a severe hangover. He was a motor cycle despatch rider at Fortress Headquarters and, unlike the men of the infantry battalions at their battle stations, had been allowed out on Sunday night. Sunday was the twenty-first birthday of his particular friend, Private Briggs, and it was soon apparent that Briggs was to attain his majority in no ordinary way.

The drinks in the Nathan Hotel were strong and many, and all the Chinese hostesses entered into the spirit of the thing. The party culminated in a rickshaw race which Hanshaw won by a distance. Hanshaw went to bed that night convinced of the might of the British Army in general and Private Christopher Hanshaw in particular.

At 6 am on Monday morning the Fortress Headquarters Sergeant-Major took a less exalted view. "Get on that motor bike of yours, Jehu," he ordered. *"Didn't anyone tell you there was a bloody war on, you 'orrible little man?"*

Suffering from a severe headache and a heaving stomach, Hanshaw kicked his motor cycle into a spluttering roar. All that day he tore round the island, narrowly escaping death from suicidal rickshaws, tram cars, taxis, shells and mortar bombs. He was delivering General Maltby's Order of the Day.

Maltby wrote this Order of the Day because, as General commanding a beleaguered outpost of Empire, it was the only thing left for him to do before the battle started in real earnest.

Maltby wrote: 'It is obvious to us all that the test for which we have been placed here will come in the near future. I expect each and every member of my force to stick it out unflinchingly and that my force will become a great example of high-hearted courage to all the rest of the Empire who are fighting to preserve truth, justice and liberty for the world.'

Maltby would be the first to admit that he is not skilled with words. For twenty-nine years he had followed a profession in which, to use a threadbare platitude, actions speak much louder. He read the Order of the Day again with critical self-derision: it was banal, it was cliché-ridden, it might have come out of a horse opera written in glorification of the Indian Wars in America. General Custer, thought Maltby grimly, might well have written something like this before he set out for the Little Big Horn.

For all that, it would have to do. . . .

The Japanese attack came at a good time for Signalman Eddie Hutchinson and Signalman 'Snickie' Allen: they were in the 'clink'.

Every soldier in Hong Kong knew that the detention barracks was a place to be avoided and only a very few professional hard cases went back to sample it a second time. This was the old-fashioned 'glasshouse', as opposed to the new fangled 'Military Corrective Establishment' where erring soldiers are psychoanalysed, educated to near-matriculation standard and see television twice a week. The detention barracks at Hong Kong was a place of trial but not of error: everything was done at the double; there were no Chinese boys to swab out the barrack rooms; webbing equipment had to be scrubbed to a dazzling whiteness by its owner; being shaved in bed was a relic of a happier past. This establishment may not have turned a bad soldier into a good one, but it went a long way towards discouraging the type of military crime which carries with it the dread word 'detention'.

First parade was normally at 6 am, but on the morning of December 8th, 1941, the prisoners found themselves unwillingly assembled at 5.30. Staff-Sergeant Webb looked them over with an eye from which all vestige of hope had long since departed. They were, thought Webb, as tasty a bunch as he had seen in seventeen years of soldiering: three signalmen, eight Royal Scots (invariably well represented in this establishment); four gunners; three sappers; four Middlesex; two RASC drivers. On the end of the line, looking as if butter would not melt in his mouth, was a cherubic-looking RAMC private, who in a fit of unaccountable rage, had taken a swing at his sergeant-major.

Their crimes embraced all the ramifications of military law: absence without leave—the proximity of pay night to Monday morning invariably produced a good haul in this sybaritic station; striking NCOs; insubordination; barrack-room pilfering; misdirected sexuality in out-of-bounds brothel areas; reluctance or downright refusal to obey orders. They were, in fact, a fair cross-section of military misdemeanour which has characterised the British Army over the centuries. As Kipling said:

> And I'm here in the clink for a thundering
> drink and blacking the corporal's eye. . . .

Of such men Wellington said with feeling; 'They may not frighten the French, but by God they frighten me!'

Staff-Sergeant Webb eyed his charges for a full minute before speaking. Then, in a voice like an articulated lorry in low gear, he said: "Pay attention, you lot! You've been granted a *pardon*"—he made it sound like a curse. "It's my personal belief that an 'orrible mistake has been made, but having regard to the fact that this 'ere country of ours is, with effect from 0445 hours, at war with Japan, it has been decided that soldiers undergoing detention will be returned to their units forthwith. It is my belief that perhaps this is a good thing after all because any Jap coming face to face with 'orrible looking

55

articles like you will indubitably run like 'ell." Staff-Sergeant paused to let his pronouncement sink in. There was a delighted grin on almost every face. "Any questions?"

There was a thoughtful silence. Then Signalman 'Snickie' Allen asked: "What happens if the Japs win, Staff?"

"In that unlikely event," said Staff-Sergeant Webb weightily, "you'll probably get about three years apiece. Squaad! DISMISS!"

Staff-Sergeant Webb little knew that he had spoken the almost exact truth. But in the terrible years to come these incorrigible rogues, commanding officers' headaches and taxpayers' dilemmas—starved, beaten, humiliated and worked nigh unto death—somehow stayed on top of the Japanese, and in some indefinable way seemed to be the victors rather than the vanquished.

Two British soldiers—Signalman Leslie Mildren and Signalman Charlie Hobson—well knew that the programme of entertainment that they had arranged for the night of December 7th, 1941, might well qualify them for admission to Staff-Sergeant Webb's establishment. This solemn thought did not perturb them greatly: they had been on cable laying duty all day on Saturday and Friday's pay was still intact.

The pay of a British soldier in Hong Kong rarely stayed intact for long and was inevitably spent on the three commodities that bachelor Atkins treasured most: drinking, women and gambling. Neither Mildren nor Hobson had romantic attachments of a pressing nature that Sunday night, but they were both thirsty (cable laying is thirsty work) and felt like a gamble, Mr Loo Sweng's gambling and drinking establishment at Lo Wu was just what the doctor had ordered. At 7.30 pm that Sunday evening Mildren and Hobson, suitably dressed in civilian clothes of a startling design, hired a 1935 Buick from Hua Hong's garage (repairs, self-drive hire and loans at low rate of interest) and headed for Loo Sweng's casino.

The beer at the casino was ice cold and the service was deft. Mildren and Hobson drank conscientiously and made serious inroads into their week's pay in two popular Chinese games of chance, Ma Jong and 'fan-tan'. At 3 am, Mildren records, three Japanese lieutenants bowed courteously, collected their winnings and left the casino. Hobson said to Mildren: "Just like a bloody Jap—picks up his winnings and ——s off when he's holding a bit."

At 5 am, just a quarter of an hour after Japan's declaration of war with Great Britain and the United States, Signalman Hobson coaxed Hua Hong's Buick into motion and they set off on the thirty-mile journey back to barracks. As dawn was breaking they exchanged a courteous 'good morning' with the sentry, preparatory to washing, shaving, changing into uniform and attending 7 am muster parade.

"Dunno what's good about this morning," said the sentry sourly. "Them —— Japs just started a —— war. . . ."

To two young women—Beryl Skipwith and Lena Longcraine, both heartbreakingly pretty and newly married—that black Monday morning seemed to sound the knell of hopeful young married life. Before their weddings they had both lived to the full the heady and sybaritic life of peacetime Hong Kong (the coming of war in 1939 had made little appreciable difference): the cocktail parties, the dinner-dances, the races, the water picnics.

They had both led sheltered lives as the daughters of prosperous and prominent citizens. They were, needless to say, pursued endlessly by long queues of officers from all three services and young businessmen, who laid constant siege to their affections. It was, of course, tremendous fun weighing them up: the good-looking, the amusing, the rich, the eligible; those with prospects and those without; those who could support one in the manner to which one was accustomed and those who merely said they could; those with honourable intentions (difficult to assess in the Far East) and the other sort.

These two young women never met in Hong Kong and have not met since. Today they are conventionally happily married matrons, living in conventional small country villages, with an aggregate of five children between them. They are both quite uncommonly good-looking, if not still heartbreakingly lovely (but their husbands think they are and that's good enough). They have the serenity which stems from terrible experiences in Hong Kong and the love of the young men they married in that blackest month of all black years, 1941. In 1960 their husbands go to work at nine and return home at six; they do not regard themselves as in any way unusual.

The men they married were poles apart: Captain Patrick

57

Skipwith, adjutant of the 8th Coast Artillery Regiment, was a serious-minded young regular officer, dedicated to the Army and gunnery. He had early impressed upon his bride that married life for a professional soldier was full of ups and downs: anxiety, heart-breaking separations, divided loyalties.

Skipwith had, in fact, wrestled fiercely with his conscience before getting married at all. He remembered the bigoted and liverish utterances of a senior officer before the war: young officers, declared this gentleman with bibulous intensity, should not get married. He should have only three thoughts in his mind: his horses, his men (they seemingly came second to horses) and his guns. If he had his way, soldiers shouldn't be *allowed* to marry. . . .

Desmond Longcraine, Far East representative of Gestetner Ltd (duplicators and office equipment), was cast in a very different mould, being neither serious minded nor dedicated. In the phraseology of the women's magazines, he was tall, dark and handsome; he sported the sort of sun tan that is only seen on the beaches at Miami, and had the sort of teeth that figure only in toothpaste ads. His black moustache, trimmed to the merest line, gave him the appearance of the almost perfect matinée idol. He was eyed speculatively by mothers of young girls; adoringly by the young girls themselves; hopefully by middle-aged women who should have known better. He had for a brief period been engaged to the daughter of the Governor of Arizona. It was generally agreed that no party was complete without him.

Desmond Longcraine had never felt himself seriously drawn to the military way of life, but Sunday night found him in the uniform of the Hong Kong Volunteer Defence Corps. The uniform was of the hit or miss variety, having been issued by a harassed quartermaster with little appreciation of the ramifications of accurate tailoring: it was at first sight difficult to discern if the trousers were short longs or long shorts (Longcraine is still in doubt about this); the jacket had been designed for a man with a fifty-inch chest; the cap, universally known as a 'fore and aft', but more universally associated with an essential piece of feminine anatomy, sat straight and defiantly on his head.

"Darling, you *do* look nice," said Lena Longcraine with all the sincerity of the very newly-wed wife.

"Yes, don't I?" said her husband. "Every inch a civilian."

Skipwith departed to the orderly room of his regiment and found himself caught up in the toils of artillery mobilisation. At 8 am on the morning of December 8th his telephone started to ring and rang continuously all that day as adjutants' telephones always do. Driver Desmond Longcraine, half-heartedly digging a trench, looked up and saw three aircraft. Assuming that they were friendly, he paused to light a clandestine cigarette. When they dropped three bombs in uncomfortably close proximity he dug with newly-found enthusiasm. . . .

Their wives had both joined the Auxiliary Nursing Service; if they had not they would have been evacuated with all the other families in June, 1940.

Before the Japanese attack the nursing service had been fun in an undemanding sort of way: about four hours in every week were spent learning bandaging, splinting, the vagaries of the thermometer, the correct keeping of temperature charts and the application of bed pans. It was a form of war work that might well have earned the very proper contempt of the sweating handmaidens of Mars in England: landgirls, factory workers, fire service telephonists, ATS drivers, WRNS boat crews and WAAF plotters in bomber stations, but one could hardly be expected to take the war seriously in Hong Kong—had not the Air Chief Marshal Sir Robert Brooke-Popham himself said that war in the Far East was a remote contingency?

On Monday morning the two girls reported themselves to their respective hospitals. Severe-looking matrons regarded their make-up and lacquered nails with ill-concealed disapproval and told them pointedly that the time for *playing* at nursing was past.

And then suddenly nursing wasn't amusing any longer. . . .

There were English civilians—conventional Far East businessmen—who found themselves hurled into the maelstrom of war that morning. For them the abandonment of comfortable and well-appointed bungalows and flats; the swift transition from well-cut Palm Beach suits to tropical uniforms that fitted where they touched.

Geal Humphries, cashier of the Hong Kong and Shanghai Bank and (*honoris causa*) Bombardier, Hong Kong Volunteer Defence Corps, told an incredulous chief accountant that war had been declared and hurried to his post with 5th Anti-Aircraft Battery; Eric Bryden, chartered accountant of the old established firm of Low, Bingham and Matthews, shovelled papers dealing with depreciation, tax rebate, profit, loss and sinking funds into an office drawer and departed hotfoot to No 2 (Scottish) Company, Hong Kong Volunteer Defence Corps.

Robert Geer, of the insurance division of Jardine, Matheson and Co gazed out of his bungalow window and observed that it was a beautiful morning. At ten minutes to eight he had a leisurely shower and started to shave. At exactly eight o'clock he heard a series of explosions which caused him to sink his razor deep into his upper lip. As Geer wryly phrased it, he shed blood in the defence of Hong Kong very early in the proceedings.

The night before Geer and his friend, Stanley Cooke of Gilman and Co. Ltd., had been on the commonplace Englishman's night out in Hong Kong: drinks at the club, a cinema, more drinks at the Hong Kong Hotel, still more drinks in someone's house, dinner at the Parisian Grill and more drinks at somebody else's house. They had returned to their respective houses and taken their uniforms out of their wardrobes, fervently hoping that they would not have to put them on.

Clutching cotton wool to his upper lip, Geer telephoned Cooke's house. A Chinese boy announced, "Mr Cooke in bath."

"Well, get him out of it," ordered Geer.

"Stanley," said Geer, when Cooke came on the line, "what the hell was that shattering noise?"

"Search me, old boy," said Cooke. "I'll just have a look out of the window." Cooke's house commanded a view of the harbour and Kai Tak airfield.

Cooke came back on the line. "Obviously all is not well, Bob," he announced in measured tones, "Kai Tak has just gone up in smoke."

Twenty minutes later found 2nd Lieutenants Geer and Cooke reporting to the Company Commander of No 4 (Chinese) Company, Captain Keith Valentine of Dodwell and Co Ltd.

"Your finest hour has come," said Valentine tersely. "We're at war with Japan." He looked at his two platoon commanders indulgently. "Why should Hong Kong tremble!"

"I had a distinct feeling," remarked Cooke as he went off in search of his platoon, "that this was going to be a *particularly* unpleasant Monday morning. . . ."

It seemed that nothing so sordid as war could ever invade the sanctity of the Parisian Grill. Anyone who has been to Hong Kong knows the PG: nowhere in the Far East (or indeed in the entire world) are the cocktails so delectably iced; the wines at so exactly the right temperature; the steaks so exquisitely tender, thick and juicy; the Chinese dishes so mouth-wateringly piquant; the vegetables so joyous to the eye and palate; the service so deft. This is a gastronomic paradise; the chef is a priest of gluttony.

Since 1937 the Parisian Grill had been secure and ever-lasting. But on the morning of December 8th the proprietor, Emil Landau, knew where his duty lay: with the 1st Battery, Hong Kong Volunteer Defence Corps at Cape D'Aguilar. He exchanged the sharkskin suit, hand-made shirt and shoes, which became him like a faultless uniform, for ill-fitting khaki drill, puttees and heavy ammunition boots. The incon-gruity of the occasion was thrown into sharp relief when he placed a steel helmet on his sleek, black hair. To his wife, Russian-born Rose Landau, he said: "Remember that what-ever happens you must keep up the standard of the Parisian Grill for as long as humanly possible."

Rose Landau did just that. The Landaus were to know heart-breaking separation, fear, despair and torture before the Parisian Grill was to re-open in 1945. In 1960 they are still there and the food, drink, service and décor are as im-peccable as ever. . . .

At least two soldiers evinced no surprise at the Japanese attack. One of them was Major-General Maltby, who had seen it coming from his first day in Hong Kong. The other was Sergeant (the 'Onourable 'Orrible) Marable of the 1st Middlesex.

In 1938 Marable had been an unwilling member of the Guard of Honour supplied three years earlier by the 1st Middlesex to greet Major-General Tanaka, then Japanese Commander of Land Forces in South China. Marable had paraded in what the Army calls red-hot drill order: he could have shaved in the toe-caps of his boots; his hair was cut

61

almost to the bone; his brasses shone with a dazzling brilliance; he had shaved so conscientiously that he subsequently came out in a rash; he was the embodiment of military perfection— all for a —— Jap.

"I could see it coming then," confided Marable darkly to Corporal Goddard; "that there Tar-nackers 'ad a dead nasty look in 'is eye. . . ."

So Hong Kong went to war. . . .

CHAPTER FOUR

AT 7.50 AM on Monday, December 8th, 1941, Hong Kong was looking its best. The sun shone brightly out of a beautiful, cloudless, azure blue sky.

At precisely 8 am 36 Japanese fighters hurtled out of the sky. They attacked down to sixty feet and, contrary to the optimistic assessment of Jap air power by the Far East Intelligence Bureau, showed a high standard of low-level bombing. By 8.5 am Hong Kong's entire air force—three obsolete torpedo bombers and two antiquated amphibians—had been destroyed. Of his air force Maltby wrote ruefully in his despatch: 'The aircraft were no match for enemy fighters and I gave orders that they were not to be employed unless the opportunity occurred, either at first light or at dusk, for a torpedo attack on an enemy capital ship or a large cruiser. In any case, all were put out of action in the first raid made by the enemy. . . .'

Japanese air supremacy in Hong Kong had been gained in five minutes.

Flushed with success, the Japs then rained leaflets all over the Colony. These were crude and childish in design and caused nothing but amusement to the soldiers who read them. Most of them depicted bloated pictures of John Bull and Uncle Sam trampling on cowering natives. Apparently they were directed principally at the Indian troops, but both Lt-Colonels Kidd and Cadogan-Rawlinson, commanding officers of the Punjabis and Rajputs respectively, reported that their men remained stoically unimpressed by this method of warfare. Japan's department of psychological warfare failed miserably from the start.

The air assault on Kai Tak marked the beginning of seventeen days of alternate elation and despair: heartening success and crippling failure; confidence and apprehension; complacency and defeatism; firm defence and disorderly rout.

It was inevitable that the first Japanese thrust should be directed at the brigade commanded by Brigadier Cedric

Wallis, consisting of the 2nd Royal Scots, the 2/14 Punjabis and the 5/7 Rajputs.

Wallis had been elevated to the rank of brigadier by the fortunes of war. His predecessor had left for the United Kingdom and as senior commanding officer the choice of Wallis was an automatic one. Wallis must have viewed his promotion with mixed feelings; he had relinquished command of the 5/7 Rajputs, after nearly thirty years' service with the regiment, to take over a brigade at short notice.

Few brigadiers can have been introduced to high command with such an apparently impossible task as the one that confronted Wallis. He was responsible for a defence line that stretched for ten and a half miles. This line was universally known as the 'Gindrinkers' Line' because its extreme left was in the famous Gindrinkers Bay, named after the fabulous water picnics which took place there in peacetime. These were sumptuous affairs indeed and the amount of gin consumed was invariably prodigious. But there was no time for gin drinking here in December 1941.

The defence of the Gindrinkers' Line would have been a formidable task for two infantry divisions: Wallis was charged with holding up the initial Japanese advance with one brigade, and a sadly understrength brigade at that.

The plan to hold the Gindrinkers' Line had been originally outlined in 1937, but it had never been practised because troops had never been available in sufficient numbers. It seems barely credible that such a plan should be made at all when it was known that it could never be implemented. It was about as feasible as planning to hold the approach to London with forces strung across Ascot racecourse.

Wallis, therefore, had to do the best he could with the meagre forces—barely 2000 men—at his disposal. A considerable amount of manual labour had to be done on the Gindrinkers' Line because it was still in its partially completed form of four years previously. It seems that, in the spacious year of 1937, no one paused to consider the impracticability of defending ten and a half miles of mountainous country with one battalion of rather less than one thousand men (the peacetime garrison consisted of four battalions and of these only one was located on the mainland). But 1937 was a year of make-believe; it was also Coronation Year and no one could be expected to take the preparation of defences too seriously.

Certain military cynics in Hong Kong contended that the idea of the Gindrinkers' Line was only thought up in the first place to give the Army something to do.

In 1941 jokes about the impregnability of the Maginot Line were only just funny, and Wallis realised that feverish work was required to get the line ready at all, let alone impregnable. The urgent necessity for speed called for this work to be done at the height of the malarial season and the hospitals were soon overflowing. As a result of this crippling disease, the Royal Scots were reduced from a strength of 711 to 600. In Hong Kong jokes about reinforcements had ceased to be funny at all. . . .

When these three battalions finally occupied their battle positions, it was immediately plain to Wallis that his force was pathetically thin on the ground. The biblical significance of the situation was not lost on Wallis. The trouble was that it seemed likely that Goliath and not David would be carrying the catapult. . . .

To one company of this pint-sized force fell the most hazardous task of all.

A soldier more imaginative and highly strung than Major George Gray, commanding 'C' Company of the 2/14 Punjabis, might have been worried about his assignment. But a surfeit of imagination and undue sensitivity would have been grave hindrances in the past twenty-nine years of Gray's army service.

At the tender age of sixteen he had enlisted as a trooper in the Sussex Yeomanry; he celebrated his nineteenth birthday as a newly gazetted second-lieutenant at Gallipoli, his twenty-first with Allenby's force in Egypt. The Punjab riots of 1918, the Third Afghan War in 1919 and seventeen years of intermittent skirmishing on India's North West Frontier had made him immune to any surprise that the Army or fate might spring upon him.

Gray was forty-five, powerfully built and tough. He loved the Army, although not blindly or unreasonably: his feelings for it could best be likened to the patient and affectionate feelings of a man for a nagging shrew of a wife; more specifically he loved his Indian Regiment of up-country stalwarts, whose outlook on life was not so very different from his own. Gray was still a major at forty-five because promotion in the pre-war Army was mortifyingly slow and subalterns with eighteen years' service were by no means rare; also, he was not Staff-trained and admission to the higher ranks in peacetime necessitated an extended education at Camberley, culminating in the privilege of adding to one's name the letters PSC (Passed Staff College, but referred to by the irreverent as Practically Senior to Christ).

Gray's orders were categorical: he was to maintain observation posts on the frontier and report Japanese troop movements; he was to cover the demolition of all bridges, thus denying their use to the enemy; he was to withdraw in an orderly fashion and fight delaying actions when necessary. When Gray asked how he was to know when a delaying action was necessary, he was told by a severe-looking staff officer that he must use his discretion. He was not, however, to become involved in pitched battle which might result in unnecessary casualties.

Gray went back to his mixed company of Punjabi Mussulmans and Pathans in a thoughtful frame of mind. His orders had been cloaked in the usual military ambiguity to which he was no stranger. The term 'orderly withdrawal' was a difficult one to define; but in the long run it could only mean retreat. To fight a delaying action meant that you had to withdraw, inflict casualties on the enemy—but have none inflicted on your own force. Gray had heard a story about a young officer in the 1914–18 war who had 'withdrawn' too precipitately, only to find himself facing a court-martial charge for 'shamefully abandoning his post in time of war'. It looked like being one of those jobs when the man on the spot was wrong, whatever he did. . . .

Gray passed on his orders to the four Indian Viceroy's Commissioned Officers who were his platoon commanders: four magnificent men whose service totalled over a century and who amply substantiated the widely spoken theory that the VCO was the backbone of the old Indian Army. Two were Punjabi Mussulmans, the other two Pathans. All four had served with Major Gray *Sahib* for many years and knew, unquestioningly, that what he said and did must be right.

To command successfully an Indian Army company—be it Gurkha, Punjabi, Pathan, Mahratta, Sikh, Baluchi, Dogra or what will you—the sahib in command is always right. British soldiers can disagree with their officers in a variety of ways, ranging from argumentative discussion to dumb insolence, but the Indian never did. He would charge, defend his position to the last man, advance, retreat, dig-in—and die, if the Sahib said: '*Hukm hai*' (it is an order).

The Senior VCO (Viceroy's Commissioned Officer) of the Company, Subedar Shah Mohamed—thirty years a soldier, straight as a ramrod, a fierce and magnificently moustached disciplinarian—listened impassively to Gray's orders. Personally, he disliked the idea of covering sappers—good enough men in their way and clever technicians, but scarcely soldiers. A Punjab regiment should always be in the forefront of the fighting instead of wet-nursing destroyers of bridges. He also disliked the word withdrawal which he associated with retreating, a manoeuvre abhorrent to Punjabi regiments in general and to Subedar Shah Mohamed in particular. Retreating, in Shah Mahomed's opinion, was another word the senior sahibs used for running away.

Shah Mahomed, privileged by virtue of twenty years' friendship with Gray, ventured first a question and then an opinion.

"Are we not then to stand and fight the Japanese *soors*[1], Huzoor[2]?" he asked.

"Probably we will fight them," replied Gray. "But our first job is to observe and report; our second to protect the engineers while they blow the bridges; the third to *delay* the enemy."

"It is no job for a Punjab regiment to protect men who blow up bridges, Huzoor," complained the Subedar. "That is the sort of work to be done by the ******s." (He named a down-country Indian regiment, never famous for its martial qualities.)

"Nevertheless, Subedar Sahib, those are my orders—and yours too," said Gray. Shah Mahomed saluted and marched away, fierce disapproval in every crashing step of his ammunition boots.

To understand the Subedar's feelings, it is necessary to know something of the men under Gray's command: splendid physical specimens of Indian manhood from the plains of the Punjab and the rugged hills that divide India from Afghanistan; born fighting men, unimaginative, ruthless

[1]The standard Indian Army term of abuse. Literal translation: 'Pigs'.
[2]Sahib; master; literally: presence.

and brave; hard of head and sinew; faithful in life and loyal unto death. . . .[1]

On December 5th, Gray marched his company to the village of Fanling, where he established company headquarters. Observation posts were set up in the neighbouring hills and it was soon apparent that the enemy were massing in considerable force. Demolition parties of Royal Engineers had already placed charges on all bridges to the north and east of Fanling. Infantrymen and Sappers waited for what now seemed inevitable.

At 1 am on the morning of December 8th, Major Gray, having satisfied himself that all sentries were alert and all weapons sited to do the maximum damage to an advancing enemy, went to bed. At ten minutes to five the field telephone by his camp bed rang insistently. It was Lt-Col L. Newnham, GSOI[2] at Fortress Headquarters, and the text of the message was simple: 'Britain and Japan are at war.' Gray dressed by the simple expedient of putting on his steel helmet: having lain down fully clothed, there was nothing else to put on.

Gray went straight to Major John Bottomley, officer in charge of the detachment of Royal Engineers responsible for the demolition of the bridges. "Time to start the firework show, John," he said. "We're at war with Japan."

Subedar Shah Mahomed changed his opinion of the sappers in the ensuing two hours, for theirs was hard and dangerous work. Two bridges at Lowu were destroyed by a party commanded by Lieutenant I. B. Tamworth, in full view of the enemy and under heavy sniper fire. Infantrymen tend to forget the contributions made by supporting arms, but even Shah Mahomed had to admit that these Engineers displayed cold-blooded courage of the highest order.

When the explosions from the bridges had died down, an eerie and uncanny silence descended over the whole area. 'There was complete silence,' records Gray, 'and nothing happened until about 7.30 am when it was reported to me from an observation post that several thousand Japs were pouring over the frontier on my right flank. This proved to be a pardonable Muslim exaggeration, but it was clear to me that at

[1] In captivity the Japanese subjected many Indian prisoners to appalling tortures and indignities in an effort to make them turn against their British officers, but to no avail whatsoever.
[2] General Staff Officer, 1st Grade.

least two battalions of Japs were after me.' Some indication that this was indeed total war was provided by the appearance of large numbers of enemy planes on their way to Hong Kong.

Gray's men had yet to meet the enemy, a state of affairs which annoyed Subedar Shah Mahomed considerably. Gray halted his men in the village of Tai Po and looked northwards towards the hills. Immediately to Gray's front was a track, running obliquely down the hillside like a long scar.

"They will come down that track, Subedar Sahib," said Gray to Shah Mahomed. "We will give them something to remember us by."

Gray positioned his men in Tai Po market, normally boisterous and bustling with Chinese commercial exuberance, but now totally deserted. Every light machine gun and rifle pointed at the track. The trigger finger of every man itched almost unbearably as they waited. Reservists, all thoughts of carefree civilian life forgotten, cuddled their cheeks into their rifle butts; young and unseasoned soldiers strove to control the trembling of their hands and the fluttering of their hearts.

A whole battalion of Japanese marched down that track, followed by a battery of artillery with pack mules. They marched in column of route, without making any attempt to take cover—'for all the world,' reported Gray, 'as if they were making a triumphal march through London.'

"When will we open fire, Subedar Sahib?" inquired a young Mussulman in company headquarters.

"When the Major Sahib gives the order, *bewocouf*[1]," snapped the Subedar, although if the truth be known, his trigger finger itched as persistently as anyone's.

At three hundred yards Gray shouted with the full force of his lungs: "FIRE!"

It was as if an ants' nest had been stirred up. Bren gunners fired in long bursts, as fast as new magazines could be placed on the guns. Riflemen worked their bolts and pressed fresh clips into their magazines as fast as their hands could fly to their pouches. For a full two minutes Gray's men poured a murderously accurate fire into the screaming, squirming, struggling mass of Japanese. The mules took fright and bolted into the middle distance. The surviving Japs disappeared precipitately over the brow of the hill.

[1]The standard Hindustani translation of 'bloody fool'.

A great roar from a hundred Indian throats echoed round the hills—a blend of Punjabi Mussulman and Pathan war cries is as frightening a sound as any man can hope to hear. Gray, normally a somewhat taciturn man of few words, found himself yelling 'Shabash!'[1] over and over again. He calculated that the Japanese must have suffered upwards of one hundred casualties and not one of his men had received so much as a scratch. Subedar Shah Mahomed, usually sparing with his praise, smote the man nearest to him with such congratulatory force upon the back that he fell down, partially winded. "Shall we let them come again or fix bayonets and charge, Huzoor?" he asked.

Gray thought for a few seconds. He had covered the successful carrying out of the demolitions; he had fought a delaying action in its fullest meaning. Now all that was required of him was an orderly withdrawal to the Gindrinkers' Line. . . .

"Neither, Subedar Sahib," he said regretfully. "We're getting out of here."

But as he spoke another burst of firing came from the left flank. . . .

Jemadar Khan Sherin, commander of the Afridi Platoon had troubles of his own. His platoon had been posted wide to the left flank in the hills to the left of Tai Po.

The Afridi is naturally cruel and unscrupulous by nature, but probably as good a fighting man as any in the world. The Afridi is tough and cruel because he has to be to survive. The land he half heartedly tills is unproductive and the soil enough to break the strongest heart. From an early age the Afridi tribesman learns that armed raids on other more prosperous farming communities are more amusing and profitable than the cultivation of his own land. For the Afridi is a fighter first and farming comes a bad second to war in his dangerous calculations: fighting is a sport to the Pathan, just as football is to the Englishman. If no war offers itself, he could always keep his hand in with a blood feud, a vengeance killing or a vendetta. Sniping at British Army columns was, of course, an ever available amusement.

With the coming of a real war, many Pathans—Afridis, Mahsuds and Khattaks—came South to join the 10th Baluchis, one of the six Punjab Regiments, the 12th Frontier Force

[1] Well done!

Regiment and the 13th Frontier Force Rifles. The fact that their fathers, brothers, brothers-in-law, uncles and cousins continued to snipe at British columns worried them not at all. Somewhat surprisingly, the Pathan reacted remarkably well to army discipline.

Jemadar Khan Sherin had fought in another world war and in three frontier campaigns. War, he felt, could hold no more surprises for him. But what he saw that morning caused him to blink, swear an oath of such frightfulness that he could not repeat it even to himself, and peer anxiously through his field glasses. Something like a hundred Japanese were advancing in extended formation towards his position. The forward elements prodded Chinese women in front of them at the point of their bayonets.

Thinking that his eyes might be deceiving him, Khan Sherin handed the glasses to his platoon havildar[1], Youssuf Khan, a scarred veteran with an alarming squint. Youssuf Khan, too, stared unbelievingly, and then exclaimed: "By Allah! The infidel yellow pigs are driving women before them! Will we kill them too, Jemadar Sahib?"

Khan Sherin, like all his countrymen, was not over burdened with scruples. An Afridi is not over particular who or what he kills, be it on two legs or four. But the Major Sahib was more humane and might object to his opening fire on women, although he personally had no strong thoughts about it—if ordered to by an officer, Khan Sherin would have shot his own grandmother without suffering excessive remorse.

His platoon position was connected to company headquarters by field telephone. When Gray came on the line, Khan Sherin said: "Huzoor, there are enemy advancing on my front and they are pushing women before them. What will I do?"

"Give 'em hell," came the succinct reply from Gray. "When you've stopped their advance, join the rest of the company jaldi"[2].

"Will I also kill the women, huzoor?"

"It's their bad luck. Now, get on with it."

Havildar Youssuf Khan squinted down his sights and expressed a colourful alternative use for the women.

Jemadar Khan Sherin, always an admirer of his company

[1]Sergeant.
[2]Quickly.

71

commander but now his life-long friend, barked the order: "FIRE . . . !"

It was first blood to the defenders. Although the action of Gray's men only merited three lines in the Intelligence Summary, they had scored a notable victory.

That evening the sepoys of 'C' Company, 2/14 Punjabis squatted round their camp fires and fought the battle over again:

"We killed a thousand of them. . . ."

"Don't exaggerate, Shere Khan—two hundred perhaps."

"I personally slew sixteen."

"What manner of *soor* are these that they drive women before them?"

"The Japs will remember 'C' Company for a long time."

"*Wah, Wah!* How the Major *Sahib* yelled!"

But disaster, irretrievable and far reaching, was only twenty-four hours ahead. . . .

Over the centuries soldiers have foregathered and talked of war and the stories have lost nothing in the telling, provided that the beer has been kept flowing freely. Mostly it is good and stimulating talk of gallant deeds. But inevitably there is something on the debit side which is one particular regiment's responsibility.

Thus, in North America the Black Watch fought magnificently but the Chepstow Fusiliers spent their time raping Red Indian women; at Lucknow, in the Indian Mutiny, the Duke of Cornwall's Light Infantry held the residency, but the Putney Grenadiers lay supine in their billets, drunk on looted rum; the East Surreys stood firm at Suakin against five thousand fuzzy-wuzzies, but the Royal Rutlands fled in panic at the first assault; the Devons captured Wagon Hill, but only after the Walthamstow Sharpshooters had refused to attack it; the Lancashire Fusiliers stormed ashore at Gallipoli, and won seven VCs before breakfast, but the Duke of Reading's Own refused to leave the beaches; the Argyll and Sutherland Highlanders marched across the Johore Causeway, 90 strong, having fought their way down Malaya, but the West Wittering Rifles legged it to Singapore without firing a shot—and so on and so forth, *ad nauseam*.

It was a tragedy that the hasty withdrawal from the mainland must be placed fairly and squarely at the door of the

Royal Scots. The Royal Scots—the First Regiment of Foot—
'Pontius Pilate's Bodyguard'—had a lot to answer for in the
initial fighting. True, they reformed later and fought gallantly
on the Island. But their early efforts added nothing to the
proud fighting record of Britain's oldest infantry regiment.
They became known to the Middlesex as, not the First of
Foot, but the Fleet of Foot. That insult has been wiped out in
blood since: at Anzio, Kohima, on the Normandy beaches and
at the Rhine crossing. But soldiers are slow to forget and there
are Middlesex men still who use that shameful appellation.

On the night of December 9/10th, a platoon of 'A' Company
of the Royal Scots held the position known as the Shingmun
Redoubt. It consisted of five pill-boxes linked by fire trenches
and tunnels surrounded by barbed wire and covered some
twelve acres of rocky hillside. It was, according to Lieutenant
Norman Brownlow, the assistant adjutant of the battalion, 'a
swine of a position to hold': the pillboxes and fire trenches,
sited in the piping days of peace, were not designed in such a
way that close quarter fire could be brought to bear from them.
An all-out Japanese attack took the Scots by surprise and they
were overrun, falling back in disorder and confusion.

This platoon was commanded by Lieutenant 'Potato'
Jones, a social lion whose junketings in the Hong Kong Hotel,
prior to the Japanese attack were legendary. But 'Potato'
Jones was not the only British officer like that: there was also
the Colonel who, only a few days before December 8th, issued
a blistering reprimand to Maurice, the head waiter of the
Hong Kong Hotel, because the temperature of the champagne
was not to his liking but remained steadfastly unmoved when
he discovered that his men were woefully short of entrenching
tools and hand grenades.

In overall command of the Royal Scots forward position was
the second-in-command of the battalion, Major Stanford
Burn. In a campaign in which personal tragedies were to become commonplace and everyday events, Major Burn's was in
a special category of misfortune.

Major Burn was a regular officer, Sandhurst trained and of
most exemplary character. Nothing, however, in his seventeen
years of well ordered, uneventful and expensive service had
prepared him for the terrible events of that night. The Japanese
attack—carried out by fanatical and hardy soldiers wearing
rubber-soled shoes—followed tactics about which Major Burn

(and, let it be freely admitted, the rest of the British Army) knew nothing whatsoever. They had learned about defended localities; set-piece attacks; reconnaissances in force; the advance to contact; the strategic withdrawal and a host of other military manoeuvres. But there was nothing in any textbook that covered this first overwhelming and terrifying assault.

Major Burn, gallant, hidebound and totally untutored in Japanese methods of warfare, was powerless to stem the tide. Later, with great bravery, he tried to find the solution to the problems which beset him. He eventually succumbed to a bullet from his own revolver and, by God's grace, found the solution to everything.

Lieutenant-Colonel G. R. Kidd, Commanding Officer of the 2/14 Punjabis saw an opportunity for his battalion to further enhance their early glory and suggested an immediate counter-attack on the Redoubt. This was ruled out by Brigadier Wallis on the grounds that the ground was rugged and precipitous and the enemy on the Redoubt probably far superior numerically to any force we could bring against them without seriously weakening other parts of the line.

Eventually it was decided that any attempt to recapture the Shingmun Redoubt was out of the question—Brigadier Wallis, as a subaltern in the Kaiser War, had been thrown into useless and costly attacks himself by generals ensconced in well appointed chateaux far behind the line. He therefore decided to cut his losses by withdrawing 'B' and 'C' Companies of the Royal Scots from their present perilously exposed positions.

But there was worse to come for the Royal Scots. In the early hours of the 11th December Japanese troops began to feel their way forward to the Royal Scots' new position on Golden Hill. The Japs were highly trained, fanatically brave and extremely difficult to detect. Their uniform, consisting of quilted material with cross stitching, was adapted to the insertion of twigs and grass, thus blending perfectly with the surroundings. As one Scot ruefully put it: 'You couldn't see a Jap until he was on the end of your bayonet.'

The attack came as dawn was breaking—a favourite Japanese time. An invariable Japanese tactic throughout the war was to send small 'jitter parties' to unnerve the defenders during the night and to launch an all out attack at dawn. On this black occasion these methods paid handsome dividends.

The attack came as dawn was breaking, all along the line

held by 'B' and 'C' Companies. The Japs swarmed forward in screaming waves, heedless of casualties. Their frenzied yells of '*banzai*!', their stunted figures and their repulsive faces made them look like creatures which had erupted from hell.

It would have been a shattering experience, even for battle-hardened troops. By 7 am the enemy were in possession of Golden Hill. Both Royal Scots company commanders were killed and more than sixty men. The remainder fell back in ignoble confusion.

It.was a crippling reverse. The Shingmun Redoubt and Golden Hill were key positions which dominated a large portion of the left flank; their losses endangered the whole of the Gindrinkers' Line. The ignominious departure of the Royal Scots gravely affected subsequent events and their failure to hold their positions was the direct cause of the withdrawal from the mainland.

Brigadier Wallis urged Lieutenant-Colonel Simon White, MC, Commanding Officer of the Royal Scots, to launch an immediate counter-attack, but to counter-attack effectively soldiers must be fresh and confident. The Royal Scots were neither. White had fought at Passchendaele and had seen battle-drunk soldiers herded forward at fearful cost to obtain dominance of a hundred square yards of stinking mud.

Wallis wisely did not enforce the order. In his report to General Maltby he said, 'it seemed useless to force a battalion commander to execute a plan in which he had no confidence.'

Complete disaster was prevented by a vigorous counter-attack by 'D' Company, led by Captain David Pinkerton, an officer of tremendous personality and almost frightening personal courage. Throughout the whole battle Pinkerton was a tower of strength and to be seen everywhere where the fighting was thickest. He seemed to be everywhere at once. He fired bren guns and two-inch mortars. He hurled countless hand grenades. He wielded a rifle and bayonet with devastating effect. He *led* his men in the fullest sense of the word.

Throughout the battle he shouted encouragement to his men and appalling barrack-room obscenities at the Japanese. He laughed, he sang, he cajoled, he joked. He ignored the advice of his second-in-command and Company Sergeant-Major to get under cover. The men marvelled that he still lived. Men fell dead and wounded all around him and he was hit himself, but hardly seemed to notice it. With his black

75

moustache bristling and a bloodstained bandage over his forehead, he strongly resembled a swashbuckling buccaneer of the Spanish Main.

Pinkerton's action saved the day and to a large extent the reputation of the Royal Scots. 'D' Company regained possession of Golden Hill, and although they were not able to hold it in the face of counter-attacks by vastly superior numbers of the enemy, they had effectively checked any further Japanese forward movement in the area.

Pinkerton was awarded the Military Cross for his gallantry on this occasion. He was wounded again later in the siege, but such was the indomitable courage and mighty constitution of this officer that he survived four years of imprisonment and returned to his Regiment in Scotland—as one of his brother officers put it 'somewhat larger than life and as good as new'. It was a cruel stroke of irony that he was killed by a stray Egyptian sniper's bullet in the Suez Expedition of 1956. He was a man whom the Royal Scots, and indeed the British Army, could not easily spare.

As always is the case when a regiment suffers a blot on its name, there were many extenuating circumstances. The battalion, normally 711 strong, went into action with only 600 effectives. They were badly hit by malaria and many casualties from this demoralising disease were sent back to duty without the normal ten days convalescence. It seems, too, that sex had played a big part in the recreational programme of the Royal Scots and they were further depleted by venereal disease.

They were attacked by vastly superior and fanatically brave Japanese forces after a concentrated mortar bombardment which very early on killed two of the most experienced company commanders and many other officers.

The loss of so many officers, the depleted ranks, the fact that many senior NCOs had been sent home at the outbreak of war, indifferent reinforcements from slothful peacetime garrison duty, poor morale—all these factors contributed to the battalion's undistinguished performance in the initial fighting. However much the truth is cloaked in excuses—and there are many—the unpalatable fact remains that the Royal Scots fell back in considerable disorder and it was some days before they could be moulded into an efficient fighting force again. Their eviction from the Shingmun Redoubt was only the beginning

76

of their shame in the eyes of many Middlesex men: many of the Scots regaled men of the Middlesex with terrible stories of close quarter battle, but brought back with them bandoliers still filled with ammunition.

And yet the Royal Scots must not be too harshly judged: it is easy to condemn the conduct of a single battalion from a comfortable billet in Salisbury Plain or Cairo or Bombay. The men who let the Japs in on the mainland and retreated in unmilitary disorder suffered terribly in the ensuing four years in Jap prison camps and the crime they committed, if crime it can be called, was irrevocably wiped out in misery and degradation. In other wars men ran away and lived to fight another day: the Royal Scots may have run away, indeed official dispatches discredit them with having done so, but every man among them longed to fight again and to wipe out that insulting nickname 'The Fleet of Foot'—as indeed they did in the subsequent fighting on the Island. Many of the survivors died miserably in captivity.

Of the 2nd Royal Scots Maltby wrote: 'It was unfortunate that the enemy captured by surprise the most important Shingmun Redoubt, and the Golden Hill position, occupied by the 2nd Royal Scots. These two incidents were the direct cause of the hasty withdrawal from the mainland. The gallant action of 'D' Company and their stubborn fighting on the Island did much to retrieve their prestige.'

As a race we British are quick to criticise and are unsurpassed in the art of being wise after the event. We are, of course, a nation of sportsmen: every Saturday millions of us scream abuse at the referee and instructions to footballers; on race-courses the length and breadth of the country, we heap vituperation on trainers and jockeys. Only a minute percentage of us know anything about the sport we disseminate with such authoritative oratory. To a large extent, it is the same in war. Armchair strategists and historians may revile the Royal Scots for what happened in those terrible early days, but only the Royal Scots really know because they were there.

Perhaps, after all, such things are best forgotten. . . .

In the fighting on the mainland the Royal Navy's sole representative was the Insect class gunboat *Cicala*—built in 1916, 615 tons, 238 feet in length, beam 38 feet, maximum speed 14 knots, complement 2 officers, 38 British and 18 Chinese ratings, armament two 6-inch guns, one 2-pounder pom-pom and eight Lewis guns—which steamed into the mainland battle with the tigerish fury of a belligerent mongoose confronted by a large and predatory snake—a maritime David in pursuit of a landlubberly Goliath.

Cicala's Captain was, in his own words, a 'one-armed dug-out'. Lieutenant-Commander John Boldero, DSC, had first seen action as a diminutive fifteen-year-old midshipman at Jutland aboard HMS *Inflexible*. As a nineteen-year-old Sub-Lieutenant he had taken part in the coastal motor boat attack on the Bolshevik Fleet in Kronstadt, subsequently winning the Distinguished Service Cross.

Boldero's naval career was ended in 1922 by one crushing blow of the Geddes 'axe': at the age of twenty-two, a veteran of seven years' salt water active service, he found himself 'on the beach'. It was a prospect that can hardly be expected to have appealed.

1922 was a lean year for axed naval officers, but Boldero managed to get a job afloat and for the next four years he served aboard an automobile ferry in Vancouver. From 1926 until his recall to active duty in 1939 he worked for the Shanghai Waterworks Company.

He felt badly out of practice for the responsibility of war, but he need not have worried unduly. Naval routine and discipline had changed but little in seventeen years, and in any event the ships in Hong Kong were of World War One vintage. To Boldero, who had an almost lyrical love for small ships, his recall was more like a home-coming and he was appointed to the command of the 2nd Motor Torpedo Boat Flotilla.

The new war started badly for Boldero. On the night of 1st April, 1941, when out on night exercises, his right arm was so badly crushed in collison with a destroyer that it had to be amputated close to the shoulder. His left arm was so badly bruised that for some weeks he was unable to raise it above the level of the shoulder. In cricketing parlance, he was out first ball: disabled without hearing a shot fired in anger. A lesser man than Boldero would have accepted the situation philosophically and continued the war from a desk, squirting ink at the enemy and pelting him with paper. Boldero, however, was not made that way.

Boldero's recovery made a mockery of medical science and

endangered the professional reputation of more than one naval doctor. At a time when men were being rejected for the fighting services because they had duodenal ulcers, hammer toes, flat feet, real or imagined defective hearing, haemorrhoids, astigmatism, colour blindness, dyspepsia, migraine and self-inflicted halitosis, the one-armed Boldero discharged himself from hospital—just eighty-four days after the amputation of his arm—and assumed command of *Cicala*. He had unanswerably silenced all suggestions that he take a shore job by saying that he had not yet mastered the art of signing his name legibly with his left hand. In any case, he pointed out with quarter-deck terseness, there were more than enough shore-based officers in Hong Kong without his adding to their number. If Their Lordships at the Admiralty did not like it, then they could do the other thing.

Officers with fighting experience of small ships were scarce in Hong Kong, and the Commodore, Captain A. C. Collinson, sensibly placed no obstacle in the way of Boldero's return to a seagoing command. The Commodore had, in the making of this decision, displayed a very special brand of bravery: the Naval Commander-in-Chief, Far East, had specifically ordered that Lieutenant-Commander John Boldero, DSC, should NOT repeat NOT return to sea. Like Nelson, Collinson turned a blind eye to the telescope and, as things turned out for *Cicala*, it was as well that he did. . . .

Inevitably, Boldero's appointment to HMS *Cicala* caused a furore of correspondence ashore. To any right thinking naval staff officer, a one-armed captain of one of His Majesty's ships of war was unthinkable. Naval bureaucracy then swept into action: heavily flagged files, bristling with flags labelled important, immediate and 'for immediate action', set out on their feverish inter-departmental voyages. After a succession of minutes, memos and medical reports, Boldero's appointment was placed under the heading of 'Harbour Service', but by some mysterious method of accounting he received command pay for a sea appointment.

There were other problems of a more domestic nature for Boldero. The stump of his recently amputated right arm still hurt abominably and he found it impossible to lie down in comfort on his bunk; every turn in sleep produced a spasm of agonising pain. The bunk was of the regulation size for a lieutenant-commander. A visiting staff officer pursed his lips austerely and eventually decided that a case, subject to Admiralty approval, could be made out for the installation of a wider bunk, normally the prerogative of a Commander. After a further fortnight of intensive correspondence Boldero got a wider bunk; but he had to wait another four years for the third stripe and the shining 'scrambled eggs' on his cap peak. . . .

Whoever else was caught napping on the morning of December 8th, 1941, HMS *Cicala* was not. By 10 on the night of the 7th every libertyman, drunk or sober, was aboard and the ship at two hours' notice for steam.

At 5 am on the morning of the 8th the telephone on *Cicala*'s gangway shrilled insistently and the coxswain, Chief Petty Officer 'Tom' Thums, answered it. On the other end was the Commodore, Captain C. A. Collinson, and his voice crackled over the wire with compulsive insistence.

"Get the Captain," commanded Collinson.

Thums said: "Aye, aye, sir," and bolted below.

The new bunk had proved a great success and Boldero was enjoying the best sleep he had had since the amputation of his arm. The appearance of CPO Thums, breathing heavily and perspiring freely, told him that *Cicala*'s comfortable sojourn in harbour was about to be abruptly terminated. He threw on a dressing gown, thrust his feet into slippers and hurried to the bridge.

"We're at war with Japan," said the Commodore, who was not given to verbosity on the telephone. "Raise steam and prepare for action."

By 6.45 am *Cicala* was ready for sea. Her instructions were to utilise her anti-aircraft armament in the protection of shipping and port installations. At 8 am the crew, all at action stations, heard the crash of bombs falling on Kai Tak airport.

"Blimey!" exclaimed a startled young ordinary seaman, "what was that?"

"Bombs," said Able Seaman Wilkinson tersely. "What d'you think they were? —— Christmas cards?"

At 8.30 am Boldero received a signal, ordering him to proceed to Castle Peak Bay. Castle Peak is situated near the frontier of the New Territories, to the north-west of Hong Kong island. From the bay a warship could dominate the road along which an advancing force might be expected to ap proach.

Cruising casually offshore on that glorious morning, the mere mention of war seemed almost indecent.

The anti-aircraft gun crews scanned the sky and saw nothing but a breathtaking expanse of blue; other men apprehensively swept the shore with binoculars and saw the apparently deserted hills of the New Territories. As an afterthought they searched the skies for the Royal Air Force. Inevitably, someone asked where our planes were. The men of *Cicala* were not to know that Hong Kong's air power consisted of a mass of twisted and tortured rubble.

At exactly 11 am the peaceful scene was rudely shattered by the appearance of two Japanese seaplanes. They screamed out of the sky and hurled their bombs at *Cicala*. But John Boldero found that he had lost none of his skill over the years: he twisted and turned the little gunboat with such dexterity that all the Japanese bombs fell wide. 'It was,' records Boldero, 'a frightening, but at the same time, an intensely exhilarating experience. *Cicala* was fitted with triple rudders and could be turned almost on a sixpence.'

Hideous were the comments of the engine room staff as Boldero gyrated the gunboat like a puppet ballet dancer; horrid, too, were the imprecations of the anti-aircraft gun crews who failed to make a hit. But the Jap seaplanes disappeared in frustrated disgust, leaving *Cicala* in triumphant isolation and monarch of all she surveyed. The only victim of the *blitzkrieg* was a vast shoal of fish which had come to the surface. Presently an encouraging odour from the galley told the ship's company that fish would figure on the menu for dinner that day.

"Think yourself bloody lucky them Japs come over," said Able Seaman Wilkinson, his mouth comfortably full of fried fish; "if they hadn't, we'd be eating tinned stew and beans."

At 2.30 pm the seaplanes were back again. Plummeting down, they made five more attacks. Like a professional welterweight matched with a punch-drunk giant from a cheap provincial boxing booth, *Cicala* bobbed and weaved, side-stepped and pirouetted. Once again the seaplanes departed, encouraged on their way by roars of contemptuous lower deck invective:

"Couldn't hit a battle wagon at ten yards. . . ."
"Just let the bastards come again, that's all."
"Some bloody air force. . . ."

But now a new sound made itself heard: the truculent crump of gunfire on the mainland. The six-inch gun crews, who had yet to fire a shot, hopefully scanned the mainland for the appearance of Japanese troops. But by nightfall no target had presented itself.

The six-inch gun crews got their chance early the next morning. A large party of Japanese were sighted on the road at Brother's Point and the forward six-inch gun opened fire gleefully. Four shells hurtled into the Japs and caused them to make a hasty and undignified dispersal.

'Made 'em hop a bit," commented CPO 'Tom' Thums with relish.

An hour later an even better target presented itself. A motor bus and lorry, both packed with Japanese troops, were sighted near Brother's Point. The six-inch guns spoke again and the two vehicles were seen to burst into flames. The guns' crews burst into exultant cheers: it seemed that *Cicala* could do no wrong; she appeared to lead a charmed life against air attack and was clearly putting the fear of God into the Japanese army. The celebratory bottles of beer sent round by Boldero were consumed with appropriate gusto.

The morale of the British ratings aboard *Cicala* would have gladdened any captain's heart. The enthusiasm of the Chinese, however, was clearly waning. They did not like the bombing and said so with dogged and vociferous persistence. Their elected spokesman, a mournful-looking petty officer, said to Boldero: "Chinese no likee bombs. Want to go ashore." Boldero informed him uncompromisingly that they were far safer on board *Cicala* than on shore. It was unfortunate that the words were barely out of his mouth when the same two persistent seaplanes reappeared and dropped six bombs and attacked intermittently during the rest of the morning. Miraculously, *Cicala* remained unscathed, but the morale of the Chinese ratings dropped to zero.

On the afternoon of December 9th the Commodore came alongside in a motor torpedo boat and was ceremoniously piped aboard *Cicala*. Captain Collinson had experienced moments of guilt and apprehension about the appointment of Boldero to a seagoing command so soon after the amputation of his arm, but he need not have worried: Boldero had not only defied medical science, he had also defied the most determined efforts of the Japanese Air Force to sink his ship.

Throughout December 10th *Cicala* harassed the Japanese in every possible way: she brought a vicious and continuous flanking fire to bear on Japanese troops who were swarming towards the Royal Scots and she broke up every attempt of Japanese working parties to carry out road repairs. Indeed, the Japs on the mainland never knew where this indomitable little ship was going to turn up next.

The enemy air force set out to destroy this impudent gunboat. At 4.15 pm on the afternoon of December 10th nine aeroplanes appeared and commenced diving on *Cicala* in quick succession, dropping one or two bombs each time. A near miss wounded Able Seaman Wilkinson, who was manning the Lewis gun on the standard compass platform. Wilkinson let out an oath of such frightfulness that Boldero affirms to this day that it seriously affected the aim of the Jap airmen.

In all, seventeen dive-bombing attacks were made but somehow *Cicala*'s luck held. At least two Jap planes were damaged by her anti-aircraft fire and limped away from the battle. They did not know, as CPO Thums succinctly phrased it, 'whether they were on their arses or their elbows'.

But *Cicala* did not escape entirely unscathed: the after compartment was holed on the port side, about two feet from the stern above the port rudder. Owing to the action of the balance flap which was fitted to Insect class gunboats, no flooding occurred. The wireless aerials were whipped away and one bomb actually fell on the deck but failed to explode. There was considerable splinter damage, but apart from Able Seaman Wilkinson (who was uttering terrible threats against all things Japanese) there were no more casualties. Boldero sent a laconic signal 'closing on dockyard for inspection. Nothing serious'—and *Cicala*, White Ensign fluttering defiantly, steamed jauntily into harbour as if she would cheerfully go through the whole performance again if necessary.

Apart from a few hours snatched in the corner of the bridge, Boldero had not slept since *Cicala* slipped out of harbour at dawn on December 8th. The stump of his right arm throbbed and ached almost intolerably. He had been given a supply of pain-killing pills, but they had long since run out. It was not until he had satisfied himself that repairs to his ship were under way that he consented to go to the naval hospital.

At the hospital a young surgeon-lieutenant regarded him with professional disapproval. "I ought to admit you, sir," he said.

"Not on your life," said Boldero readily. "I've been carved up by you butchers once and that's more than enough. Give me some more of those pills and I'll get back on board."

The Japanese had not seen the last of HMS *Cicala*. . . .

In every artillery officers' mess in England is a celebrated picture of World War One. It depicts exhausted, bandaged infantrymen on the side of a Flanders road. A troop of field guns hurtle past them at full gallop. The caption reads: 'The guns, thank God, the guns!'

The gunners on the mainland did not gallop into action on horseback, but they did the next best thing. They answered every call of the weary and bewildered infantrymen for artillery support and gave it unstintingly.

An infantry soldier will often profess contempt for the artillery: gunners, they protest, have none of the dirty work; they sit far behind the front line and occasionally, to justify their existence, they lob a few shells over. Of course, it goes without saying that they live in luxury and never get involved in hand-to-hand fighting: if a sticky fighting patrol is wanted, the poor bloody infantry do it, while the gunners sit on their tails drinking potent tea. The plaintive wail 'it's all right for the gunners!' has been echoed by infantrymen in every theatre of war, but they will be the first to admit that effective artillery support is essential to any operation. To the foot-slogger in the front line the sound of supporting artillery fire is the sweetest music in the world. The infantry may not like the gunners but they can't manage without them.

The Royal Scots, the Rajputs and the Punjabis were well served by the gunners who supported them. These were the Sikhs and Punjabi Mussulmans of the Hong Kong and Singapore Regiment of Royal Artillery.

The HKSRA were something of a *corps d'élite*. The Indians who joined the regiment did so on the clear understanding that they were saying goodbye to their own land, for the regiment served only in Hong Kong and Singapore. The men were rather better paid than the rest of the Indian Army and service in the regiment was very popular; indeed, the recruiting authorities in India had drastically cut the numbers to be taken because they complained that all the best recruits were enlisting in the HKSRA.

In India the recruit did not go to the Recruiting Officer, the Recruiting Officer went to the recruits. The Recruiting Officer rarely, if ever, came away from a village empty-handed. When news got round that he was in search of men for the HKSRA, the response was immediate and frequently over-whelming.

Major James Crowe, one of the battery commanders, whose active service career had started with the Chanack Incident of 1921, had recently returned from India with a batch of new recruits. In a village near Amritsar, the largest Sikh community in India, he had been royally received by ex-Subedar-Major Balwant Singh, a doughty veteran of over seventy who had manhandled the old screw guns on the Tirah expedition of 1896. Balwant Singh produced a bottle of Johnnie Walker whisky and prodded forward twelve stalwart grandsons for enlistment. Crowe sat back and drank appreciatively, secure in the knowledge that his journey had been necessary.

No time was wasted in filling up forms and oath taking; nor were any lectures of exhortation required. Each recruit had his name, height, chest measurements and village written on his chest with a skin pencil. The medical officer recorded the man's medical particulars on his back. Many a disappointed recruit, who had initially failed to satisfy the medical officer, persuaded a conveniently situated friend to erase the details of physical defects and came round again. If the doctor had had a long and trying day, it was frequently possible for a man to join the august ranks of the HKSRA at the second attempt. At first sight all Sikhs look alike, and if a workmanlike job had been made of the eradication of the skin pencil, a rejected recruit could try again with a reasonable chance of getting away with it.

The HKSRA in Hong Kong and Singapore were, to all intents and purposes, a self-contained Indian community. Wives and children sailed from India to join their menfolk.

All through that long, sunny Sunday of December 7th the Sikhs and Punjabi Mussulmans stood to their guns. Riding

85

round his battery's positions (he had acquired a horse by methods which he was not prepared to divulge in full), Major Crowe looked with pride on his men. He had recruited many of them personally and knew every man by name. No fewer than four of the venerable Balwant Singh's grandsons were in his own battery; no doubt, thought Crowe, the old man wished he were there himself.

Sunday passed peacefully. The evening meal of *chappattis* and rice was eaten. The British officers did the rounds of gun positions and sentries; then they retired to the mess tent and played poker by the light of a smoking hurricane lamp.

The Hong Kong and Singapore Regiment of Artillery were ready. . . .

Many were the urgent calls for artillery support in those terrible early days. Muzzles recoiled and roared, sweating gunners rammed shells into the open breeches as fast as they could pick them up, breechblocks were slammed home. The sky was filled with the snarling whine of shells.

Not once during the next three days and nights were the howitzers of the HKSRA wholly silent. Morning, noon, afternoon and night the batteries fired in the same orderly and unhurried manner. A steady flow of reports went back to Headquarters, Royal Artillery: '1120 hrs. Enemy OP on GRASSY HILL destroyed. . . .'; '1138 hrs. Enemy working party and light gun engaged by 2nd Mountain Battery. . . .'; '1252 hrs. Enemy infantry at WO LIU NANG engaged. . . .'; '1430 hrs. Engaged enemy massing for attack on R. Scots. Fire reported effective. . . .' The HKSRA, trained to a fine peak of perfection by a handful of devoted and dedicated British officers, were making their presence felt.

But in common with every other unit in Hong Kong the HKSRA were woefully ill equipped: ammunition was rigorously rationed; there was a grave shortage of field telephones, which are so vital to artillerymen; there were so few drivers that locally enlisted Chinese were put at the wheels of the regiment's trucks, a course of action which necessitated the presence of a valuable gunner as a permanent guard on the driver in case he took it into his head to drive the vehicle away; rifles were in such short supply that only half the men had them; the Thompson sub-machine gun—a devastating killing weapon at close quarters—was issued to the regiment when actually in battle and then only one to each section; there were only eight wireless sets and these were equipped with weak batteries; it was, in fact, the same melancholy pattern of inadequacy which prevailed throughout Hong Kong's fighting services—a nightmare of improvisation and frustration.

With the best will in the world and the best gunners in the world (and the Indian is probably unsurpassed in the art of practical gunnery) an effective and continuous artillery barrage cannot be maintained with rationed shells. The battery commanders of the HKSRA resembled wartime housewives in England with a family of voracious children demanding to be fed.

It speaks volumes for these splendid men that no reasonable call for artillery support went unanswered and that they brought their guns intact from the mainland.

The 5/7 Rajputs were involved in some of the bitterest fighting on the mainland, but they would not have had it otherwise: ever since its formation in 1825 this battalion had gone where the fighting was thickest.

They had been present at the Sikh Wars of 1849; when the Indian Army mutinied in 1857 the 5/7 Rajputs had remained unswervingly loyal; they had fought in China, on the North West Frontier of India, in Flanders and Iraq.

The outbreak of the Second World War found them fretting restively in the stultifying heat of the Malabar Coast. Endless and monotonous training took place in manoeuvres which they knew by heart. It was a grim station indeed: the weather was vile and the amenities basic in the extreme; there seemed no immediate prospect of the battalion proceeding on active service. Indian battalions went to the war in the Middle East while others did tours of duty on the North West Frontier. But it seemed that the 5/7 Rajputs were condemned to stagnate in India. In a way, this was no bad thing, for a good battalion bogged down in routine training invariably goes into action with a frustrated fury that bodes ill for the enemy.

Eventually the order to move came, but it was received without enthusiasm. For a well-trained battalion with a fierce hunger for battle to be sent to Hong Kong, a 'fleshpot' garrison station, seemed the ultimate insult. If the prospect of war had seemed remote on the Malabar Coast, in Hong Kong it seemed unthinkable. There was little social activity on the Malabar Coast, but in Hong Kong it seemed never-ending.

Soon, however, the Rajputs found themselves digging and wiring in the Gindrinkers' Line. They worked hard and uncomplainingly, but it was a little difficult to take active service really seriously when the battalion band, resplendent in peacetime scarlet uniforms, played at the Saturday race meeting on 6th December.

The 7th Rajput Regiment was not, as their title suggests, entirely composed of Rajputs. In addition to these sturdy, serious-minded and phlegmatic men, there were also Punjabi Mussulmans: more carefree, volatile and humorous. The Rajput is a Hindu, the Mussulman a Mahomedan; but contrary to the popular conception of Indians, which contends that Hindu and Mahomedan are constantly at one another's throats, there were no inter-racial feuds in the 5/7 Rajputs: they were a fine battalion with unshakeable morale who desired nothing more than to get to grips with the enemy at the earliest possible moment.

They had not long to wait. On December 10th, shortly after the disastrous fall of the Shingmun Redoubt, Brigadier Wallis ordered Captain Robert Newton's company of Punjabi Mussulmans to strengthen the line. Newton was an officer of very singular gallantry, but at first sight he resembled an exuberant schoolboy captaining his house rugger XV rather than a company commander embarking on the bloody business of war. Fair haired and slightly built, he had the sort of pink and white complexion coveted by many women but achieved by only a few, and he seldom had to shave very seriously. His men would have cheerfully lain down and allowed him to walk over their faces if it had afforded him any satisfaction.

There was nothing schoolboyish about Newton in action. The Japs, flushed with early success, advanced swiftly towards Kowloon. Newton took up position and waited for them. To his men he said: "Now then, who's going to win the Victoria Cross? Stand fast and shoot straight. There will be much killing to be done soon."

Newton's Mussulmans grinned. This was a real *sahib*, even though he looked as though he should still be in the schoolroom: his spirit was one of confident self-reliance and of belief in the worth of his men. It seemed that he gave every man a share of his tireless energy and unshakeable cheerfulness.

Ubiquitous and strong, Newton never seemed to sleep: every man under him had the feeling that the company commander knew not only what the individual soldier did, but what he thought; with such a man at their head they could not and would not be defeated.

The Japs, expecting another walk-over, swept down on Newton's men in howling waves. They attacked frontally, seemingly heedless of casualties. Having seen Englishmen break before their onslaught, they did not expect resistance from a rabble of downtrodden Indians, the dupes of swaggering white men who beat them and humiliated them. The attacking Japs did not know that the Rajputs had howled with unrestrained mirth at the leaflets which had been dropped upon them, exhorting them to desert the tyrannical British and fight for Japan. But to the Japs Newton's company was but a tiresome little obstacle to be brushed contemptuously aside.

The Japs ran straight into a withering and deadly fire that rocked them to their heels and tore great gaps in their ranks. Newton, steel helmet at a rakish angle, yelled like a dervish: he was all the schoolboy now, cheering his team on to the inter-house championship.

Shocked and bewildered, the Japs reeled back to their starting point. Now Newton became very much the shrewd soldier, although his language was of public school and Sandhurst. "Put their tails down a bit," he announced gleefully to the artillery observation officer with him. "Get on to your chaps and tell 'em to knock the blighters for six."

The gunners of HKSRA needed no second bidding. Soon 6-inch howitzers were pumping shells into the Shingmun Redoubt, whither the Japs had precipitately retired. The morale of the 5/7 Rajputs had never been higher: they had taken on a superior enemy force and given them a salutary whipping.

But back at his headquarters on Hong Kong Island, General Maltby was a worried man. The reports he received were indicative of steadfastness and gallantry, but gallantry alone would not be enough on the mainland. True, the Japs had received a mauling at the hands of Newton's men, but they had substantial reinforcements to call upon. The mainland brigade had none.

Tactically, the situation was far from reassuring: the line was alarmingly thin and if an immediate counter-attack were launched by Newton's company it would become thinner still. The Rajputs and Punjabis were full of *élan*, but the Royal Scots, shaken and bewildered by the first onslaught, were not in good shape; they resembled a first class football team unaccountably knocked out of the Cup Final by an unconsidered Third Division side. A company of Winnipeg Grenadiers, hastily moved over from the island, were untried in battle and Brigadier Wallis was in no hurry to put them to the test.

To Newton's intense chagrin, the counter-attack was called off, for Maltby knew that the mainland could not be held for much longer. Maltby resembled a businessman with a small bank balance and no capital who was being forced into bankruptcy by a rival with virtually inexhaustible resources. To Lieutenant-General Sakai, the Japanese Supreme Commander, the men mown down by Gray's Punjabis and Newton's Rajputs were, so to speak, on the expense account.

Lieutenant-General Sakai, on the other hand, had not a care in the world. At his well-appointed headquarters near the border he ate quantities of prawns, drank copiously of saki, and made elaborate plans for his triumphal entry into Hong Kong.

For this great day, he decided, he must have a horse—a *white* horse. Already he had acquired a magnificent animal, and two soldiers, specially detailed for the job, were grooming its coat until it shone, plaiting its mane and tail and polishing a set of saddlery to an extraordinary brilliance.

Sakai was not unduly worried about casualties because none were reported in the Japanese Army below the rank of captain. Like a fat, Oriental and elegantly moustached bookmaker with a hard-won reputation for paying out promptly, Sakai regarded his losses as small bets which were scarcely more than a minor irritation. He had 60,000 men at his disposal.

The crack 38th Division had been kept in reserve for the assault on the Island: two battalions of the 228th Regiment; all three battalions of the 230th Regiment; two battalions of the 229th Regiment. In addition there was the Divisional Reserve, composed of one battalion from the 228th Regiment and one battalion from the 229th Regiment. There was an imposing force of artillery, a unit of light tanks, engineers, signallers and ample transport. In spite of his sanguine confidence, Sakai was leaving nothing to chance.

The 38th were being fattened up for the assault in villages near the border. Although discipline was fierce, Sakai did not believe in self-denial for soldiers not in the actual fighting line. Consequently, whole villages were declared brothel areas and the off-duty activities of the 38th were accompanied by the screams of countless outraged Chinese women.

Comfortably flatulent from a surfeit of prawns, Sakai waited for the inevitable withdrawal of the British forces from the mainland. On the afternoon of the 10th December he visited all units of the 38th. The expression on his fat, creased face was one of mingled greed and affection, like a man who has set his heart on a long-coveted prize.

The withdrawal could not be long delayed. In his despatch Maltby stated: '. . . unless the Japanese launched a major offensive against the Gindrinkers' Line, I saw no reason why the period between their crossing of the frontier and the evacuation of the mainland by my forces should not extend to a period of seven days or more. I gave no guarantee and still maintain that this was a fair estimate and might well have been accomplished had not the key to our position on the mainland been captured by surprise by the enemy.' But Maltby well knew that while an operation might be, strategically, a tidily conceived plan, tactically it was liable to become a series of accidents.

At midday on December 11th, Maltby decided to withdraw all troops from the mainland and to concentrate all his forces on the island. 'The notice I could give,' he went on in his despatch, 'was regrettably short but unavoidable owing to the rapidity with which the situation had deteriorated.' It was all too soon to deteriorate still more. . . .

Orders were given for the withdrawal of all troops under cover of night: the Rajputs and Punjabis were to retire to Devil's Peak, the remainder to Kowloon Peninsula, whence they would embark for the Island. It was to prove a hazardous undertaking.

The departure from the mainland was complete and devastating. The Cement Works and the China Light and Power Station were destroyed; the docks were thoroughly demolished; all remaining British merchant ships were scuttled (and in an excess of zeal, one Swedish vessel as well); the RAF evacuated the aerodrome, having completed the job of destruction initiated by the Japs.

The withdrawal of the Royal Scots, Rajputs, Punjabis and one company of Winnipeg Grenadiers was a desperately difficult operation. It was a manoeuvre that had never been practised, any more than the evacuation of the British Expeditionary Force from Dunkirk had been practised; the withdrawal of the mainland forces was, in fact, a Dunkirk in miniature.

To make matters more difficult, the moon on the night of December 11th, with rare perversity, elected not to come out. The night was pitch black and the desperately tired troops had to break off contact with the enemy and move, in many cases, across the front of the advancing Japanese.

The Royal Scots and the company of Winnipeg Grenadiers had a comparatively easy task. They retired towards Shamshuipo and were taken across to the Island in launches and ferry boats. So far the evacuation had proceeded according to plan. General Maltby heaved a heartfelt sigh of relief when he heard the news.

The Rajputs and Punjabis, however, soon found themselves in evil case. They had to move along the line of the Passes—Kowloon Pass, Shatin Pass, Grasscutters Pass—to Devil's Peak.

This would have been a sufficiently strenuous march for fresh and lightly armed troops in broad daylight. For exhausted men, carrying all their stores, machine guns and mortars, it was a massive feat of endurance. Their progress along knife-edged hill tracks was, of necessity, slow and laborious: men bumped into one another in the impenetrable blackness; mules, carrying precious food and water, took fright and galloped into the middle distance.

All ranks were feeling the strain of lack of water, food and sleep. The two Indian battalions had both endured four days and nights of fighting, marching and continous vigilance. But inspired by the example of their British officers, they plodded wearily and uncomplainingly on. Their eyes were glazed with weariness, but never a man spoke. On a march such as this, British soldiers will take time out to grumble and swear; the Indian saves his breath and marches on in silence.

The Japanese were hard on their heels. Indeed, for much of

the march the Punjabis were in close contact with the enemy and actually fighting a rearguard action. It is to the everlasting credit of these dour and stoical men that they arrived at Devil's Peak, not only intact, but in possession of all their military stores. This was a march worthy of Hannibal.

But their troubles were not over yet. . . .

The rearguard of the 2/14 Punjabis, under Lieutenant Nigel Forsyth, were cut off from the main body at Shatin Pass, lost their way and found themselves in Kowloon City. They were soon involved in fighting with Chinese fifth columnists as well as with advancing Japanese patrols. Arrived at the ferry wharf, Forsyth found himself confronted with the unenviable task of shepherding thousands of refugees on to the ferries which were going over to the Island.

Forsyth's command was swelled by stragglers: Royal Scots and assorted gunners who had been cut off from their units. Forsyth's orders were crisp and unequivocal: they were to hold the Japs at bay until the last ferry had departed. Then, and only then, would they embark for the Island themselves. . . .

This mixed force covered the withdrawal of thousands of assorted civilians and Forsyth earned the unstinted praise of all who saw him (he was recommended for a high decoration, but, with military perversity, he received nothing better than a reprimand for getting lost in the first place). The Japs hurled themselves at the wharf in infuriated waves, but every attack was beaten off. Eventually Forsyth embarked his men on the last ferry boat. With tommy gun blazing, he stood in the stern of the boat. Some of the more enterprising Japanese forward elements actually tried to leap on to the craft from the quayside. Forsyth had the double pleasure of not only seeing them miss their footing and plunge screaming into the water, but of spraying them with well-directed bursts of fire.

The Chinese in Kowloon City did not help much. A distinguished authority on oriental affairs has written: 'One must not hate the Chinese as a race, for they have infinite capacity for good.' At the time of the Japanese entry into Kowloon, their capacity for evil was even more infinite.

Chinese fifth columnists with lamps operated by a mirror and dry cell battery signalled British positions to the Japanese artillery. Others, more daring, sniped our troops. They transformed a well-nigh impossible military situation into a hideous shambles.

The large majority, however, had more material ambitions and contented themselves with looting. Shops and houses were broken into and systematically ransacked. As looters the Chinese are in a class by themselves: houses were reduced to empty shells; doors, window frames and floor boards were ripped away; every stick of furniture and every personal effect was taken.

For Ellen Field, December 11th was a day of fearful terror.

Ellen Field was (and is) brunette, *petite* and pretty. In 1960 she is, scarcely believably, a grandmother.

Her husband, a ship's engineer of a coastal freighter, had been called to his unit of the Hong Kong Volunteer Defence Corps; leaving her in a flat in Kowloon with three children aged six, four and one year. The flat was luxurious and equipped with every possible labour-saving device. On that morning, Ellen Field knew that she was looking at it for the last time.

The Japanese were actually on the outskirts of the town when Ellen Field started to pack. In spite of the fact that she had two *amahs*, she was a mistress of every domestic eventuality. One suitcase, she decided, would have to suffice for the whole family's luggage. Into this one suitcase went some of her own clothes, a supply of nappies, a teddy bear and two dolls. The two eldest children, who appeared to think that this evacuation of their home had been planned for their own amusement, sat and jumped on the solitary suitcase to make it shut.

Accompanied by the two *amahs*, Ellen Field set out on the two-mile walk to Kowloon City Pier. The *amahs* wailed hysterically and were, if anything, more trouble than the children. Soon the anguish of the *amahs* communicated itself to the two older children. Ellen Field said to the *amahs*: "If you two are going to yell all the time, you can go away and I'll take the children by myself." The wailing of the *amahs* subsided into muted moans of self-pity. Clutching the smallest child in one hand and the suitcase in the other, Ellen Field led her family to the pier.

Here was a scene of indescribable confusion. Thousands of Chinese jostled, screamed and fought on the quayside. Clearly it was a case of every man (and woman and child) for himself; an overworked devil would take the hindmost. . . .

John Lee, most conventional of Colonial civil servants and Immigration Officer in Hong Kong, had been sent across to Kowloon to supervise the issue of permits to cross to Hong Kong Island. His instructions were to ensure that no one crossed without one. As soon as he set foot on the mainland he knew that his task, drafted and drawn up by a well-meaning bureaucrat, was a hopeless one before he started. The Chinese, never at their best in an emergency, had unanimously decided that it was a matter of *sauve qui peut* or, more contemporarily, 'Blow you, Jack, I'm all right'. For every one person queueing for a permit, there were a hundred who were not. The Chinese were not worried about permits: they had only one idea in their heads and that was to get away to the island and out of the path of the oncoming Japanese.

Lee telephoned the Commissioner of Police and told him that the issue of individual permits was completely out of the question. By the common compulsion of fear, Chinese were swarming on to the ferry and into launches and sampans. The Japs were barely two miles away.

Heedless of the clamour all around them, fifteen determined and grim-faced men went about their business. They were the remnants of a Royal Scots' platoon under a burly sergeant.

The sergeant felt the shame of the Shingmun Redoubt episode acutely. He had told his men in the most uncompromising terms that they were making a last stand. He informed them that any of them who could not stay in the position alive would stay there dead. The men nodded grimly: they feared the sergeant more than the Japanese.

They died to a man. It was the first step in the wiping clean of the Royal Scots' slate. . . .

Ellen Field had lost one of the *amahs* in the crush and was now carrying both the youngest children. The other *amah* clutched the eldest. The suitcase had been torn from Ellen's hand and the contents trampled underfoot. The baby sucked a rattle and gurgled ecstatically.

She never really knew how she got into the launch, but she has a vague memory of a soft and persuasive Canadian voice.

Just as the launch, filled to overflowing, cast off, she heard the voice again: "Somethin' else I can do for you, ma'am?" She looked into the pink and cherubic features of Private Aubrey Flegg of the Winnipeg Grenadiers.

Flegg was just twenty; a courteous and slow-speaking farm-boy from Ontario. Cut off from his company, he had wandered in the direction of the ferry. He had encountered the fierce sergeant of Royal Scots and offered his services. The sergeant, who had a low opinion of Canadians, instructed him to "get to hell oot o' it".

Flegg proved himself to be a tower of strength on the passage to the island. Amid the seething, panic-stricken horde of Chinese, he held the two youngest children and entertained them with the most accomplished baby-talk. In his haversack he carried apparently inexhaustible supplies of sweets. Every ten minutes or so he remarked guilelessly to Ellen Field: "Gee, but you're mighty pretty, ma'am." To an elderly Chinaman, whose panic-stricken wailing demoralised everyone within three feet of him, Flegg said chidingly: "That's no way to act, Joe."

John Lee, having abandoned all hope of issuing permits, reported to his volunteer unit on Hong Kong Island. He was greeted by an irascible sergeant-major who asked him where the hell he'd been and whether he thought the war was a bloody picnic.

One man, left on the wrong side, was determined at all costs to rejoin his unit. He was old, small and desperately frightened. Sweeper Bhokar of the 2/14 Punjabis was a man with a mission.

To those unacquainted with Indian Army procedure the term 'sweeper' requires some explanation. Water sanitation was virtually unknown in India and to enjoy the luxury of pulling a plug necessitated a stay in one of the larger hotels in Bombay, Delhi or Calcutta. On field service an Indian Army officers' mess was usually a tent or, when in close contact with the enemy, a tarpaulin stretched over a deep trench. Adjoining the mess there was always another and smaller tent, inexplicably known as a 'Kitchener'. This was the officers' lavatory or, as it is more universally known today, toilet.

The 'Kitchener' tent houses a wooden device on four legs

which was universally known as a 'thunderbox'. The 'thunder-box' was equipped with a hole in the middle and underneath this was a deep enamel pot.

Within calling distance of the 'Kitchener' was to be found the officers' mess sweeper. Sweepers were men of low caste, sometimes known as 'untouchables', and by virtue of their lowly status, noncombatants. It was the responsibility of the mess sweeper to ensure that each successive officer found the 'thunderbox' pure and unsullied when he entered to perform his natural functions.

Bhokar had ministered to successive generations of British officers in the 14th Punjabis since the Mohmand Expedition of 1908. He had got to know the officers solely from their eliminatory habits: there were, most conventional of all, the 'after breakfast *sahibs*'. There were the mid-morning *sahibs* and the after tiffin *sahibs*; there were the midnight *sahibs* and the *sahibs* who made a determined dash for the 'Kitchener' after the early morning cup of tea. Bhokar knew them all as well as he knew himself.

At the age of fifty-two Bhokar found that his marching was not what it used to be. In the tramp of Forsyth's men through the darkness he had fallen farther and farther behind. Apart from a sympathetic "*Shabash, buddha!*"[1] from the weary Punjabis who passed him, no one could do anything for him.

But Bhokar was fiercely determined to catch up with the officers' mess. The *sahibs* would want their 'Kitchener' tent and he didn't want to get caught out. In thirty-three years' service he had never failed them.

Bhokar found himself alone on the quayside. The Japanese were all around him and he could not swim. But he found a fortuitous life-belt and paddled himself across. When the Punjabis reformed on the Island, the 'Kitchener' tent stood proudly by the shelter which did duty as an officers' mess. Squatting unconcernedly nearby was Sweeper Bhokar. He had not let the *sahibs* down. . . .

Last to leave the mainland were those most stubborn of fighters, the 5/7 Rajputs. Mindful of their previous drubbing by the Rajputs, the Japs attacked them with a considerably larger force, but the result was the same. Continuous attacks were beaten off. Despairing of ever dislodging the Rajputs,

[1] "Well done, old man!"

the Japs withdrew and subjected them to merciless dive-bombing and mortar fire.

The irrepressible Captain Newton was in the forefront of the fighting, but acquitting himself as well was an officer of entirely different calibre. Captain Mateen Ahmed Ansari was an Indian: a fiercely proud scion of a well-to-do Hyderabad family. Ansari, until called upon to show magnificent qualities of leadership in battle, had been something of an *enfant terrible* and a constant headache to his superior officers.

From his first day with the battalion Ansari had been remote, touchy, surly and morose. He did not like the Army and he lost little time in letting everyone know it. Worse still, it was discovered that he was a staunch Indian Nationalist and on arrival in Hong Kong he made friends with a set of undesirable Indian civilians. Ansari very promptly found himself 'on the mat'.

His Commanding Officer, Lieutenant-Colonel Roger Cadogan-Rawlinson, was an Indian Army officer of the older school. To him an unsociable officer, who shunned his comrades in mess was bad enough; but Ansari was a Nationalist which was infinitely worse. Here was a shady affair—an officer of the Regular Indian Army who dabbled in politics. The Colonel told Ansari in the most uncompromising terms that he would either mend his ways or go.

Ansari's face was expressionless as he saluted smartly and marched out of the orderly room. Later that evening Cadogan-Rawlinson sought counsel with his second-in-command, Major 'Bruno' Browning, over a whisky and soda.

"He's bad medicine, John," said the Colonel decidedly.

Browning, more tolerant, disagreed. "He'll probably do well in action, sir," he said.

The Colonel snorted derisively. "Action! The only fighting that chap will ever do is when he punches someone's nose in the mess!"

By a strange quirk of fate, both the Commanding Officer and the second-in-command were proved right. A few nights later a heated argument on the vexed subject of Indian nationalism developed in the officers' mess. A British officer—a tough, hard-living ex-tea-planter—and Ansari disagreed violently and eventually bloodily. Afterwards Ansari found himself something of a hero and was incredulously delighted when the ex-tea-planter, black of eye and broken of teeth, shook hands with him. This, he suddenly realised with cynical amazement, was belonging to the Regiment—the be-all and end-all of military endeavour. In the past he had steadfastly declined to take part in the puerile after-dinner activities of his brother officers: 'High Cockalorum', rugby scrums, 'Are ye there, Moriarty?' and the like. After a single outburst of bad temper and a gory exchange of fisticuffs he found himself accepted. It was all very strange. But Major Browning, who had witnessed the incident, smiled a secret little smile. All Ansari needed now was some *real* fighting. . . .

He was very soon to get it. When the Japs swept down on his company of Rajputs, Ansari's men scarcely recognised this calm and unruffled warrior as the indolent and faintly supercilious young man whom they had known in barracks. In the last battle on the mainland, Ansari's company accounted for over a hundred Japanese.[1]

'C' and 'D' Companies of the 5/7 Rajputs—heavily and bloodily committed to battle since 8th December—were the last off the mainland. For three days they had held up a numerically vastly superior force of Japanese at Devil's Peak. The official despatch states baldly that 'a strong enemy attack . . . developed against 5/7 Rajputs, but was successfully beaten off'. There was considerably more to it than that.

The Rajputs had given the attacking Japanese plenty to think about: under ceaseless shelling, mortaring and bombing they had held their ground against continuous and determined Japanese infantry attacks. Every night was rendered livid by bursting shells and mortar bombs; the glint of tracer bullet; the frenzied yells of the attackers who hoped to wear down these stubborn Indians by sheer weight of numbers. But somehow the Rajput companies, most gallantly led by Captains Ansari and Newton, held their ground.

The Japanese concentrated all their fury on this, our last position on the mainland. All day long the Rajputs were under vicious and sustained artillery and mortar fire. All night the suicidal waves of infantry were flung against them. But somehow the line still held.

But in spite of all this gallantry the sands were fast running out. Maltby foresaw the greatest difficulties, indeed the im-

[1]After the capitulation, Ansari died as a prisoner-of-war in exceptionally gallant circumstances. He was starved and abominably tortured by the Japanese in their efforts to seduce him from his loyalty to the British. When all else failed, he was beheaded.

possibility, of maintaining this gallant little force with ammunition and supplies in their isolated position. At 4 a.m. on 13th December he ordered their withdrawal to the island, where clearly every man who could hold a rifle would be needed.

The evacuation of the Rajputs from Devil's Peak was in the nature of a miniature Dunkirk. The antiquated destroyer *Thracian*—Hong Kong's largest warship, built in 1916, maximum speed twenty knots, total armament three 4-inch guns—came in as close as her captain, Lieutenant-Commander Pears, RN, dared.

Stung to fury at their failure to eliminate this obstinate force, the Japs rained shells and mortar bombs on the Rajputs as they waded out to *Thracian*, rifles held above their heads. Not a single man who could walk left his weapon behind.

Petty Officer Peter Paul of *Thracian* watched the Rajputs as they came aboard. He could see that they were very far from being beaten men. Their discipline as they struggled aboard the destroyer, Paul records, was wholly admirable; comparable, indeed, to that of the Guards at Dunkirk.

The faces of these Indians were grim, tight-lipped and unsmiling. In the battles on the mainland, as each successive Japanese attack was hurled back, there had been laughing and cheering; but now there was silence, ominous and complete. There was, too, a peculiar greyish tint to their skins, appropriate to men who had been bombed and shelled almost beyond the point of human endurance. But in not one brown face was there evidence of defeat.

All right, these faces seemed to say, so they've driven us back by bombing and shelling—but these bombs and shells were delivered by men we cannot see. Back on the island it will be a different story; put us back in the front line on the island and we'll take the Japs on again any time they like. We did it on the mainland and we'll do it again—just give us a chance to fight men we can see.

Captain Bob Newton was the last man to board *Thracian*. His face had subtly changed: it was no longer boyish and clear-complexioned, but deeply etched with lines—the face of a man who had experienced the uttermost extremes of exhaustion and endeavour. But it was not a beaten face. . . .

It was 9.20 am on the morning of 13th December when the last Rajput set foot on Hong Kong Island at Aberdeen.

General Maltby, an Indian Army man himself, went to Aberdeen to meet the Rajputs. He saw at once that the ranks of the two companies were sadly depleted. Seeing these men, the words of congratulation in Hindustani did not come easily because he found a strange difficulty in speaking. But the men saw and understood: the General *sahib* had come to meet them and after a rest they would do anything that he asked of them.

The fact that Lieutenant-General Sakai was in a bad temper was early apparent to the orderly who called him, the staff officers with whom he came in contact and the two grooms who were working on his white horse. Everything was wrong: the prawns were not cooked right; last night's *saki* had left him with a heaving stomach and a sick headache; the white horse seemed to look like any other flea-bitten grey; his sword scabbard had not been properly polished; his moustaches, instead of curling imperiously upward, had developed a tendency to droop; his highly polished field boots seemed unaccountably full of feet; he was constipated. It was a bad look-out for someone.

He vented his wrath on the commander of the battalion which had been bloodily and expensively repulsed by the Rajputs; he heaped invective on a soaking and bedraggled major who had failed to prevent the crossing of Forsyth's force (the major had fallen into the water and narrowly escaped drowning). Sakai stormed about his headquarters like a petulant fishwife and everyone kept well out of his way. For the first time since the invasion of Hong Kong had started, things were not going according to plan and the general was out for blood.

The casualty lists were, for the first time, assuming significance. After the initial triumph of the Shingmun Redoubt, the stubborn resistance of the Rajputs had infuriated Sakai.

Later in the day Sakai's temper simmered down. He had first toyed with the idea of launching an all-out offensive which would put the whole stubborn and misguided garrison of the Island to the sword. The resistance of the Rajputs was just a flash in the pan: the rest of the defenders must be demoralised by the shelling, the bombing and the uncertainty of waiting. Chinese fifth columnists were even now spreading defeatist propaganda and many civilians must be thinking in terms of surrender. The soft and spoon-fed population of Hong Kong were in no state to withstand a prolonged siege.

With these thoughts to guide him, Sakai composed a letter to the Governor of Hong Kong and gave instructions that it was to be delivered on the following morning.

At 9 am, while the last Rajputs were still in transit, a launch bearing a white flag of truce put off from Kowloon pier. On board the launch were four of Sakai's staff officers bearing a letter addressed to the Governor. The letter demanded the immediate surrender of the Colony and threatened severe and indiscriminate artillery fire and aerial bombardment in the event of refusal. The demand was tantamount to unconditional surrender and was rejected with a curt 'No' from Sir Mark Young.

Clanking their swords, the Japanese staff officers re-boarded their launch and headed for Kowloon, hissing threats of total annihilation.

In the little Kowloon Hospital the endless work of mercy went on. There was not enough room for all the civilian casualties; there never had been enough room. Originally built to accommodate a hundred bed patients, by the evening of December 12th it contained at least a thousand Chinese. Old men and women; young men separated from their wives; young women separated from their babies; they poured into the hospital in a never ending stream. Here was an old woman with a great gaping gash from hairline to throat; here was a small boy with a smashed kneecap; here a young mother, three fingers blown from her hand, rocked a baby to sleep—she did not know that the baby had been shocked out of life by the blast of the bomb that had mutilated her hand.

They lay on beds, under beds, on the floor, in the corridors, on stretchers, on tables; they sat on chairs, staring dumbly in front of them; they moaned, howled, wept and laughed hysterically; they died when the nurses' backs were turned for a moment. Over the whole hospital hung a sickly smell, compounded of blood, unwashed bodies and incipient gangrene.

Outside could be heard the noises of battle, coming ever nearer: the crump of shells, the stutter of machine guns, the sullen whine of ricochetting rifle bullets. The three doctors and fifteen nurses paid no heed to any of these things: tottering with fatigue, bespattered with blood, they worked on.

That afternoon the matron, Miss Dorothy Gean, had called all the nurses together. Without dramatics she told them that the mainland was to be evacuated. Miss Gean was a middle-aged, grey-haired woman with a somewhat severe face: the type of matron whose appearance in a ward sends a shiver of apprehension through the young nurse on duty and causes patients to extinguish furtive cigarettes. But Matron Gean had an unsuspected heart of gold under her somewhat forbidding exterior; only the children knew about the sweets secreted in her apron pocket.

A young nurse called Vera Brett asked if everyone was going over to the Island. Even as she spoke, the last of the Rajputs were in transit across the channel.

The Matron smiled her rare and oddly attractive smile. "Everyone," she said slowly, "except us. . . ."

Sybil Spencer had had perhaps seven hours sleep in four days. She sat in the small nurses' rest room and examined her face in a small mirror. Automatically she said to herself: "I look terrible."

She was conscious of a paralysing feeling of exhaustion. She found that every time she sat down her eyes closed; the backs of her legs ached intolerably; her temples throbbed. Her normally trim white uniform was creased, crumpled and streaked with blood.

She found herself thinking of all sorts of pleasant things that had happened to her, so long ago now: the swimming parties at Repulse Bay: the Russian dinner at the Balalaika, a famed Kowloon nightspot, where a Filipino dance band played into the small hours of the morning; the *borge* and cream and the thirty-two dishes of assorted meat and fish; the young Canadian officers who had danced so much better than the British; her last home leave and the Crazy Gang at the Palladium; the new evening dress, as yet unworn, in the nurses' quarters. Sybil Spencer cried briefly and unobtrusively. Then she bathed her eyes in cold water and went back to the crying, the maimed, the dying and the dead. . . .

At 9 am the following morning everything suddenly seemed much quieter. At that precise moment the last of the Rajputs were landing at Aberdeen and Lieutenant-General

Sakai's representative was crossing the harbour with his demand for surrender.

There was just as much noise in Sybil Spencer's ward. On all sides she could hear the piteous cries of 'missee Nurse!' She was in the act of putting a dressing on a gaping wound on a woman's thigh when she heard the commotion outside: heavy footfalls and high-pitched, lisping voices.

A Japanese soldier kicked open the door and stood facing her. He was small and bow-legged. Slung on his shoulder was a long rifle with bayonet fixed. He wore spectacles and when he opened his mouth Sybil Spencer saw that he had a complete set of gold teeth. At first sight he seemed almost unbelievably comic.

He came so close to her that she could smell the rank, stale liquor on his breath. Just behind her an old woman, both hands swathed in bandages, let out a high-pitched, prayerful wail. The Jap nudged Sybil Spencer with the butt of his rifle and pointed to the door.

"You come," he said. . . .

The indecently unemotional voice of a BBC announcer said: *"The evacuation of the mainland is complete. Hong Kong is now settling down to an old-fashioned siege."* Tokyo Radio predicted that the fate of Hong Kong would be decided in a matter of days.

CHAPTER FIVE

Now Hong Kong Island was finally and irrevocably on its own and the impact on its inhabitants was immediate and varied. Englishmen, who had maintained to the last that it would never happen, rolled up their sleeves and swore to sell their lives dearly: they had not built up prosperous businesses to see twenty years of endeavour go to waste; the Chinese fifth columnists licked their lips in pleasurable anticipation and thought up subtle and hideous schemes: the spreading of false rumours, inducing desertion from essential services, inciting to riot.

A prominent Chinese merchant indulged in vociferous defeatist talk and promptly found himself under arrest; men back from the mainland fighting exploded all the preconceived notions of the Far East Intelligence Bureau. The Japanese attack on the mainland had finally convinced everyone that the Japs meant business. Suddenly everyone started to take the Japanese very seriously indeed. They had ceased to be funny little yellow men with bandy legs, gold teeth and wearing spectacles.

The British Press, in the main, took it on the chin. The *Daily Sketch*, for instance, said: 'It will need more than Japan's third-rate air force to save the shockingly over-confident yellow Napoleons from the consequences of their folly', and later, 'We are not in the least disheartened or alarmed at any of the preliminary catastrophes suffered either by America or ourselves at the hands of Japan. We anticipated them.' Obviously, it would take more than Japan to throw a scare into the *Daily Sketch*.

The Times, too, was buttressing the Island fortress. 'The British have not in any way been taken by surprise,' it announced, presumably to make upper-class breakfasts more palatable.

But the *Dail Mail* was in more sombre mood. 'Britain's loneliest outpost—the fortress of Hong Kong—is today fighting for its existence against the full weight of Jap military, naval and air power ... the island must depend on its own resources, with little or no hope of relief.' Then, as if everyone didn't know, it proclaimed, 'We must face the fact that the war in the Far East has so far gone badly.'

The *Daily Telegraph*, however, were sternly optimistic. 'Hong Kong, easternmost outpost of the British Empire, is being shelled and bombed and is facing the siege for which it has been preparing for years. Food stocks have been built up which will last for at least three months and there is no shortage of heavy guns. The Union Jack flying over Government House typifies the determination of everyone to fight to the last drop of blood. Whatever the colony's fate, two things are certain: the population is in for a hard time and the Japanese will have to pay dearly for any headway they may make.'

The *Daily Express* were cautiously non-committal: 'There is room to believe, I understand,' wrote a well-informed journalist, who must have been listening in on Lieutenant-General Sakai's operational orders, 'that a much bigger offensive than the present harassing attacks may be undertaken very shortly.'

It was left to the *Daily Mirror* (and Jane) to keep morale on the Home Front at a high level. A brave headline roared: 'Sir Mark Young told the Japs (politely)"GO TO HELL".'

The Germans and Italians were jubilant; the Americans, shocked and reeling after Pearl Harbour, could offer little save distant sympathy; the Russians, with Hitler hammering at the gates of Stalingrad, had more than enough troubles of their own. Only in Singapore did complacency continue to reign supreme. 'We shall,' said the *Straits Times* with bland confidence, 'be rejoicing before 1943 comes round. . . .'

Now these things befell Hong Kong. . . .

It was obvious to even the wildest optimist in Hong Kong that a Japanese landing on the island could not long be delayed. On December 13th the Japs started a cat and mouse game. Lieutenant-General Sakai well knew that to assault the island immediately would invite heavy casualties and the casualty lists had already caused him some concern: the rough handling his men had received at the hands of the Rajputs at Devil's Peak had given him food for thought.

Sakai knew, moreover, that the anti-aircraft defences of the Island were inadequate—indeed, he knew exactly where every gun was located—and it seemed likely that Hong Kong could be bombed from the air, almost with impunity.

But on that day one Japanese seaplane failed to return to base and the credit for this belongs solely to Sapper Bill Bailey of 22 Field Company, Fortress Engineers.

Bailey's company commander, Major Dan Grose, had never forecast an illustrious military future for him and he had been unwillingly appointed cook. Bailey's culinary efforts had made him a wide-open target for the company wags who gleefully produced that ancient barrack-room chestnut: 'Who called the cook a bastard?' to which the devastating *riposte* is, 'Who called the bastard a cook?' Like many small men, Bailey had an exceptionally loud voice and his stentorian bawl of *'Come an' get it!'* sent shudders of apprehension through the stomachs of 22 Field Company.

On the 13th, dinner had been eaten and groused at: Bailey had produced a confection which he had imaginatively described as 'Cornish pasty'. The popular opinion was that it was all Cornish and no pasty. While the other men of the company went about the multifarious tasks of the sapper—laying anti-personnel mines, installing booby traps and strengthening fortifications—Bailey was placed on the Lewis gun and informed that he was solely responsible for the company's anti-aircraft defence. The Sergeant-Major had grimly threatened him with slow immersion in one of his own stews if any harm came to them from the air.

It was yet another glorious sunny afternoon. Comfortably replete (he liked his own cooking, even if no one else did), Sapper Bailey scanned the clear blue sky. On the whole, he considered, this seemed a cushy enough assignment—it was certainly vastly preferable to digging trenches in the hot sun.

Two sappers paused to pass the time of day with Bailey.

"We'll be all right now," said one, "wiv old Bobba-ji[1] on ack-ack."

"I'd rather be bombed than eat another of them ruddy pasties," opined the other.

Before Bailey could think of a suitable retort, the seaplane dived at them out of the sky. The two sappers dived for cover. Bailey swung the Lewis gun into position and fired a long burst. The two sappers looked up and rubbed their eyes. The seaplane, black smoke pouring from its tail, was spiralling into the sea.

On receipt of the glad news, Major Grose presented Bailey

[1] Thomas Atkins' Hindustani for cook.

with fifty cigarettes. From then on Sapper Bailey became a man of some standing in 22 Field Company, but it was agreed that as a cook he made a bloody good machine gunner. . . .

During the rest of December 13th enemy artillery fire increased in intensity: a 9.2-inch gun at Mount Davis was knocked out by a direct hit, and at dusk that evening Belcher's Fort was heavily shelled and set on fire. Other fires, which spread with vicious swiftness, were started at West Point and Kennedy Town. The pall of thick black smoke, which was shortly to envelop the Island, had started already.

Chinese fifth columnists resumed their vile work with renewed enthusiasm and persuaded large numbers of army transport drivers to desert and take their lorries with them. They tapped telephone calls and circulated false rumours about imaginary landings at different points on the Island. They fastened avidly on rumour, uncertainty, fear and defeatism. It was no wonder that panic spread through the Chinese civilian population like a carrier of some filthy disease.

The looters, not to be outdone, went about their trade with a will; they stripped clean every damaged or deserted house: a building was no sooner vacated than it was reduced to an empty shell.

A few, but only a very few, Europeans remained unaffected by the fact that the Japanese were in possession of the mainland and must shortly launch an offensive on the Island. Second-Lieutenant Stanley Cooke was on town patrol on the afternoon of December 14th, checking the unauthorised parking of vehicles. Near the foot of the Peak he observed an English-woman, a determined and unquenchable bridge player, alighting from the car. Clearly the lady, so far as outward appearances were concerned, was leaving nothing to chance: she was tastefully dressed for the occasion in a wide-brimmed hat accoutred with a bewildering array of *fauna*, and gloves with frills at the wrists.

Mad bitches and Englishwomen, thought Cooke inconsequently. "I'm afraid you can't leave your car there," he said.

The lady regarded him with immeasurable scorn. "And why not?" she demanded with glacial menace.

"The Japs are in Kowloon," Cooke reminded her gently. "They may be here soon."

The lady glared at him, as if scenting impertinence. "That," she said, "is a matter of supreme indifference to me." She shot him a look of concentrated venom and sailed majestically into her bridge party.

Meanwhile, the shelling continued. . . .

On the morning of December 15th, to the relieved amazement of everyone, the expected 'morning hate' on the Island failed to materialise. The shelling, uncannily accurate because all targets had been pin-pointed in the spacious days of peace, had become almost as commonplace as the air raids on London and Liverpool. But at 8 am on that morning a sodden and disquieting silence descended over the Island: not a single Japanese gun spoke; not a plane appeared in the clear blue sky.

The feeling of relief soon gave way to one of uneasy apprehension. The Japs were in full possession of Kowloon and everyone (with the possible exception of the more determined bridge schools on the Peak) knew that the Japs must be preparing for a landing on the Island. If anything, the enemy inactivity increased rather than lessened the strain.

"What d'you think they're up to, sir?" Iain MacGregor asked General Maltby, as they breakfasted together at Flagstaff House.

"Putting the wind up us," remarked the General, "and not making such a bad job of it either."

"The Japanese," declared the lady bridge player forcibly, to anyone who would listen to her, "have no manners. . . ."

On the evening of the 14th, Lieutenant-General Sakai had sent for the officer in charge of the psychological warfare department, an earnest and bespectacled young captain. This captain, it seemed, had a comprehensive knowledge of the English character, which he had gleaned from a close study of their racial characteristics before the war. He knew all about such diverse things as public schools, greyhound racing, Ascot and the Cup Final.

The captain developed his theme with relish. The British soldier, he said, not entirely inaccurately, thought only of four things: beer, home, cigarettes and women.

Sakai reminded him that his assessment of the Indian soldiers' war aims had been sadly at fault: the crudely and melodramatically designed leaflets, far from causing the Indians to throw their hands in, had produced exactly the reverse effect. The bulk of the casualties suffered by the Japs had, indeed, been inflicted by the Punjabis and the Rajputs, allegedly downtrodden lackeys of the British. How did the captain explain away that one?

The captain, feeling a cold wind blowing round his promotion prospects, could explain it and said so. But, he went on, his face gleaming with honest dedication, he had a scheme for undermining British soldiers' morale which was a sure fire winner.

The General waved the captain away. Whatever his new scheme was, he assured him, it had better be good.

Sakai next sent for Major-General Ito Takeo and they went into a lengthy huddle. He told him that a signal honour would shortly come the way of his 38th Division. When the psychological warfare section had had their bit of fun it would be Ito Takeo's turn. . . .

The psychological warfare section installed a loud speaker apparatus of enormous power and volume on the Kowloon ferry wharf. Presently a loud hissing noise—presumably the Japanese equivalent of 'testing'—was heard all over the Island. Then the voice spoke:

"British soldiers!" it boomed, "you must know it is useless to fight us. Why do you not go home to your wives and children? You cannot resist the might of the huge Japanese Army. We have many thousands of men, guns, aeroplanes, ships. Go home, British soldiers, go home!"

The men of the Middlesex in their pill-boxes listened, enthralled.

"No good me going home—we bin bombed aht."

"He wouldn't say that if he knew my mother-in-law."

The voice became cosy and intimate.

"Christmas will soon be here and the children will hang up their stockings. The carol singers will be singing Good King Wenceslas and Hark the Herald Angels Sing. Throw down your arms and there will be peace and good will to all under the great Japanese Empire. Father Christmas will be coming down the chimney . . ."

"Wouldn't get dahn ours," said a private soldier morosely, "my mum's bin on to the sweep for a bloody year but he ain't been yet. Next Friday, missis, for sure, 'e sez . . ."

". . . and the joyous cries of the children will echo in every home . . ."

"'E wouldn't think they was joyous cries if 'e 'ad our nipper. Every —— morning at three o'clock—a-o-o-o—o—aow— eeeee! Gettin' 'is first teeth, see? Cor, wot a bull an' cow . . ."

"Think of the Cup Final and the Boat Race," continued the voice inexorably. "The chorus girls at the Empire. The naked girls at the Windmill Theatre, swaying backwards and for-wards . . ."

"That's all 'e knows abaht it—they ain't allowed to move."

"I saw one move once—she got a wasp on 'er left tit. Cor, wot a carve-up that was . . ."

"Henley, and the oars slipping in and out of the water . . ."

"Blimey!" said a lance-corporal who had not been paying attention. "That sounds a bit of orlright."

"What do?"

"The 'ores slipping in and out of the water."

"*Oars*, you ignorant ——"

"That's wot 'e said."

"Don't you never think of nothink else?"

"Fish and chips. Roast beef and Yorkshire pudding. Girls to dance with. Kisses in the darkness of the cinema. Piccadilly Circus, Leicester Square, Widdicombe Fair and Birmingham. A pint of bitter and mild at the Savoy Hotel . . ."

"Now, that proves the bloke's dead ignorant," said Private Cullen, universally known as 'The Major' because of a strange tendency to address everyone as 'old boy'. "They ain't got no draft wallop in the Savoy."

"'Ow do you know?"

"Cos I bin there, that's 'ow. A geezer took me in there an' asked me wot I was goin' to 'ave. 'Pint of bitter,' I sez. A waiter bloke, all done up in a white coat, said: 'Sorry, sir, only bottled ale.' I'm telling you, old boy, this Jap's got it all arse about face. . . ."

"And now," continued the Japanese voice, in the tone of a man determined to introduce culture into a swinish rabble, "we will have some music. When you have heard this I am sure that you will take my advice and throw down your arms. Listen now, British soldiers. . . ."

Across the channel came the penetrating voice of Al Jolson. The men of the Middlesex joined in enthusiastically. 'Rocka-bye', 'Toot-toot Tootsie' and 'Carolina in the Morning', were quickly followed by 'Swanee'.

"How I love you, how I love you, my dear old Swan-e-e-e-e-e-!" sang the Middlesex in blissful and frustrated chorus.

"Wot about 'Mammy' then?" demanded a vintage corporal, who preferred Mr Jolson's older renderings.

Soon the honey-sweet soprano of Deanna Durbin trilled with heavenly and professional perfection round the Island. She sang, 'It's Foolish but it's Fun', 'The Lights of Home', and, inevitably, 'Home Sweet Home'.

"Wouldn't mind 'avin' 'er in this —— pill-box."

"My ole woman sings a bit in the kitchen but she don't sound like that. . . ."

It was hardly surprising, having regard to this conversational exchange, that the psychological warfare section found that they had yet another flop on their hands.

By 10.30 am that morning the Japanese had gone back to a more practical form of warfare. The captain in charge of the psychological warfare section had retired fussily to the rear with a new problem on his hands: America was in the war, too, and he was planning a big campaign. The Americans, as everyone knew, persecuted Jews and Negroes; the phrases came easily to his facile tongue: 'American Negroes unite against your American enemies! You fight for them now, but back in America they will rape your wives and your children and burn you alive. Why be a shoe-shine boy all your life?' This was big stuff: the Japanese captain, chewing over the choice phrases as if they were exotic sweets, planned for his next campaign against the Americans in the Pacific. . . .

The shelling increased in intensity. Three pillboxes on the North Shore were knocked out and a fourth badly damaged. A high velocity gun of small calibre, firing from a concealed position on Kowloon waterfront, drilled forty holes through one of these pillboxes, killing every single man inside. This, then, was part of the softening-up process, for no army, not even the Japs with their vast reserves of manpower and disregard for casualties, would hurl infantry against a position before it had been all but pounded to pulp. This was only the beginning.

By now the Island defences had been reorganised and the Island was divided into two Brigade areas. The senior Canadian officer, Brigadier John Lawson, MC, commanded the force known as West Brigade, which comprised the Middlesex, the Royal Scots and the 2/14 Punjabis.

Of the 2nd Royal Scots, Maltby says bluntly in his despatch: 'This battalion was not in good shape, as they had lost many of their best officers killed or wounded.'

West Brigade was disposed as follows: Brigade Head-quarters was on the road, one hundred yards west of Wongnei-chong Gap; the Punjabis held the shore-line from the Naval Yard westwards to Telegraph Bay; the 1st Middlesex carried on from Telegraph Bay to Stanley Peninsula and were also responsible for the coast between Causeway Bay and the Naval Yard. The Royal Scots were in the area around Happy Valley racecourse.

East Brigade, commanded by Brigadier Cedric Wallis, comprised the 5/7 Rajputs, the Winnipeg Grenadiers and the Royal Rifles of Canada. The Rajputs held the coastline from Causeway Bay eastwards to Dai Wan; the Royal Rifles of Canada were along the coast from Dai Wan to Stanley; the Winnipeg Grenadiers were in the Repulse Bay-Deepwater Bay area. Headquarters of East Brigade was at the point where the Shek-O Road joins Island Road, overlooking Saiwan.

The commandant of the Hong Kong Volunteer Defence Corps, Colonel Henry Rose, MC, was pleasantly surprised at the speed and precision with which his men took up their positions.

Colonel Rose—thirty years a soldier, a last war winner of the Military Cross, one of the original 'contemptible little army' sent out to hold back Von Kluck's hordes in 1914, a conventional British infantryman of the older school—had viewed his assignment to the command of the Hong Kong volunteers in 1938 with some misgivings—misgivings which were very soon to disappear. He was fortunate enough to have with him Regimental Sergeant-Major 'Wacky' Jones of the East Surrey Regiment—a fierce disciplinarian of small stature but lungs of brass—and between them they moulded what at first appeared to be something of a rabble into a finely disciplined fighting force with an *esprit de corps* which was peculiarly their own. Bright red were the faces of the Middlesex Regiment when, in 1940, No 3 (Eurasian) Company beat them hollow in a machine gun shooting competition. Purple were the faces of the marksmen of the Royal Scots when the Portuguese walked off with the rifle cup.

"There is," said Colonel Rose, "only one thing that I like to remember about the battle for Hong Kong, and that is the absolutely splendid behaviour and fighting qualities of the Volunteers throughout."

The Volunteers were ready: mixed British and Chinese companies; the Scottish company (Scots of every nationality, as Lieutenant Eric Bryden described them); the Portuguese company; the Eurasian company: businessmen, clerks, bank officials, civil servants and engineers. RSM Jones had repeatedly told them that he had seen nothing like them since he had joined the Bethnal Green Wolf Cub pack in *circa* 1910 and that he had seen better soldiers in a Shanghai whorehouse, but he would not have accepted a transfer to the Grenadier Guards. . . .

The Hong Kong Volunteer Defence Corps were positioned as follows:

1st Battery:	Cape D'Aguilar
2nd Battery:	Bluff Head, Stanley
3rd Battery:	Aberdeen Island
4th Battery:	Pak Sha Wan
5th Battery:	Sai Wan Hill
No 1 Company:	Tytam Valley
No 2 Company:	Pottinger Gap and Big Wave Bay
No 3 Company:	Jardine's Look-Out
No 4 Company:	High West, Victoria Gap and Mount Kellett
No 5 Company:	Mount Davis
No 6 Company:	The North Shore
No 7 Company:	Magazine Gap, Wanchai Gap, Middle Gap.

This was all there was in the way of Major-General Ito Takeo's 38th Division with a strength of rather more than 20,000 men. . . .

On the afternoon of December 15th, disquieting news came from observation posts on the Island. The enemy were observed to be preparing sandbagged positions on Kowloon Waterfront and the theory was put forward that mortar positions were being prepared: a theory which was sombrely confirmed shortly afterwards when mortar bombs began to fall in the vicinity of the Naval dockyard, causing several casualties. Now, added to the bombing and the shelling was the additional menace of the mortar. Unlike the defenders, the Japs were not short of mortar ammunition—a fact which became increasingly apparent as the afternoon wore on. They were also terrifyingly skilled in the use of this devastating weapon.

Still more sinister were the movements of a number of small craft in Kowloon Bay. This could point to only one course of enemy action: a landing on the Island.

At 9.15 pm that evening the Japanese attempted a landing. In concept it was bold to the point of being suicidal and was summarily and bloodily dealt with.

The attempt was carried out by fanatically brave men. Estimates of their numbers varied from one to two companies, but on this occasion not a single Jap set foot on the Island.

Many swam across the channel, pushing crude rafts made of petrol tins with their equipment. Others made the journey in a strange assortment of craft: small rubber boats, sampans and junks. An alert searchlight picked them up in its beam and all hell was promptly let loose. The sight of them must have gladdened the heart of every man within striking distance.

It certainly gladdened the heart of Master-Gunner Cousins, in charge of a detachment of 6-inch guns at Pak Sha Wan. They fired over open sights and poured shell after shell into this unwieldy armada. Machine gun and rifle fire from a platoon of the Royal Rifles of Canada added their quota of hellish din and contributed generously to the slaughter.

It was a wonderfully heartening experience for the defenders and they poured a steady and murderous fire into the Japanese. A junk, punctured by hundreds of bullets was holed, and sank; riflemen picked off the struggling Japs in the water as fast as they could work their bolts and machine gunners sprayed the water, by now reddened with blood. Obscenely bathed in the glare of the searchlight, the channel became a dark shambles of shrieking, struggling, kicking and drowning Japanese. Not until the last yelling voice was silent and the last clawing hand still, was the order to cease fire given.

It was a tremendous boost to the morale of the defenders, whose nerves had been cruelly shaken during this uneasy and protracted period of waiting. Many of the Canadians had barely fired their rifles on practice ranges, let alone in anger, and it was particularly gratifying to these young and unseasoned troops to discover how easy it was to destroy a screaming and struggling enemy in the water. There was hardly a single man of the Royal Rifles of Canada who would not have welcomed another attempted landing like this one.

HMS *Thracian* met with mixed fortunes on this night. She made her way from Aberdeen, across the enemy front to Kowloon Bay—a singularly daring manoeuvre by Lieutenant-Commander Pears. Unhappily, by some inexplicable error of navigation, she went aground.

'At first,' relates Petty Officer Peter Paul, 'I was certain we had been torpedoed. It was pitch dark, there was no moon and we were at action cruising stations. Suddenly there was a shuddering crash; the ship's bottom was ripped open and the forward compartment flooded.'

Thracian, however, was very far from being sunk. As soon as he realised that she was aground, Pears backed her out just as dawn was breaking. As the old destroyer struggled free, the most mouth-watering target that any naval gunner can have ever seen presented itself. Two large junks, packed from bows to stern with Japanese troops, lay dead ahead.

Seriously incapacitated as she was, *Thracian* permitted herself a brief gloat and then opened up with everything she had. A shell hit one of the wooden junks and it was soon blazing from end to end.

The Japs were as vulnerable as paper boats in a slow stream pursued by determined small boys armed with a supply of large stones; the first shell hit one of the junks amidships and it burst into flames. In a matter of seconds it was blazing from end to end.

A Chinese junk is not designed for swift manoeuvrability and the other one did not escape *Thracian*'s vengeful fury. Every piece of metal at her disposal was pumped into these cumbersome craft. When nothing remained but floating bodies and spars of wood, *Thracian* headed painfully but triumphantly for home.

These two successes, following so soon one after the other, were galvanic shots in the arm for the defenders. There was, however, little jubilation in Maltby's headquarters for the General well knew that these landings were nothing more than curtain raisers: the Island was still faced by Ito Takeo's fresh and formidable 38th Division (the troops used in the attempted landing were low calibre expendables); Japanese planes were still overhead and could bomb the Island with insulting ease; their navy, vigilant and menacing, watched from the sea. 'We were,' observed Gwen Dew, an American journalist, 'clay pigeons in a tiny shooting range.'

The situation was not, however, entirely black; the defenders of the Island had drawn first blood and it was reported from the Chinese General Staff in Chungking that General Yu Han Mou's 7th Army was advancing towards Hong Kong to take the Japs in the rear. This news was modified by the cautious statement that effective assistance could not be made available before early January, but it represented the nearest thing to good news that Maltby had heard yet.

Although Maltby privately thought that it would be unwise to bank on Chinese help, he circulated the news of the Chinese advance to all units. The morale of his men needed all the boosting it could get.

The effect on morale was all that Maltby had expected and there was jubilation on all sides. Even if they were alone, it seemed that Hong Kong was not a beleaguered fortress entirely without hope. The men on Hong Kong were short of nearly everything but hope—and hope was a priceless commodity. If the news about the Chinese was something of a white lie, it was better than nothing, and the *Daily Telegraph* fastened on it with enthusiasm: 'The imperturbability of the Chinese is admirable,' it reassured its readers. 'The Canadians are in fine fettle. . . .' It is not certain whether the United States Marines besieged on Wake Island did, in fact, say 'send more Japs', but there is no doubt that a young officer of the Royal Rifles of Canada said just that—and meant it.

A reference to an equally beleaguered force, Major Devereaux's US Marines on Wake Island, is not inappropriate here. A favourite axiom of the United States Marine Corps, expressed in its most colloquial form is this: 'Maybe you oughta get more, maybe you will get more, but all you can depend on getting is what you already got.'

That's how it was on Wake Island and that's how it was in Hong Kong. . . .

CHAPTER SIX

ON DECEMBER 16th the Japs started to hot things up. Obviously the Japanese artillerymen and airmen thought that Hong Kong had had it easy up to now and it was high time that a salutary lesson was administered. If the truth be known, Lieutenant-General Sakai was getting worried: as in any other army, the hierarchy were on his tail; his orders were to capture Hong Kong, and the Japanese High Command had never been famed for their patience. Although the High Command stayed well away from the battle, they made the whole thing sound easy from Tokyo. Sakai's failure to capture Hong Kong on time would not excuse him with the procession of geometrically fiercer beings behind him. In the Japanese Army, as in any other, there was always a way: take the right way and there lay promotion and a glittering array of appointments in occupied territory; take the wrong one and there was obscurity and disgrace—and, in the case of a Japanese General, *hara-kiri*. . . .

The gunners, therefore, were urged to shell the Island with unprecedented ferocity; the air force were committed to maximum effort. Mount Davis was attacked by seventeen enemy planes and subjected to heavy and accurate shelling. Anti-aircraft units did the best they could, but Goliath dominated the skies and David's sling, at best, was woefully short of both stones and elastic.

General Maltby, ever a man of integrity and scrupulous fairness, described the anti-aircraft defences of the Island with severely controlled bitterness. From beginning to end Maltby was a fierce champion of his soldiers and he had this to say about the gallant but unavailing attempts of his anti-aircraft gunners to combat this shattering menace from the air:

'There were insufficient guns to give adequate gun density at any point. The anti-aircraft defences were well known to be inadequate, but I realised that the call for the European and Mediterranean theatres of war had prevented reinforcements. Targets were numerous ('he can say that again,' observed a disgruntled and much-bombed Canadian officer) but the anti-aircraft positions extremely few owing to the mountainous nature of the country of Hong Kong Island. The enemy, with such good observation from Kowloon, was very quick on to any AA section opening up, and I consider that Lieutenant-Colonel F. D. Field, in command of anti-aircraft defences, fought his command courageously and well. The scarcity both of transport and roads severely handicapped the mobility of the guns and also the ammunition supply and administration of the sections.'

For the defenders—Middlesex, Royal Scots, Indians, artillerymen and volunteers—it was hard to remember anything except the paralysing weariness, hunger and lack of sleep. In a way, the Royal Scots and the Indians were luckier than the rest because they had experienced close combat and had *seen* their enemy face to face. But for the others the days blurred together in an exhausting sameness of bombing, shelling, unceasing vigilance, hastily snatched meals and unutterable weariness. A hungry man will scramble for food; a thirsty man will fight for water—just as an incurable alcoholic will perjure his soul for a shot of hooch. But a tired man longs only for unconsciousness—blissful oblivion and the heavenly knowledge that someone else is handling things.

The men of the Middlesex probably emerged from this ordeal best of all. They were, almost to a man, Londoners, and Londoners—dog-weary, battered but unquenchably durable—had been thumbing their noses at Hitler's *Luftwaffe* for two weary years. It was Regimental Sergeant-Major Challis, a frightening disciplinarian and ever sparing with his praise, who said of these men: "It's a funny thing about these blokes—you just can't get the bastards down. . . ."

Major Henry Marsh, commanding 'C' Company of the 1st Middlesex, reports laconically in his diary: 'Air raids appeared to be timed to take place during normal meal times and considerably interfered with the distribution of hot meals. (The soldiers' dinner hour, 1 pm—2 pm, was apparently as inflexible as the military mind.) Lack of canteen facilities became very marked, but the works manager of the British American Tobacco Company presented us with 25,000 cigarettes which were much appreciated. . . .'

"As long as they've got their fags," declared RSM Challis, "they'll hold the bloody Island for ten years. . . ."

No survivor of Hong Kong is likely to forget December 17th in a hurry. It was a day of such ludicrous incongruity that in contrast with all the misery and horror that had gone before, it seemed almost laughable. The pattern of events, it was universally agreed, could only have been engineered by a Jap. It proved, in a way that nothing else in the Pacific War could, that in childlike confidence and inordinate conceit the Japanese, as a race, are in a class by themselves.

The day started normally enough with the humdrum sounds of bombing and shelling; the steady drain of casualties; the cursing of sleep-starved men; the rumours. In pillbox, artillery gun position, in hospital ward, in private house the same question was asked: 'Will they land today?'

An artillery officer said: "Hope to God they do. My chaps haven't fired a shot yet."

A Middlesex private said: "They'd bloody well better, or I'll lose a dollar."

A Royal Scots company sergeant-major said: "Here's tae us. Whae's like us? Bluidy few, an' they're all deid."

A middle-aged volunteer said: "If they don't come today, old boy, I'm going back to the office."

Mr Ralston, Canadian Minister of Defence, said (in Ottawa): "The garrison's position is undoubtedly, for the time being, a very trying and difficult one."

The lady bridge player said: "What I can't understand is why doesn't somebody *do* something about these odious Japanese?"

The *Daily Telegraph* said: 'In a full state of siege, Hong Kong is confident of the outcome of its heroic defence.'

At midday, December 17th, 1941, the Japanese came to Hong Kong Island, but there were only three of them.

The arrival of the Japanese 'Peace Mission' was as ludicrous as the appearance of a low comedy trio of baggy-trousered acrobats in the middle of a *Grand Guignol* play. Onlookers on the quayside at Victoria rubbed their eyes, stared, pinched themselves and put it down to an exaggerated form of war neurosis.

Chug-chugging across the harbour was a small launch bearing on its bow a large white banner on which was emblazoned 'PEACE MISSION'.

Three Japanese tripped delicately from the launch: Colonel

An aerial view of the Hong Kong residential, business and harbour areas

Hong Kong's Taikoo district and in the background the hills over which the Japanese swarmed to take the city

Lieut-General Rensuke Isogai, first
Japanese governor of Hong Kong

Captain Christopher Man
of the Middlesex

Corporal Harry Pelham,
Royal Engineers

Lance-Corporal 'Tookie' Poole

Major Robert Templer,
8th Coast Artillery

Captain Alastair Thompson, who
stormed Shouson Hill with 25 Sikhs

Lieut-Commander John Boldero
of the *Cicala*

Corporal Dan Cavill, who fought with
the 'Hughesiliers'

British POWs leaving Hong Kong on their way to a Japanese prison camp

Captain Bob Newton of the 5/7 Rajputs and (*right*) his grave

CAPT. H. R. NEWTON.
5/7 RAJPUTS.
19. 12. 41.

Tada, slender and unsmiling, carring a large *Samurai* sword; Lieutenant Mizuno, squat and bespectacled, self-consciously carrying a white flag; Mr Othsu, comfortably built and soberly clad in dark civilian clothes, carrying a briefcase. They were all short men and their arrival was, at first sight, irresistibly comic. Here and there a stray shell screamed over; two Jap planes, well out of range of optimistic anti-aircraft guns, hovered with nonchalant curiosity in the clear blue sky. It was an absurd scene, yet one with a heavy overtone of covert menace.

With a brisk exchange of salutes, Major Charles Boxer met the Japanese delegation on the quayside. Steel-helmeted British soldiers stood with fixed bayonets, while a curious and apprehensive Chinese crowd watched the proceedings in open-mouthed amazement. If Adolf Hitler, Goering and Goebbels had gathered on the steps of the War Office in London, the scene could not have been more bizarre.

Major Boxer had made liaison visits to the Japanese Army in the New Territories before the war and had met Mr Othsu before. Othsu lost no time in informing Boxer of the purpose of the visit: it was a demand for the unconditional surrender of the Island. There would be a cessation of hostilities until 4 pm, by which time the Japanese expected a reply. In the event of a refusal, future bombardments would be totally indiscriminate. There was a further exchange of salutes and Boxer sped to Government House in a staff car.

During the period of waiting, Gwen Dew spoke to the Japanese. She asked Mr Othsu: "Is it true that you have bombed Pearl Harbour?"

Othsu politely inclined his head. "Yes," he said. "American navy was mostly destroyed. Soon we will take Hong Kong." He then turned to Colonel Tada and Lieutenant Mizuno and translated the question. The eyes of both officers narrowed to the merest slits and they produced thin and humourless smiles.

'I didn't like their sureness,' records Gwen Dew in her book, *Prisoner of the Japs*. 'It made my heart shiver.'

Within the hour Boxer was back. He took a document from his briefcase and handed it to Mr Othsu. With a totally expressionless face Othsu read it, explained its text to the two officers and turned on his heel. Boxer and the two Japanese officers exchanged grave salutes.

Sir Mark Young's reply said: 'The Governor and Commander-in-Chief, Hong Kong, declines most absolutely to enter into any negotiations for the surrender of Hong Kong and he takes this opportunity of saying that he is not prepared to receive any further communications on the subject.'

Later, a brave official communiqué stated: 'It can now be revealed that the Japanese who came from Kowloon under cover of a white flag brought a letter enquiring if His Excellency the Governor was willing to negotiate for surrender. His Excellency summarily rejected the proposal. This Colony is not only strong enough to resist all attempts at invasion, but all the resources of the British Empire, of the United States of America, and the Republic of China are behind us, and those who have sought peace can rest assured that there will never be any surrender to the Japanese.'

They were brave words indeed: all the available resources of the British Empire were on the Island already; the reference to the United States was nothing if not premature; help from the Republic of China was not expected until January.

Of this second surrender delegation, General Maltby had this to say in his despatch: 'The envoys seemed genuinely surprised and disconcerted when the proposals were again summarily rejected. The second delegation coming within four days of the first suggested that either (a) they disliked the prospect of attacking across the water, or (b) that the Chinese threat in their rear was taking effect, or (c) that it was an attempt to undermine our morale by thoughts of peace and quiet.'

The British Press rallied to Sir Mark Young's side. Said the *Daily Mail*: 'Hong Kong, braced and exhilarated by the roar of her great guns, tersely rejected a second Japanese request to discuss surrender terms.'

Sir Mark had yet another champion in a correspondent to *The Times*, who wrote: 'The reply of Sir Mark Young to the Japanese should be read in every public place and school throughout the Empire. It breathes a spirit that needs no comment or elaboration.'

Film producers in Hollywood were also doing their bit towards victory in Hong Kong. 'They Met in Bombay', lightheartedly adapted from the novel by Louis Bromfield, starred Mr Clark Gable and Miss Rosalind Russell as two jewel thieves. Finding that Bombay was getting too hot for them, they fled to Hong Kong where Clark Gable joined the British Army and won the Victoria Cross (presumably Errol Flynn had pressing battle commitments elsewhere). 'Some of the laughs,' said a charitable film critic, 'are intentional.'

At precisely 4 pm the shelling and bombing started again....

CHAPTER SEVEN

A T 10 PM on the night of December 18th the Japanese landed on Hong Kong Island and this day marked the beginning of the most terrible week in the Colony's history.

It was an exceptionally dark night and there were frequent showers of rain. To add to the overall misery and uncertainty of the night, Japanese artillery fire had set fire to the oil tanks near North Point and the strong wind brought the smoke in a dense and choking pall over the northern part of the Island. The result was almost impenetrable darkness. The darkness, however, did not worry the Japanese, in spite of the facile observation of the Far East Combined Intelligence Bureau who had announced that 'Japanese night work was poor'.

There was nothing poor about their work on this night. The initial attack was made on the front from North Point to Lyemun and three separate landings were effected: Colonel Tanaka's 229th Regiment, acting independently, took the left or east flank; Colonel Doi's 228th Regiment the centre; Colonel Shoji's 230th Regiment the right or west flank. The whole of this first assault force was seven battalions, or rather more than 7500 men.

None of these troops had been used in the fighting on the mainland, but had been groomed for stardom in the first landing. All were tough and seasoned fighters—they had been effectively 'blooded' in China—and every man was a sworn and dedicated killer.

It was a tragedy that the initial fury of Tanaka's men took completely by surprise the 5th Anti-aircraft Battery of the Volunteers. The 5th Battery—a heterogeneous mixture of British, Chinese, Eurasians and Portuguese—had started the war well by shooting down two Japanese aircraft; they had, in fact, been the first volunteer unit to go into action. Their morale, reports Bombardier Geal Humphries, was of a very high order and they considered themselves ready for anything.

But on the night of December 18th they were not ready for Tanaka's men and had no chance of hitting back at the enemy who enveloped them in their first furious rush. The men of the 5th Battery did not know that the Japs had landed at all.

Bombardier Geal Humphries counts himself the luckiest man in the Hong Kong Volunteer Defence Corps, for barely half an hour before the arrival of the Japanese he had been switched to another sector of the Island.

The massacre of the 5th Battery was the first of a melancholy series of frightful incidents that proved beyond all shadow of doubt that the defenders of Hong Kong were opposed by a brutal and dehumanised enemy without the most elementary standards of decency.

The 5th Battery—twenty-nine men in all—were surrounded in Lyemun Fort and it was at once clear that they were outnumbered by something like ten to one. To the helpless men trapped in the fort a Japanese called out in English: "Surrender and we will save you!"

The twenty-nine men had no choice and surrendered because any further attempts at resistance would have resulted in their complete liquidation. But on that night it was better to die quickly. . . .

The Japanese formed a semi-circle round the entrance to the fort. Then an officer rapped out an order and the soldiers stood in grinning expectancy. They nudged one another and laughed: this promised to be something like *real* sport . . . the Jap officer shouted: "Come out all men, and you will be released!" The Japanese soldiers stopped grinning and became tense and alert.

Several men walked hesitantly to the entrance, but were peremptorily waved back by the officer. He smiled benevolently at them. "One man, one time," he ordered.

As the first man came out, the Japanese soldier nearest to him lunged with his bayonet. The man let out a thin squeal and fell, clutching his abdomen. The Jap stabbed at him on the ground, placing his foot on the volunteer's chest to facilitate removal of his bayonet. Instantly a barking clamour broke out among the other Japs, which was instantly silenced by the officer. "Next man!" he called. With a ludicrous travesty of disciplined movement, each man adopted the 'on guard' position.

The hideous procession went on until twenty-nine torn and bloody bodies lay on the ground. Some, luckier than others, had died almost at once: these had received thrusts through the heart or throat which had killed them almost instantaneously. But others, victims of more slipshod butchery, had taken the point through lung, liver, shoulder or lower abdomen: for them death was a long drawn out affair of coughing, retching, moaning and screaming. The luckiest man of all was one who, seeing what was coming, made a break for it and was cut down by rifle fire.

Japanese soldiers stood looking at the pile from which came the groans of men soon to die and men who wished they could die now. Then the officer rapped out an order and the dead and the near dead were thrown over a wall into a pit. The soldiers, laughing merrily among themselves, as if at some private joke, picked up stones of varying sizes and threw them into the pit. A comparatively lucky man, with a fearful bayonet wound at the base of his neck, was decapitated by a single swipe of the officer's sword. Quite soon the worst mutilated volunteers started to die.

Two men—Gunner Chan Yam-kwong and Bombardier Martin Tso Hin-chi, both civilian clerks in one of the big business houses—did not die.

Chan Yam-kwong had been bayoneted *across* his abdomen. The bayonet went through his shirt and into his wrist. The blood from his wrist went all over his shirt and he fell down: by this time his opponent, one of the more careless butchers, had turned his attention to another target on the mistaken assumption that Chan Yam-kwong was dead.

Martin Tso Hin-chi was bayoneted in the thigh and pretended to be dead. Both men were thrown with the others into the pit.

For three days and nights the two men lay in the pit. The groans of the dying grew fewer and soon there was silence.

There was worse to come (this phrase will be repeated several times in this narrative because each successive atrocity seemed, if possible, to be more bestial and horrifying than the one that had gone before).

Drunk with blood and victory, Tanaka's butchers swept on to the next slaughterhouse: the Salesian Mission at Shaukiwan, which had been hastily turned into an Advanced Dressing Station for wounded. It was commanded by Major Stanley Banfill of the Canadian Medical Corps and with him were Captain Osler Thomas, a volunteer medical officer; two

British nurses, Mrs Tinson and Miss Fearon; and some twenty assorted medical staff: medical orderlies, clerks, ambulance drivers, storemen and cooks.

There was no hint of war in the Mission at 7 am on December 19th; indeed, no one in the Dressing Station even knew that the Japanese had landed. An encouraging odour of bacon from the cookhouse told the men that breakfast was almost ready.

The men were sitting down to breakfast when the duty sentry rushed into the dining hall and announced that the Dressing Station was entirely surrounded by Japanese. Still in ignorance of the fate of the men of 5th Battery, Major Banfill made the decision to surrender the post. He had, in fact, little choice in the matter because his force was outnumbered by something like twenty to one.

The men walked out of the mission, their hands held in the air. Outside, they were roughly prodded into line with rifle butts. The two nurses were led away under separate escort.

The men were then ordered to strip to their trousers and vests and marched about two miles up the road towards Lyemun Barracks. There they were halted with their backs to the Japanese. The Japs, bayonets fixed, chattered and laughed shrilly.

Two men had miraculous escapes from the orgy of hacking and stabbing which then started.

Corporal Norman Leath of the Royal Army Medical Corps was, for the first time in nearly twenty years, saying his prayers. He was praying that the bayonet reserved for him would go straight through his heart and not, like the man who writhed and moaned next to him, between the shoulder blades.

Leath suddenly felt a terrific blow on the back of his neck; to this day he does not know what hit him. The force of the blow shot him into the air, spun him completely round and he fell to the ground face downwards, blood pouring from his eyes, ears and mouth. This, thought Leath, must be death, and he remembered offering up another prayer of thankfulness that it had been comparatively painless.

But Norman Leath was not dead; although his body felt completely paralysed, his brain remained perfectly clear: it told him with hammering insistence to lie perfectly motionless.

All around him he heard the gasping groans of the men who

had been bayoneted and the laughter of the Japs, one of whom actually trod on the back of his hand. Then there was a new sound of revolver shots and with each shot one man less was left to groan. Soon both the groaning and the shooting ceased, but Leath still lay face downwards, not moving a muscle. Now that the numbing shock of the terrible blow had worn off, his head and neck were separate torments of raging pain.

Corporal Norman Leath did not die. For eight days and nights he alternately hid in ditches and walked. During this time no food passed his lips and he drank only muddy water from streams. When he finally arrived at North Point Internment Camp, more dead than alive, he was informed by a British medical officer that according to all the laws of averages he should be headless: the blow that Leath had felt on the back of his neck had been caused by the blade of the Japanese officer's sword.

Captain Osler Thomas, medical officer attached to the Hong Kong Volunteer Defence Corps, did not die. When the orgy of bayoneting started, Thomas and two other men broke away and ran for it. They were followed by shots and both the other two men were hit, just short of the deep ditch towards which they were heading. Thomas fell into the ditch and feigned dead; the bodies of the other two were thrown on top of him.

Thomas lay in that ditch for a day and a night. For the next four days, dressed in Chinese clothes, he hid in a hut. Eventually weakness and dysentery forced him to make his way to the internment camp.

Chan Yam-kwong, Martin Tso Hin-chi, Osler Thomas and Norman Leath lived to testify at the War Crimes trial of Colonel Tanaka and Tanaka went to the scaffold. Just before the rope was placed round his neck he must have wondered how two of his men could have been so lax in their bayonet training as to leave two small and insignificant Chinese clerks alive. He must have wondered still more how an officer under his command could have fouled up such a comparatively simple routine task as beheading Corporal Norman Leath.

The only thing in favour of Tanaka's butchers is that the two nurses were unharmed and unmolested.

But, inevitably, there was worse—much worse—to come....

To the tired and depleted men of 'D' Company, 5/7 Rajputs it came as no great surprise to find that they were in the thick of the fighting once more: possibly, indeed, they would have felt insulted if they had not been. But their line on the seashore between North Point and the Docks was pathetically thin; their pillboxes had been mercilessly shelled and scarcely one remained undamaged; they were desperately tired, having enjoyed only one night's rest since their evacuation from the mainland. But they still had Captain Bob Newton commanding them and that made up for a multitude of deficiencies.

Bob Newton, that indestructible warrior, was, of course, as good as new and delighted to find himself in the forefront of the battle once more. But he had the usual depressing array of deficiencies so inescapable from military endeavour in Hong Kong: no communications to ask for reinforcements (even if any had been available); food, supplies and ammunition were dangerously low. Opposing him were the crack assault troops of Colonels Doi and Shoji, going into action for the first time—fresh, well fed and fanatical. Newton was going in ninth wicket down with a bodyline bowler at the other end.

The Japanese swarmed ashore in the face of withering fire from Newton's Rajputs. But they took no account of their dead, and as men fell, others, seemingly drunk and half-crazed at the sight of blood, took their place. Neither Doi nor Shoji had earned their promotions for the conservation of life.

Soon the Rajputs only had their bayonets and their courage to ward off the enemy. Newton, recklessly exposing himself and shouting encouragement to his men, was cut down by a burst of machine gun fire. When he could no longer shout he whispered and when he could no longer whisper he died. When his body was found his empty revolver was still in his hand and six dead Japs lay around him. His face was to the sea, and his last shout of exhortation and defiance had died in his throat. . . .

With Newton's death some of the heart went out of 'D' Company and indeed out of the whole battalion. To the men of 'D' Company, who had regarded him as well-nigh god-like, it seemed impossible that that ebullient voice was silent and those eager hands still.

Of the survivors—some thirty men in all—some stood and fought to the death until shot down or bayoneted. Some—a very few—feigned death or vanished into the darkness.

Forlorn and leaderless, these remnants of a proud company wandered hither and thither and so lived to fight again. But the bulk of 'D' Company, 5/7 Rajputs had become names to be carved on their Regiment's lengthy Roll of Honour. . . .

Also in early trouble on the night of December 18th were Captain Caesar Otway, Corporal Harry Pelham and four sappers of the Royal Engineers. They were manning the fixed beam searchlight at Lyemun Pass.

Otway had seen the motor boats, sampans and assorted small craft plying between Devil's Peak and Lyemun Pier. He knew at once that a full-scale enemy landing was in full swing.

Corporal Pelham, twenty-four years old that day, thought that this was a hell of a way to spend a birthday night. Pelham, in spite of his comparatively tender years, was a veteran of ten years' service—he had enlisted as a boy in that leanest of years, 1931—and would normally have been celebrating in the Nathan Hotel, the scene of many a corporal's birthday junketing. As it was, he was stuck out on an exposed cliff with, so far as he could judge, the entire bloody Jap army coming at him. Pelham could be excused for wondering if he would live to be twenty-five: it is still a source of wonderment to him that he did.

Captain Otway was busily engaged in locking the doors of the searchlight emplacement. The total armament of his force was his own revolver, a light machine gun and four rifles.

Suddenly twenty or thirty Japs rushed straight into the searchlight's beam: they made a magnificent target and the machine gun opened up with a long, chattering burst. This single burst reduced the Jap patrol by half; the remainder fled in ignoble confusion.

There was no time for jubilation. "They'll be back again," said Otway. "Keep your eyes peeled."

And they were. This time about twenty more Japs came running and were only beaten back when they were within twenty yards of the sappers. Again the bren gunner tore a great gap in their ranks.

The third attack was beaten off with fearful effort; a grenade killed the bren gunner and one of the other sappers; it also wrecked the gun.

"That settles it," said Otway. "We're getting out of it."

The words were hardly out of his mouth when a solitary Jap loomed out of the darkness and stood stock still, just ten yards from Pelham. Pelham, a phlegmatic man who believed in what he saw, and then only when strictly sober, saw the Jap at exactly the same moment as the Jap saw him: evidently he was either an individualist to a marked degree or a suicidal one-man wave of destruction.

Pelham is a keen viewer of Westerns on television. "It was," he says, "like something out of 'Gun Law'. We fired simultaneously."

Pelham, who had never performed with distinction on the rifle range, put his bullet into the Jap's stomach. The Jap's bullet hit him in the back of the hand. Then at least fifty Japanese rushed yelling at their position. "GET OUT OF IT!" bawled Otway at Pelham and the other sapper.

Pursued by bullets, Pelham hurled himself down the almost sheer cliff into the sea. The cold salt water was agreeably numbing to the pain in his hand and he struck out strongly.

Before he had been swimming long, the realisation came to Pelham that both the sea and the inlying shore were full of Japanese—more than once he had to swim under water to escape detection by the landing parties. By a supreme stroke of irony, he found himself at one moment swimming in the lonely and defiant glare of the searchlight which he had served with such loving care.

Three times Pelham attempted to make his way ashore and three times he had to take to the water again to get away from the Japs; they were swarming ashore at a dozen different points. Eventually, after nearly three hours in the water, Pelham scaled an almost perpendicular cliff and collapsed on the top of it, flat on his face. His limbs felt like leaden weights; the slow drying of his body was horribly painful; the wound in his hand throbbed with agonising persistence. But he was still alive, though there seemed to be no good reason why he should be.

Suddenly a sound came to Pelham through the darkness which made him wonder whether the events of the past two hours had not unhinged his brain. Two obviously drunken voices were singing in a travesty of harmony 'Red River Valley'.

"Now come sit by my side if you love me-e-e-e!" carolled the voices with deadly penetration; "dew not hasten to bid me adieu-u-u-u-u!"

Pelham walked forward a few painful paces and saw the two Canadians.

They sat, leaning against one another, and drinking from a bottle. On the skyline was a truck. They were both unarmed.

"C'mon an' join the party, mac," one of them invited.

"Thash right," echoed the other. "Me an' my buddy here are sittin' this goddam war out. Have a drink!"

With a dazed feeling of unreality, Pelham took the proffered bottle and took a long swig. It was rye whisky and comfortingly warming. He said: "Where are you going in that truck?"

"We ain't goin' no place, pal," said the first Canadian with a resounding hiccup. "Like I said, we don't want any part of t'is war. You want the truck, you help yourself. And gimme that bottle back."

Pelham got into the driver's seat and pressed the starter; nothing happened. Then he took the handle and swung it with the same defeating result.

"Forgot to tell you, mac," sang out one of the Canadians. "The —— truck's outa gas!"

Pelham started to walk, he knew not whither. Just as dawn was breaking he ran into a patrol of Royal Scots. Later that day he met Captain Otway and each expressed mutual astonishment at the other's survival. The only other sapper to survive the attack on the searchlight was never seen again.

Old men, women and children counted for little in the Japanese scheme of things, but Colonel Doi's men ran up against the old men defending the Power Station and acquired a healthy respect for them.

Before the war, some units of the Hong Kong Volunteer Defence Corps had been regarded as something of a joke (although by December 19th it was a joke that was no longer funny). One of these was the 'Hughes Group', universally known as the Hughesiliers and by the more irreverent as the 'Methusiliers'. The 'Hughesiliers' were a static unit and their specific function was the defence of the Power House.

The Hughesiliers were formed between the wars by Colonel

A. W. Hughes, a doughty *taipan*[1] and Chairman of the Union Insurance Company of Canton. With his departure to England just before the outbreak of war, command evolved on Major the Honourable J. J. Paterson. The official description of the Hughesiliers, as outlined by General Maltby in his despatch, is that they were 'men of 55 and over who felt the call to duty though they themselves were outside the terms of the Compulsory Service Act'. There was considerably more to them than that. . . .

It had been said of 'J.J.' Paterson that if he had not existed, then Somerset Maugham would have had to invent him. Chairman of Jardine, Matheson and Co., Senior Member of the Legislative Council, he was a man to be reckoned with—as Colonel Doi was shortly to find out to his cost. 'J.J.' was the prototype of the class of Englishman who, in India, was referred to as the *burra sahib* and in Malaya the *tuan besar*. In Hong Kong he was in a class by himself.

He was (and is) a big man in every sense. Whether in business, in politics (where his explosive utterances and unconventional opinions were quoted the length and breadth of China) or in hospitality, he did things in a big way. Officers of all three services, who now mow their lawns and help with the washing-up, still recall with amazed nostalgia the fabulous parties in 'J.J.'s' house at Fanling and the spacious magnificence of his private box at Happy Valley racecourse. Hong Kong, the present day *taipans* declare, has never been the same since he departed to a farm in Kenya.

In the First World War 'J.J.' served with the Camel Corps in the long drawn out campaign against the Senussi and marched into Baghdad with Allenby. His services had been recognised by no fewer than six mentions in despatches; he was shortly to earn a seventh.

During the battle 'J.J.' Paterson was a constant tower of strength. In subsequent captivity he regarded the Japanese with unfailing distaste, as befitted the scion of a noble house who found himself confronted with grinning, unwashed ya-hoos without the smallest idea of how to behave.

Almost every Hughesilier had served in the First World War; not a few, indeed, had taken part in the Boer War. Among them were Edward des Voeux, nephew of a former Governor of Hong Kong, Secretary of the Hong Kong Club,

[1]Literal translation of Chinese word *taipan* is 'Big Manager'.

bullion broker of international repute, 70 years old—and private in the Hughesiliers; 'Tam' Pearce, Chairman of J. D. Hutchinson and Co., Secretary of the Hong Kong Jockey Club, 67 years old—and private of the Hughesiliers; Captain 'Pop' Burch, sixty years old and Chairman of the import and export house of Moutrie and Co.

There was 'Pop' Hingston, a ribald and wicked old man: a septuagenarian sprite with an unquenchable zest for life. He used terrible language, exploring the uttermost depths of obscenity and blasphemy in his everyday speech. He had fought with the Canadians at Vimy Ridge, although he had been over age even then. Hingston, incredibly, was head chef at the ritzy Hong Kong Hotel; a most admirably skilled man at his craft. The Hong Kong Hotel had been famous for its food for sixty years; 'Pop' Hingston had been responsible for it for the past twenty. In the Power House he produced *ragouts* of bully beef of a most appetising piquancy; in the prison camp his *fricassée* of salt fish and coolie rice was talked about for years afterwards—and still is.

Certainly the most picturesque of all the Hughesiliers was Captain Jacques Egal, a wine merchant from Shanghai. Egal was the French aristocrat of fiction and seemed to have stepped straight out of the pages of Dumas. Clearly, he had been born three hundred years too late: he should have worn lacy ruffles at his wrist and carried a rapier instead of a Lee Enfield rifle.

His curling white moustaches and luxuriant mane of white hair were of another age. His impeccable tussore suits, his faultless linen, his cravats embellished with a pearl pin and his silver-topped walking stick drew respectful glances from everyone who saw him. No doubt Egal's ancestors had mounted the guillotine with a look of frozen contempt for the ragged revolutionaries; in a prisoner-of-war camp Egal had regarded the Japanese in much the same way and been brutally beaten up for his pains.

Also attached to the Hughesiliers were some thirty British technicians of the Hong Kong Electric Company, all middle-aged men and nearly all veterans of the Kaiser's war.

After they had overrun Newton's Rajputs, Doi's men swarmed towards the Power House and by 1 am on the morning of the 19th had it completely surrounded. But the Hughesiliers saw to it that its capture presented no easy task. 'J.J.'

Paterson told his men: "By rights, half of you ought to be dead now. If a man can't stay in his position alive, he'll stay in it dead. Those are your orders; now give 'em hell."

Many of the hands gripping the butts of rifles were rheumy; nearly all the eyes that squinted down the sights were myopic. But from every window came a devastating hail of fire and somehow the Power House still held. The movements of the defenders were slow and their breathing was heavy—the muscles of many of them could no longer work in co-ordination with their eyes and their nerves—but at 4 am not a single Jap had set foot in the Power House.

"This is plain bloody ridiculous," said a disgruntled *taipan*, who had had his share in Flanders. "How the hell do they expect to hold up the whole damned Jap army with a bunch of old fossils like us?"

"What the hell are you grousing about?" demanded 'Pop' Hingston, who had cooked many a delectable meal for the *taipan*. "D'you want to live for ever?"

Somehow the Power House still held. . . .

Hearing of the fate of the Rajputs and the threat to the Power House, an armoured car of the HKVDC and two trucks bearing a hastily assembled force from 'Z' Company of the Middlesex, set off along King's Road. They were immediately enfiladed by murderous machine gun fire from both sides of the road. The armoured car was burned out, but its commander, Second-Lieutenant Carruthers, managed to escape. The platoon of Middlesex was reduced to six men: Corporal Dan Cavill, Lance-Corporal Wally Coleman, Bandsman Bill Tunmer, Privates Tommy Tucker, Harry Cooke and Ron Parker. They staggered into the Power House and took up their positions, shoulder to shoulder with their grandfathers-in-arms.

"As soon as we saw those old geezers," said Cavill, "we knew it was up to us to put up a good show."

They did just that. The battle raged all that night, but the additional fire power of the two Middlesex machine guns took an enormous toll of the enemy. "Thank God for some young men," said Edward des Voeux feelingly. "We're all too damned old for this sort of thing."

"You speak for yourself," retorted 'Pop' Hingston, who was thoroughly enjoying himself.

But gallantry and determination were not enough and the sands were fast running out. Apart from one ancient Lewis gun, the Hughesiliers only had their rifles and a few Mills bombs. They were men in the evenings of their lives who should have been sitting in their favourite chairs in the Club; instead, they were holding at bay twenty times their number of blood-maddened Japanese.

As dawn of the 19th broke, the Japs had still failed to dislodge this stubborn force. Suddenly, to the amazement of the defenders, there was not a Jap in sight. One moment there had been a swarming mass of them all round the Power House; now there was nothing. The Hughesiliers, drawing on their variegated last war experiences, swapped theories:

"They'll do a bit of sniping and then rush us."
"Playing a cat and mouse game, if you ask me."
"Yes, and we're the damned mice."
"Remember those bloody Boers? They did the same sort of thing. . . ."
"Perhaps they think we're too old to kill."
"We should all have had heart attacks by now, anyway."
"Not sure I haven't had one."
"They'll be back; don't you worry. . . ."

Soon mortar shells were falling in the Power House. A bomb burst among a group of Hughesiliers, killing Private Edward des Voeux. Just before the mortar bomb claimed him, des Voeux had said: "I'd just as soon be killed in here as die in some filthy prison camp. Anyway, I'm three score and ten and on borrowed time now."

The mortar barrage lasted a full two minutes and then the Japs swarmed in exultantly for the kill. "Let 'em have it, Tommy," said Corporal Cavill to Private Tucker on the machine gun.

Tucker gave the advancing Japs a long burst and saw a dozen of them fall. He continued to fire even when his right eye, blown out by a grenade thrown at close range, lay on his cheek. Lance-Corporal Coleman and Bandsman Tunmer threw their last grenades into a mass of Japanese and went down under a surge of bodies.

Soon the roof of the Power House was alight. 'Tam' Pearce looked out of a window and saw a derelict omnibus in King's

Road. To J. J. Paterson he said: "I'd just as soon be killed in a bus as roasted alive inside a burning building."

"At the time," said 'J.J.', "there seemed to be quite a bit in what he said—there was damned little choice either way."

Corporal Robert Dunlop, Privates 'Tam' Pearce, Vincent Sorby, John Roscoe and Private 'Paddy' Geoghan—their total ages came to over three hundred years—took up position in the bus and for two hours defied every Japanese attempt to evict them. Pearce, Sorby and Roscoe fell to machine gun bullets; Dunlop died from the effects of a sword slash. The last man, Geoghan—an extrovert, flaming-haired Irishman with an insatiable liking for the good things of life—roared fearful oaths and despatched five Japanese in a fine frenzy of rage before falling, riddled with a dozen bullets.

Gradually the battle of the Power House died away. The surviving Hughesiliers, their ammunition exhausted, were rounded up. They were roped together and marched away into unwilling and explosive captivity. Battered and bedraggled, there was about them a dignity that no Jap could undermine.

"I cried when I saw those old men being marched away," said Corporal Dan Cavill. "It was partly because of that and partly because I'd been in the Middlesex for seven years and we'd been taught that we were never to surrender. At the time I thought I'd rather have been killed with my mates. Yes, I just burst into bloody tears and collected a clout from a Jap's rifle butt—whether it was for surrendering or crying I never knew. It wasn't the last clout I collected—not by a long chalk."

So ended the Hughesiliers' first and last battle.

General Maltby had this to say about the Hughes Group in his despatch: 'This force was instrumental in holding the Power Station this night and fought in the streets next day until the late afternoon, when the house-to-house fighting and mopping up by the Japanese caused their surrender by encirclement. . . .

'The delay the force imposed was very valuable to me.'

No one ever laughed at the Hughes Group after that. . . .

Just as General George Armstrong Custer made American history on June 25th, 1876, so did Brigadier John Lawson, commander of the Canadian contingent in Hong Kong, take his place in Canadian history on December 19th, 1941. The two soldiers died in almost exactly similar circumstances, for both were cut down by hordes of their enemies with a smoking pistol held in each hand: Custer facing the Sioux Indians on the Little Big Horn; Lawson surrounded by Japanese at Wong Nei Chong Gap.

Although the last battles of these two soldiers were so much alike, the men themselves had little in common: Custer was brave, ruthless, headstrong and arrogant; Lawson matched him in bravery but in none of his other characteristics. Lawson, in fact, was not a professional soldier at all, although he had won a Military Cross fighting with the Canadians at Passchendaele. Between the wars he had been a schoolmaster and an executive of the Hudson Bay Company.

The senior army officers in the Hong Kong campaign can all count themselves unlucky so far as military recognition went after the battle: they were all victims of circumstances and could only do what they thought was right against appalling odds and with no outside help. Thus, General Maltby acquired a Companionship of the Bath (considering the weight of his responsibility, little more than a consolation prize); Brigadier Cedric Wallis got a mention in despatches; Colonel Henry Rose (who took over Lawson's brigade after his death) collected nothing to add to his 1914 Military Cross. Lawson, though, was the unluckiest of all because Maltby, Wallis and Rose still live.

John Lawson had been given command of the Canadian contingent—the Winnipeg Grenadiers and the Royal Rifles of Canada—as a result of a visit to Canada of Major-General Grasett (himself a Canadian) on his way home from Hong Kong. Grasett had optimistically told the Chief of the Canadian General Staff in Ottawa that the addition of two Canadian battalions to the Hong Kong garrison would make the Colony strong enough to withstand a Japanese attack for a long period (he did not, however, specify how long). The response of the Canadian Government, presumably lulled into a false sense of security by Grasett's comforting assessment of conditions in Hong Kong, was to select the Winnipeg Grenadiers and Royal Rifles of Canada from a list of nine battalions listed as 'not recommended for operational training'. History, alas, does not relate the precise function for which they *had* been

138

recommended: whatever it was, it was *not* for close quarter fighting against crack troops of the Japanese Army.

Maltby realised that this was the old, old story—the mixture as before. The Royal Navy had to make do with antiquated and obsolete craft; the Royal Air Force had nothing capable of flying at more than 100 mph with a following wind; the Royal Artillery were short of officers, telephones, wireless sets, guns and shells; the best infantry NCOs had been sent home and the battalions had no mortar ammunition; there was no radar. Perhaps, the General thought, he was lucky to get anything at all: Hong Kong was, as the War Office were at pains to point out, only an 'outpost of Empire'. Obviously it was thought that Hong Kong did not rate more than two half-trained and (in the case of some of the men) untrained battalions.

The British and Canadian Governments took a more exalted view: the presence of the Canadians, they argued with massive condescension, would make all the difference to Canada's interests in the Pacific—with revolting smugness they made Canada sound like a big business concern threatened by a take-over bid; their arrival would reassure General Chiang Kai-shek of the British intention to hold Hong Kong to the last man and the last round; they would have a great moral effect on the whole of the Far East; they would provide a strong stimulus to the garrison and, indeed, to the whole Colony. They condemned 500 young Canadians to death as surely as if they had mown them down with machine guns.

The Canadians duly arrived in Hong Kong in November, 1941. They arrived without lorries or carriers, on which their mobility depended. This did not unduly perturb anyone in London or Ottawa, because it was understood that these two battalions would be required only for garrison duties—after all, they were not recommended for operational training, let alone active warfare. As neither battalion had ever done anything except garrison duties up till now, this seemed at the time to be a reasonable enough supposition.

The British Army lecturer from Singapore did not help much. A superbly laundered being with a pronounced gift for oratory, if nothing else, he told the Canadians about the Japanese successes in China. These, said the lecturer, could not be seriously taken into account because of the poor quality of the Chinese resistance. The bombing was poor and the Jap

Air Force had had little practice in night flying. Now, are there any questions so far?

"Yes, sir," said a Canadian private. "Is it okay if we smoke?"

Across the frontier, went on the lecturer with a decisive sweep of his pointer, are only 5000 poorly equipped Japanese troops whose fighting qualities are very much in doubt. They are inexperienced in night operations. They have very little artillery and their standards of gunnery are poor. Getting back to their Air Force for a moment—and the lecturer appeared to have a bad smell under his nose—their aircraft are, for the most part obsolete (he forebore to mention our own machines) and the pilots, to a man, are short-sighted. A short-sighted pilot, went on the lecturer with relish, is obviously quite useless for dive-bombing purposes.

The Canadians dispersed from the lecture in cheerfully vociferous groups, having received this glib assurance that Hong Kong was impregnable. It was difficult to contradict this assumption without damage to morale.

Such was Brigadier John Lawson's command.

From the start the Canadians were, in the words of a popular song, bewitched, bothered and bewildered: within a fortnight of their arrival they had been hurled into battle against a relentless and determined enemy. They dug trenches; they were dive-bombed, mortared and shelled; they marched hither and thither, not knowing where they were going or why.

Of the Canadians Maltby wrote without bitterness: 'These two battalions proved to be inadequately trained for modern war under the conditions existing in Hong Kong' (he might have added 'or anywhere else'). 'They had very recently arrived in Hong Kong after a long sea voyage and such time as was available had been devoted to the completion of the south shore defences and making themselves *au fait* with and practising the problems of countering a south shore landing. In this role they were never employed and, instead, they found themselves counter-attacking on steep hillsides covered with scrub, over strange country, and as a result they rapidly became exhausted.'

It is small wonder that Lawson became known as the unluckiest officer in the Canadian Army. He had been told in Canada that his men would be employed on garrison duties; in Hong Kong he had been told that they would be used in a static defensive role. On the morning of December 19th he had no idea where any of his men were. He only knew that his Brigade Headquarters was entirely surrounded by the swiftly advancing men of Colonel Shoji's 230th Regiment. . . .

Bandmaster Walter Kifford of the 1st Middlesex also died on this day. Only a short fortnight before, conductor's baton in hand, he had produced music of exemplary perfection at the last dinner in the Middlesex Officers' Mess. The band of the Middlesex had performed at a host of social functions in the Colony: at cocktail parties at Government House, at the Happy Valley race meetings, at Captain Christopher Man's wedding reception. They had become an integral part of the glittering social scene.

On December 19th Kifford wielded not a baton, but a rifle. With four of his bandsmen—Bandsmen Davies and Dillon and Drummers Enderby and Klintworth—he had been attached to Lawson's Brigade Headquarters for Intelligence duties. Davies and Dillon, trombonists both, had discarded their instruments for a light machine gun; Enderby and Klintworth, drums forgotten, carried rifles and hand grenades. All four had, at one time or another, incurred Kifford's displeasure at band practice but he had no fault to find with them now.

Screaming their exultant 'banzais !' Shoji's men surged into the headquarters. Every man who could hold a rifle—Kifford's bandsmen, clerks, cooks, signallers, storemen and drivers—fought it out to a finish. Shoji's men took no prisoners and bayoneted every recumbent body they could see, dead or alive.

Alone in his office, Lawson decided to use his telephone—just once. He got through to Maltby and announced calmly: "They're all round us. I'm going outside to shoot it out." His voice, Maltby remembers, was completely matter-of-fact and unemotional.

Lawson then smashed the telephone switchboard and went outside, a revolver in each hand. Like George Armstrong Custer, he was still firing his two revolvers up to the very moment that he was killed.

Lawson's body was not found for six days. No one to this day knows whether he was killed by sword, bayonet or bullet. It is known, however, that he took eight Japanese with him, for both his revolvers were empty when he was found and the Japs lay all around him.

Twelve years ago, five Canadians visited Hong Kong's War Memorial and looked long at one name:

CSM J. R. Osborn, vc
1st Battalion the Winnipeg Grenadiers
19-12-41.

These men remembered Osborn: they recalled how they had involuntarily put their caps on straight at his approach and jumped at the sound of his parade ground voice, clearly audible at three hundred paces. The sergeant-major is only a carved name on the memorial now, for he has no known grave.

But on December 19th, 1941, it seemed possible, nay probable, that John Osborn would live for a million years. "And so," said these five Canadians whose lives he saved, "he should have."

Greater love hath no man than this. . . .

'B' Company of the Winnipeg Grenadiers—already sadly depleted in numbers and commanded by a nineteen-year-old second lieutenant—had been charged with the capture of Mount Butler, a task for which their happy-go-lucky garrison service in Jamaica had scarcely fitted them.

The youthful company commander fell, cut practically in two by machine gun bullets, before they had advanced twenty yards. 'B' Company, partially trained and bewildered as they were, found themselves leaderless. The advance was checked and slowed down to a virtual standstill almost before it had started.

'B' Company, however, were going to take Mount Butler or Company Sergeant-Major John Robert Osborn was going to know the reason why. Osborn was forty-two years old: lean, granite jawed and uncompromising. By the very nature of his life, Osborn was tough: as an able seaman in the British Navy he had fought at Jutland; he had been a farmer in Saskatchewan; he had worked on the railroad in Manitoba. To Osborn Mount Butler was a challenge and with him he had sixty-five raw young soldiers who, to a man, fervently wished themselves back in Jamaica.

Osborn virtually *lifted* those men up the slope in the face of a withering fire that reduced his total strength to thirty. He roared unprintable obscenities at the Japanese and fearful derision at the more recalcitrant attackers. Such was the fighting spirit that Osborn infused in these men, that the Canadians were in full possession of the hill just half an hour after starting their advance. Osborn had lost his steel helmet; his bayonet dripped blood; he had an ugly gash in his right forearm. But his men were on Mount Butler and he had every intention of ensuring that they stayed there.

"Now, you bastards," said Osborn to his men with affection, "we're here and we're goddam well staying here. Any guy who thinks different, say so." Not a man spoke.

The Japanese, shaken by the impetus of Osborn's charge, drew off to lick their wounds. Osborn strode among the survivors of 'B' Company. Half way up Mount Butler they had been frightened boys; now, on the summit, they were men with a taste for killing.

"Dig, you sons of bitches," commanded Osborn; "dig like you never dug before. They'll be back for us."

They were. Little digging had been accomplished before the Grenadiers were counter-attacked from all sides. Regardless of casualties, the Japs swept up every side of Mount Butler and soon were within hand grenade throwing range. Soon a shower of grenades fell among the Canadians like fine rain.

Osborn was everywhere at once. He clubbed two Japs to death with the butt of his rifle; he wrested a sword from an officer and decapitated him with it; he fought with boots and bare fists. He picked up grenades before they exploded and threw them back into the faces of the advancing Japs. Six, seven, eight, Japanese grenades he threw back into the attacking hordes. All the time he continued to shout encouragement to his men and hideous abuse at the Japanese.

Osborn and his tiny force—by now reduced to twelve men—held Mount Butler for eight and a half hours. Soon the twelve men were only six. One grenade fell where the sergeant-major could not reach it. He shouted a warning to the men in the vicinity and hurled himself upon it as it exploded. . . .

The Jap soldier is a strange animal. Many men who surrendered at Hong Kong were wantonly and contemptuously butchered on the spot. But the Jap, treacherous and dehumanised monster that he is, admires fighting qualities in an enemy above all things: he never surrenders himself and feels comparatively kindly disposed towards an opponent who fights to the last. These five Grenadiers, whose lives had been saved by their sergeant-major, were spared and in the fullness of time returned to Canada.

John Osborn was posthumously awarded the Victoria Cross. Of his exploit the London Gazette says: '... CSM Osborn was an inspiring example to all throughout the defence which he assisted so magnificently in maintaining against an overwhelming enemy force for 8½ hours, and in his death he displayed the highest quality of heroism and self-sacrifice.'

There was a volunteer fighting that day who had never harboured any ideas about winning a Victoria Cross, or indeed any other medal. Today he has the 1939-45 Star, the Pacific Star and the British War Medal prominently displayed in his downstairs lavatory.

For Driver Desmond Longcraine, of the transport section of the Hong Kong Volunteer Defence Corps, Hong Kong's transition from playground to battleground had not, at first, been easy to take. For three years he had driven round the Island in a gleaming Buick (provided by courtesy of Gestetner Ltd.), clad in a shirt of snowy whiteness, tussore trousers with a knife-edged crease and hand-made buckskin shoes. Now he wore crumpled khaki drill, sweaty puttees and ammunition boots like boats.

Longcraine's truck, like every other item of equipment issued to the Volunteers, had seen better days: it was an ancient and asthmatic Dodge of *circa* 1924; its mileometer had stuck several years previously at 95,000; it groaned its protests uphill and frequently boiled over; it needed at least ten minutes of back-breaking swinging of the handle to persuade it to start in the morning. Yet somehow, incredibly, it always seemed to get there.

Longcraine's job was the distribution of ammunition and rations to outlying detachments of Volunteers. He knew everyone in the Colony and his arrival was greeted, as it had been at countless parties, with shouts of joy: old Desmond was never late for a party; by the same token, in spite of the temperamental habits of his vehicle, he was never late with the supplies either. Men in whose houses and flats he had enjoyed champagne and tingling Martinis, pressed upon him enamel mugs of steaming stewed tea and tins of lukewarm and gaseous beer. Nothing had really changed because with Desmond Longcraine present the party was bound to be a good one—as soon as we've seen these bloody Japs off things will get back to normal. . . .

But things didn't get back to normal. On December 18th Longcraine had paid a fleeting visit to Lena, glamorously workmanlike in nurse's uniform, at the hospital in Happy Valley. It was their last meeting for three years and eight months. . . .

On December 19th he set out on his last drive at the wheel of a vehicle for three years and eight months.

He was carrying a load of ammunition and rations destined for Brigadier Lawson's Brigade Headquarters. On his way shells whistled round his truck and Longcraine did his best to convince himself that his truck carried only rations: a direct hit could only result in the complete obliteration of his truck and himself.

At Wong Nei Chong Gap Longcraine found not a Brigade Headquarters—normally an orderly nerve centre of operations—but a charnel house: a scene of total and complete massacre.

Longcraine had never seen death at close quarters before and confesses that he only stayed long enough to be sick. But he still had his ammunition and rations: they were of no use to Brigade Headquarters, but farther on there must be men who could use them.

He drove on for about a mile and came across six dejected Canadians of the Royal Rifles of Canada, sitting by the side of the road. They looked weary unto death, grimy and despairing; their faces were grey masks of exhaustion.

Longcraine stopped the truck and leaned out of the cab. A young corporal looked up listlessly. "What's going on?" Longcraine demanded.

The corporal had a dirty bandage round his head and he had lost his steel helmet. When he spoke there was a note of near hysteria in his voice. "It's murder," he said, "plain goddam murder. We're all that's left of our platoon."

"But where are you going?"

The corporal rested his elbows on his knees and buried his face in his hands. "We ain't goin' no place," he muttered, "no place at all. . . ."

Longcraine continued along the road until he found the

remnants of a Royal Rifles of Canada company, reinforced by a few Volunteers. This little force had been under continuous shellfire and subjected to savage infantry attacks for twenty-four hours, but were in good heart. Longcraine received a rapturous reception, for the force was woefully short of both food and ammunition.

The young Canadian captain in command was infectiously optimistic. "We'll be okay now," he declared. "Let 'em all come."

In the absence of any orders Longcraine decided, having off-loaded his precious supplies, to remain with this force. Ammunition was distributed and a hasty meal eaten. Just two hours later they found themselves completely surrounded by Japanese.

Desmond Longcraine had last fired his rifle at range practice in 1940 when he scored five out of a possible fifty. But on this day he killed four Japanese and that night he fired until the rifle was too hot to hold.

As dawn was breaking on the morning of the 20th they were overwhelmed and forced to surrender. Longcraine and twenty unwounded survivors were tied up. "We were," recalls Longcraine, "most professionally trussed up like chickens—our ankles were tightly secured to our wrists in the small of our backs. We soon realised how lucky we were not to be wounded."

In this degrading attitude, the survivors witnessed a sickening and loathsome scene. The wounded were contemptuously kicked into position and bayoneted.

"We were then untied," went on Longcraine, "and roped together, for all the world like a chain gang. We were then marched the four miles to North Point."

Another peculiarity of the Japanese race quickly manifested itself. The average Jap is small and there is something about a big man—particularly if he is a prisoner—which moves him to insensate fury. All the captives were beaten up in one way or another on this terrible march—prodded with bayonets, belaboured with rifle butts, kicked and slapped across the face. But one volunteer—a veritable giant of six feet six inches—was singled out for special attention. On arrival at the hastily prepared prison camp at North Point both his eyes were closed; all his teeth were smashed; his nose was broken almost beyond surgical repair.

But this man, too, lived to give his evidence at Colonel Shoji's trial. . . .

December 19th was a day of practically unrelieved disaster in Hong Kong but the *Daily Telegraph* were determined to allay any possible tendencies towards despondency in its readers. 'Plenty of activity but no vital change is the general summary from this front,' it declared reassuringly. 'The military situation is not unsatisfactory.'

The Times, however, seemed worried. It said: 'Grave anxiety must continue to be felt until a halt can be put to this wave of Japanese successes.'

Mr Duff Cooper summed up adroitly. "Let us frankly admit," he said, "that so far the Japanese have been extremely successful."

CHAPTER EIGHT

THERE WAS a restive and frustrated spirit abroad in the 2nd Motor Torpedo Boat Flotilla. Prior to December 19th they had done routine patrols, performed as glorified seaborne taxis in the evacuation from the mainland and been bombed from the air. As Leading Stoker Ken Holmes succinctly phrased it, they had been mucked about from earhole to breakfast time.

The MTBs were trouble makers—hit and run craft with, as Their Lordships at the Admiralty cautiously put it, 'wide discretionary powers'. This, in effect, meant their job was to sail in and beat up everything in sight. Like everything else in Hong Kong, they were old and slow (maximum speed thirty knots) and obsolete. But a daring offensive spirit permeated every crew and they were spoiling for a fight. They were soon to get it—a fight comparable to a maritime charge of the light brigade; for there were guns to the right of them, guns to the left of them and guns in front of them. There were, alas, tragically few guns behind them.

On the morning of December 19th Captain Collinson gave orders that the MTBs were to attack enemy shallow-draft vessels which were ferrying troops from the mainland to the island. These were the two battalions of the Divisional Reserve and artillery units.

At 6 am the MTBs prepared for sea. First Lieutenants shouted orders: "Clear away springs. . . .!" "Uncover guns. . . .!" Then the engines roared into life and the flotilla formed into line. No 2 MTB Flotilla was heading for the war at last.

The flotilla made a rendezvous at Green Island and Lieutenant-Commander George Gandy, a veteran of the Dover Patrol, ordered the MTBs to attack in pairs.

MTBs 07 (Lieutenant R. Ashby, RNVR) and 09 (Lieutenant Kennedy, RNVR) tore into the Japanese landing craft, with Lewis guns blazing. They ripped forward at maximum speed, their bows lifting proudly and menacingly.

Some of the small craft used by the Japanese were caught in the MTBs propellers and died in a yelling scurry of foam. A large landing craft was sunk and the soldiers in the water were sprayed with Lewis gun fire: no orders had been given for the picking-up of survivors and in all probability would have been ignored if they had, for the MTB crews had heard about the massacres at Sai Wan and the Salesian Mission.

Another landing craft caught fire. Blazing from end to end, the flames fried its passengers with heartening thoroughness. Those who escaped from the inferno of fire were shot in the water. A third landing craft, deciding that discretion was the better part of valour, put about and ran for the beach, pursued by bullets and lower deck invective.

The Japanese response from the shore was swift and deadly. Shore batteries opened up and converted MTB 07's engine room into a dark shambles. 09 took her in tow and the first attacking wave made way for the second.

But when the second pair—MTB 18 (Lieutenant J. B. Colle, RNVR) and MTB 11 (Lieutenant J. C. Collingwood, RN)—went into the attack the Japs had stopped ferrying across the harbour. 18 and 11 ran into a hail of shells from shore batteries on all sides of them. Both boats forged ahead courageously, but their crews were practically blinded in a rainbow of tracer and star shell.

18 received a direct hit on the conning tower which killed her captain and first lieutenant (Sub-Lieutenant D. McGill, RNVR). Another shell hit her amidships and soon the decks were slippery with oil and blood. Completely out of control and burning heavily, she crashed into the sea-wall near the Kowloon docks.

11 was also hit but Collingwood, by superhuman courage and seamanship, managed to get her back. Six of her crew were killed and many others cruelly burned. MTB 11 presented an extraordinary spectacle: all the men were black with oil; the starboard turret was shattered; there were gaping holes in the canopy; the hull was holed in no fewer than fifteen places—some large gaping gashes, others only big enough to admit a fist.

By now the Japanese were shelling from all sides and aircraft were attacking the MTBs with light bombs and machine gun fire. Collinson ordered the remaining two MTBs not to press the attack further, but Lieutenant D. W. Wagstaff, in command of MTB 26, either never received the signal or chose to ignore it. 26 ploughed resolutely towards the harbour into a maelstrom of bombs, shells and machine gun fire. She was last seen, single Lewis gun firing defiantly, stopped dead off North Point.

The gallant action of the MTBs was a Balaclava of the sea: the attack was pressed home with incredible gallantry and against crippling odds. It almost marked the end of British sea power in Hong Kong, for *Thracian* was in drydock.

Almost—but not quite. There was still the ubiquitous and impertinent *Cicala*. . . .

The Royal Navy, always the most resourceful and adaptable of the three services, were soon to find themselves fighting on land for the first time since the storming of Zeebrugge on St George's Day, 1918. On hearing the news the sailors shrugged philosophically, tucked their voluminous bell-bottom trousers into their gaiters, donned steel helmets and drew rifles. "We've got the bloody Army out of trouble before," they declared, "and we can do it again."

Early disaster befell one Naval party composed of ratings from *Thracian*, among them Petty Officer Peter Paul. Thirty strong, they were hurriedly assembled and sent in two lorries in the direction of Wong Nei Chong Gap as reinforcements for Brigadier Lawson's hard pressed Canadians. They never got there.

The Naval party ran into a cunningly sited ambush, some three miles south of the gap. The first burst of fire killed the driver of the leading lorry, which ran off the road down the hillside. Six sailors were killed by this first fusillade and five more when the lorry ran off the road.

The occupants of the second lorry fared no better. They scrambled out and attempted to take up defensive positions, but were cut down like chaff before they had covered ten yards.

Some—tragically few—of this party survived the massacre. Six, Petty Officer Paul among them, rolled down the slope and eventually contacted a party of Royal Scots some eight hours later.

The fate of the remaining four men was a grim one. They took refuge in a nearby house and held it against repeated attacks for two hours. When their ammunition was exhausted they tied a handkerchief to a rifle and waved it out of a window.

The first three sailors were taken out of the house and bayoneted. The fourth, Able Seaman Ronald Mattieson, struck the rifle out of the hands of the Japanese soldier deputed to kill him and dived head first over a cliff. He fell and rolled for fifty feet, finishing up with a broken collar bone at the entrance to a small cave. This cave was to be his home for the next thirty days. . . .

Major 'Monkey' Giles, who had been in charge of Naval Intelligence, found himself out of a job for the very good reason that naval operations had come to an abrupt standstill with the virtual annihilation of the MTB Flotilla. He therefore went to the Commodore for orders.

"You'd better go and command some sailors," said Captain Collinson.

"They won't like having a marine in command of them, sir," said Giles.

"Well, go and command some soldiers then."

"They'll like it even less."

The Commodore had had a difficult morning. "Well, for God's sake go and command *something*," he said testily. "Now, buzz off. I've got work to do even if you haven't."

Eventually Giles contacted Lieutenant-Commander Pears, his friend for twenty years, and offered his services. Pears welcomed him with enthusiasm.

"Only too delighted to have you with us, old boy," he said. "Whatever you're like as a fighting soldier, you'll be a damned sight better than me."

Giles collected his command: bewildered young 'hostilities only' ordinary seamen; horny handed three badge able seamen (who had long since ceased to be surprised at anything); petty officers; sick bay attendants; telegraphists. He also had the not inconsiderable assistance of Corporal Leonard Trim, twenty years a marine and some time heavyweight boxing champion of the Portsmouth Division.

Giles had serious doubts about the fighting qualities of only one man. He was a writer[1] from Naval Headquarters: small, bespectacled and desperately anxious to please. He was holding a rifle for the first time in his life, much as a timid man handles an axe. The barrel was thickly encrusted with dirt.

[1] In the Royal Navy a clerk is a writer.

151

"You'll have to clean that before you start fighting," said Giles with a touch of severity.

"Yes, sir," said the writer. "Please, sir, how?"

"God give me strength," said Giles. "With a pullthrough, of course."

"Yes, sir," said the writer earnestly. "Where's the pull-through?"

Giles clapped his hands to his head. "In the butt trap. Now, don't tell me you don't know where the butt trap is."

"Sorry, sir," said the writer. "Where is it?"

"Now look," said Giles kindly, "I'm afraid you'll have to go back to Headquarters."

The writer seemed about to burst into tears. "Oh no, sir," he protested, "anything but that."

Major 'Monkey' Giles is not likely to forget this, his first command in war. Later they all acquitted themselves gallantly in some of the bitterest fighting on the Island. But best of all he remembers the diminutive, frightened, desperately deter-mined writer with the blinking, short-sighted eyes and the filthy rifle. . . .

This, then, was to be the pattern of much of the future fighting: units composed of Royal Scots and dockyard workers; Middlesex and Royal Rifles of Canada; Winnipeg Grenadiers and Chinese clerks; gunners and marines; Punjabis and Portuguese businessmen; Rajputs and engineers —thrown together by the misfortunes of a war which was increasing in savage violence every minute. . . .

All too soon it was December 20th. . . .

CHAPTER NINE

COUNTER-ATTACK . . . this is the phrase dinned into lance-corporals commanding sections; subalterns commanding platoons; captains commanding companies; lieutenant-colonels commanding battalions; brigadiers commanding brigades; major-generals commanding divisions; lieutenant-generals commanding a corps; generals commanding an army. In the broadest layman's language it means that when a position is lost, no effort must be spared in its recapture: unless the enemy is speedily ejected from newly-won ground he digs himself in and makes a firm base from which still more annihilating advances can be planned.

Shrewdly delivered counter-attacks have won wars or at least lengthened them by agonising months. In 1918, with victory seemingly assured, the Allies reeled back from a succession of body blows and bowler hats were issued as fast as Gieves of Bond Street could produce them; in 1945 Von Runstedt fell upon a complacent American Army in the Ardennes and added six months to the European War. On the credit side, Montgomery's counter-thrust at El Alamein altered the course of history, while Slim's pursuit of Japan's army of invasion in India (*sic*) exploded yet another Nipponese myth.

But to counter-attack effectively there must be air support and a crushing preponderance in artillery. There must be fresh, well-fed and eager battalions of assault infantry. There were none of these things in Hong Kong on December 20th, 1941.

There was no air force and artillery support was limited to eight field guns, stringently rationed for ammunition. There was no such rarity as a fresh and well-fed infantryman in Hong Kong because every soldier had been fighting, marching and dodging shells for eleven days on a near-starvation diet.

The Japs, on the other hand, were firmly established in the Wongneichong Gap, in the Jardine's Look-Out area and in the Tytam Valley. These were the men of regiments commanded by Colonels Doi, Shoji and Tanaka: confident, well blooded, hardy and calculatingly vicious. They constituted a force which, even allowing for casualties, was larger than our total strength in Hong Kong. Casualties meant little enough to Doi, Shoji and Tanaka because they had virtually an inexhaustible pool of reserves to draw on and the assurance of Lieutenant-General Sakai that the total decimation of their regiments would not affect the outcome of the battle. The three Jap colonels were on a good thing and well they knew it.

General Maltby had learned about counter-attacks at Sandhurst in 1909 from old gentlemen who had formed squares against the dervishes at Suakin in 1885. As a company commander in the Jats, Maltby had counter-attacked the Turks and as a battalion commander contributed to the rout of Pathans in Waziristan. He knew that once the Japanese had established themselves ashore, persistent counter-attack was the only policy if the enemy were not to win the Island merely by landing on it. He also knew, with clear and awful knowledge, the strength of his available forces to the nearest ten men.

The forces available for this counter-attack were the 2nd Royal Scots, two companies of the 2/14 Punjabis and what was left of the Winnipeg Grenadiers.

The Royal Scots had started the battle only six hundred strong and had suffered a hundred casualties on the mainland. The measures adopted to bring them up to strength were reminiscent of the worst days of the battle for Loos in 1915: lightly wounded men were hastily patched up in overcrowded hospitals and sent back to their platoons; these were the men who, in happier circumstances, could have counted on an extended convalescence followed by a fortnight of leisurely recuperation in well-appointed and sybaritic surroundings. Many other Scots, still weak and shivering from the after effects of malaria, were hustled back as potential giant-killers.

The ideal composition of an infantry force detailed for an all out counter-attack is a combination of fresh young soldiers, new to battle, whose élan is tempered by a nucleus of case-hardened veterans. The Royal Scots, from Colonel Simon White to nineteen-year-old Private Angus McFee, were veterans to a man—veterans with a sour taste in their mouths.

The Royal Scots were victims of circumstances which had

hung over them like cliffs; since December 8th every cruel stroke of military misfortune had conspired against them. They were desperately tired after days of fighting and marching; shocked and reeling from shelling and bombing from the air. They had been without sleep and proper food for an uncalculated number of hours. But they were belligerent and they had been insulted, and a belligerent and insulted Lowland Scot spells trouble for someone.

The Royal Scots still had gallant leaders in plenty: Major Dick Pirie, who had enlisted as a boy piper twenty-three years previously and had lost none of his fierce Glaswegian independence; Captain David Pinkerton, miraculously recovered from wounds received on Golden Hill and making everyone's life a misery with his clamorous demands for more action; Lieutenant Norman Brownlow, short of stature but enormously rich in courage; Captain Douglas Ford[1] and his irrepressible younger brother, Second-Lieutenant Jimmy Ford; Second-Lieutenant Michael Fenwick, just twenty years old and only six months out of Edinburgh University.

The Royal Scots formed up for the attack to the accompaniment of desultory machine gun fire and the distant crump of artillery fire. Magazines were charged, hand grenades were primed, bayonets were fixed, cocking handles of light machine guns were placed at automatic. There was little conversation among the men; there was about them an air of dour and smouldering fury. Many of these men were condemned to be dead within the half hour, but if the thought passed through their minds it was an impersonal one. Looking at these men it was easy to understand why Louis XIV had given the Royal Scots precedence over all French units. These were the men of the 1st of Foot whose antecedents had stormed into action against the King's enemies for three centuries.

The Royal Scots advanced over open ground in the teeth of withering and accurate machine gun fire from the firmly entrenched Japanese positions. The attack was doomed before it started because the artillery support was woefully inadequate and there was scant cover for the advancing troops. But the attack was pressed home with the greatest resolution with Captain David Pinkerton, as always, in the van.

[1]Subsequently shot by a Japanese firing squad and posthumously awarded the George Cross for extraordinary courage under the vilest torture.

It was, in the words of Colonel Simon White, 'a most gallant affair'. Machine gun and mortar fire tore great gaps in the ranks of the Royal Scots but they never faltered. Many of them got within grenade-throwing range of the Japs; not a few achieved some deadly close quarter work with the bayonet.

Second-Lieutenant Alec MacKenzie had been seconded from the Scottish Company, HKVDC to the Royal Scots. He was forty years old; prior to December 20th, as a staid and chairborne executive of the export and import house of Messrs. Harry Wicking Limited, his most violent activities had taken place on the golf course. These hours on the golf course had stood him in good stead, for he was advancing at the head of his platoon and giving ten years away to the oldest man in it.

To MacKenzie's right flank a machine gun opened up and he saw five of his men fall. As the bullets zipped over his head, MacKenzie knew that that machine-gun post must be liquidated if the advance of his company was not to be slowed down to a standstill. He had to charge it in order to raise its fire from his company; but the machine gun nest was too well defiladed, its approaches too open for a frontal attack. This tactical consideration did not stop Alec MacKenzie, if, indeed, he even thought about it: he rose, hesitated momentarily and stumbled forward.

Mackenzie saw the machine gun swivel towards him; then he flung himself flat as it opened up on him. He saw the Jap, teeth bared in an animal snarl, grenade in hand. He heard the crash of the explosion and saw a single, searing flame. That was the last thing that Alec MacKenzie ever saw.[1]

But gallantry and offensive spirit was not enough. Outnumbered by something like five to one, the Royal Scots were beating their heads against a brick wall. The only two remaining company commanders were both wounded: Captain John Robertson received three bullets in the stomach; David Pinkerton, that unquenchable warrior, was hit in both legs and, cursing horribly, had to be forcibly removed from the battlefield.

Command of 'A', 'B', 'C' and 'D' companies evolved on four second-lieutenants: Brownlow, Haywood, Glasgow and Ford. These four subalterns struggled gamely forward with

[1] Alec MacKenzie is now Secretary to the Scottish War Blinded Association.

their men—by now reduced to approximately twenty per company—but it was painfully plain that the Royal Scots had become a spent force. Out of the 500 men who went into the counter-attack on the Wongneichong Gap there were 175 still on their feet. At the end of hostilities the fighting effectives of the 2nd Royal Scots numbered 4 officers and 98 other ranks.

After this gallant attempt, recriminations against the Royal Scots died on the lips of every man who had berated them. Exiled from their homeland for eight years and incompletely trained for war, they had bought their battle knowledge at a hideously heavy price.

In the earlier part of this narrative the 2nd Royal Scots have not been over kindly treated. When mud is thrown at a regiment some of it is bound to stick.

But now the slate of the Royal Scots had been wiped clean.

The end of the battalion's participation in the battle, which had ended so gloriously, came on a supremely ironic note. Throughout the fighting, in their heavy and cumbersome ammunition boots, the Royal Scots had been outfought, out-flanked and outwitted by the incredibly mobile Japanese soldiers in their rubber-soled boots. On Christmas Eve two hundred pairs of soft-soled gym shoes were sent to the Royal Scots from the base supply depot. The delivery note which accompanied this tardy contribution said: 'It is considered that greater mobility in future operations will result if all ranks wear these shoes. Acknowledge receipt.'

The battalion quartermaster signed for the gym shoes on the appropriate form, but found himself landed with ninety-eight surplus pairs. . . .

In one of the minor campaigns on India's North-West Frontier in the mid-thirties—a campaign about which the British public read nothing in its newspapers—a young British captain found himself in command of a half company of raw young soldiers. They were pinned down by a murderous and accurate fire from Pathans cunningly concealed behind rocks. Ammunition and water were dwindling to a decimal point and the relieving force were five miles away. The soldiers were tired, hungry, thirsty and frightened, but the Pathans were none of these things. The young captain, thinking aloud, said from the heart: "Oh, for a hundred Sikhs with fixed bayonets!"

Ranking high among India's great fighting men are the Sikhs, those proud and fierce bearded warriors with their strange and rigid religious customs: the hair on the head and face must never be cut; they must never smoke; every man wears a steel bracelet on his wrist; they must invariably wear white underpants (other soldiers of the Indian Army, particularly Gurkhas, go in for gaily-coloured checks and stripes but the Sikh's 'unmentionables' must always be of purest white); they scorn the use of the steel helmet and on occasions have come near to mutiny when it was suggested that they wear it.

The British soldier gets up an hour before first parade (and later if he can get away with it). The Sikh must be astir at least an hour earlier if his shoulder-length hair is to be neatly coiled under his *puggri* and his beard arranged in a state of military perfection—the most dandified Sikhs place their beards in a net such as a woman puts over her hair. A company of Sikhs on parade is a splendid sight: they are mostly six-footers and the rows of grave, proud and bearded faces from which flash fierce and unfathomable dark brown eyes create an impression of disciplined arrogance calculated to warm the heart of any commander.

In battle they charge with an élan which has struck terror into Germans, Turks, Pathans and Japs alike. Men think twice before standing up to cold steel wielded by these men who are transformed by the heat of battle into hairy nightmares. Their battle cry '*Sat sri kal!*' is as frightening a sound as any man can hope to hear. Sikhs, however, are not the easiest of men to command: they tend to be moody and (like good soldiers the world over) have a pronounced fondness for alcohol. But a British officer who has won their respect can count on extraordinary devotion and loyalty and would not exchange them for Guardsmen, Highlanders, Gurkhas, or any other type of soldier who has brought glory to British arms. Just such two officers were Captain Alastair Thompson and Lieutenant Nigel Forsyth.

A hundred Sikhs—hefty, determined and dour—is what Lieutenant-Colonel Gerald Kidd, commanding the 2/14 Punjabis, longed for to assault Shouson Hill: he also longed for a troop of tanks, a battery of mountain gunners and half a dozen dive-bombers, but Kidd was an essentially practical soldier whose dreams, if he ever had any, never strayed into the realms of fantasy.

Captain Alastair Thompson's Sikh company was reduced to one other British officer, Lieutenant Nigel Forsyth, and twenty-five riflemen. These, plus half a dozen enthusiastic but bewildered naval ratings, comprised Kidd's assault force.

Colonel Kidd was lean, grey and tough, which was not surprising in a man who had served in another world war and a score of skirmishes on the North-West Frontier. If his exterior was somewhat forbidding and froze newly joined officers into trembling immobility, he had a heart of gold and would fight tooth and nail for any officer or other rank whom he considered had been the victim of injustice at the hands of higher military hierarchy. His liver was no more unpredictable than that of any other soldier who had campaigned for thirty years in fickle climes at the dictates of an ungrateful and unappreciative government. First and foremost Kidd was a fighting soldier: if his officers had had the advantage of an extended education at the Staff College, then that was very nice for them as long as they kept their textbook theories to themselves. But they still had to prove to their colonel that they could march fifty miles in full fighting order. Kidd was not concerned with their choice of tailor or their prowess on the polo field: he was only concerned with their soldierly qualities and their ability to get the best out of their men.

He had no qualms about Alastair Thompson, Sandhurst trained and almost fanatically devoted to his Sikhs. Kidd knew that if anyone could take Shouson Hill, Thompson could.

Shouson Hill was named after Sir Shouson Chow who lived in a splendid mansion on the hilltop. Sir Shouson, eighty-three years old and a millionaire, had been one of the first Chinese to study in the United States and one of the very few to be knighted by the British Empire. Shouson Hill was to be the scene of one of the bitterest fights of the entire campaign.

The hill is a steep-sided knoll rising straight out of the ground and is covered with opulent private houses. All these houses were occupied by the Japanese. This was the objective entrusted to Colonel Kidd, two officers, twenty-five Sikhs and ten sailors.

The Sikhs, Thompson at their head, set off towards the hill

at the slow, loping trot of the well-trained soldier. Kidd and the sailors followed close behind: it would be their job to provide covering fire for the main assault which was to be carried out by Thompson.

The sides of the hill were precipitous and slippery, but the Sikhs swarmed up in the face of withering fire from the houses and the summit.

The fighting on Shouson Hill was close and savage; no quarter was given or asked for. Soon it had resolved itself into a snarling dog fight with bayonet and grenade. Thompson and Forsyth, roaring encouragement at their Sikhs, were everywhere at once. A gigantic havildar bayoneted three Japs and tossed them over his shoulder down the slope like sacks of hay; a naik despatched five more with a single burst of tommy gun fire; two sepoys, surrounded by twenty Japanese, fought back to back with clubbed rifles until they went asunder.

But this counter-attack, like all the others, was also doomed to failure: there was not a vestige of cover on the precipitous hillside; the force was absurdly small for such a herculean task; there was a total absence of artillery or machine gun support. In the later years of the war such an objective as Shouson Hill was pounded ceaselessly by artillery for anything up to two hours before being assaulted by at least two companies of infantry. It was little short of miraculous that the attackers reached the summit at all and the general concensus of opinion was that only Thompson and his Sikhs could have done it.

The 2/14 Punjabis suffered a grievous loss in the death of Colonel Kidd in this action. He fell, recklessly exposing himself in an attempt to draw fire from one of the houses. He should not, in fact, have been there at all, for it is not part of the duty of a commanding officer of an infantry battalion to lead desperate sorties on strongly fortified positions. But Kidd had never been one to order men to do things that he was not prepared to do himself.

Some people say that Gerald Kidd, almost heartbroken at the near decimation of his magnificent Sikhs and the ever present feeling of impending defeat, deliberately sought death on Shouson Hill. Others contend that the cause of his death was the complete negation of all his training as a tactician and that he had no right to rout about like a private on the battlefield: he had deliberately exposed himself to draw fire in an effort to pinpoint a Japanese strong point. Others, again, are of the opinion that to launch such an attack was a blunder, although Thompson, Forsyth and the eight Sikhs who survived affirmed vehemently that they would willingly do it again. Everyone, however, agreed that Lieutenant-Colonel Kidd had displayed soldierly qualities of the highest possible order since the beginning of the fighting and by his fearless example he had inspired everyone with whom he had come in contact. Every man in the 2/14 Punjabis mourned his loss and his Subedar-Major, that magnificent soldier Haidar Rehman, was inconsolable for many months to come.

It is easy to be wise after the event, and Colonel Kidd was of the opinion that Shouson Hill could be taken. Furthermore, he backed his opinion with personal valour that was beyond all praise. Impetuous action, the military experts will say, is better than no action at all. By the same token the proof of the pudding is in the eating and Lieutenant-Colonel Gerald Kidd swallowed every bitter mouthful of it. The fighting record of the 2/14 Punjabis has always been a glorious one; Kidd saw to it that it stayed that way.

Alastair Thompson himself was wounded in the attack, peppered by fragments of half a dozen grenades. Forsyth, by some unexplained miracle, emerged unscathed. Of the eight surviving Sikhs, five were more or less seriously wounded. Havildar Irjan Singh, his immaculate *puggri* stained with blood, carried a sepoy, whose pelvis had been shot through, on one shoulder and a light machine gun on the other.

Later that day Irjan Singh sat with Thompson over mugs of strong tea generously laced with rum. "It was a good fight, *sahib*," said the havildar. "If only there had been more of us. . . ."

In this simple statement Irjan Singh summed up what every soldier, from General Maltby to Private Stutz of the Middlesex, was thinking.

If there was any counter-attacking to be done it was reasonably certain that HMS *Cicala* was going to be in on it.

For the past two days, with as good a grace as possible, she had been carrying out a melancholy and soul-destroying task: the sinking of merchant shipping in the harbour. It was not a job that Lieutenant-Commander John Boldero viewed with any enthusiasm.

On the afternoon of December 20th Boldero received an order that was very much more to his liking. Strong enemy attacks were developing in the Deep Water Bay area and Boldero's orders were simple: to give the strongest possible support to land forces operating in the area and to inflict the maximum damage on the enemy.

"Better than sending a lot of rusty old tubs to the bottom, sir," observed the First Lieutenant Walter Davis, RNR.

"It could hardly be worse," said Boldero.

Cicala's complement had been seriously depleted by the precipitate departure of the Chinese ratings who had not found naval warfare—or indeed any form of warfare—to their liking. Two Chinese, however, had elected to stay: Telegraphists Siong and Charles Ong. Both had apologised to the First Lieutenant for the cowardly behaviour of the rest of the Chinese members of the crew. Apparently, however, it was simply explained. "They are Chinamen," explained Charles Ong simply.

"Well, aren't you?" said Davis.

"No, sir," said Charles Ong with immeasurable superiority, "Siong and I are Singapore Chinese." Davis let it go at that. Singapore Chinese or Chinamen, telegraphists were scarce.

Davis, a diminutive and grizzled Welshman, had spent twenty-five of the best years of his life on coastal freighters, pounding their guts out in the China Sea. At first he had found Royal Navy discipline a little hard to understand and Boldero, an immaculate and correct figure in spotless whites, was in sharp contrast to his last skipper who, dressed in grimy singlet and battered bowler hat, breakfasted on the bridge off jellied eels and stout. Between Boldero and Davis, men poles apart in normal circumstances, had sprung up a firm friendship and highly effective partnership. To the more conventional naval mind they must have appeared an odd combination: Boldero, one-armed and forty-one years old; Davis, forty-three years old and with a background of battered tramp steamers. Be that as it may, *Cicala* represented British naval might in Hong Kong and she lost no time in letting the Japanese know it.

Cicala steamed into the fray with her accustomed gusto and promptly came under heavy mortar and sniper fire from the direction of Brick Hill. *Cicala* took aggressive retaliatory action and her six-inch guns silenced the mortars.

"No more trouble from *that* quarter," observed Boldero with grim satisfaction.

But Japanese planes were quickly on the scene and six machines attacked *Cicala* singly, dropping sticks of light bombs. Boldero was ready for them and manoeuvred his ship with the same skill that he had displayed in previous attacks. But on this occasion *Cicala*'s luck ran out.

One bomb burst in the skiff on the starboard side just below the bridge; another went through the mess deck; a third exploded in the after compartment. The starboard side of the ship was holed amidships and the engine room casing had been blown in; the mess decks, store room and after compartment were flooded. Mortally damaged by the force of the bombs, *Cicala* shuddered and slued to a standstill.

Boldero's worst fears were confirmed when the voice of Chief Engine-room Artificer John Ousgood came faintly from the engine room: "Oil feed pipes are broken, sir," he reported. "She's sinking by the stern."

"I'm afraid she is, Chief," said Boldero.

The Jap planes screamed down for the kill. A final stick of bombs destroyed all the boats and killed the gunner's mate. With a single anti-aircraft gun still defiantly firing, *Cicala* settled down in Lamma Channel. *Cicala* had fought her last fight.

For some unexplained reason the Japanese planes did not administer the *coup de grâce* to the stricken gunboat, though the omission could hardly be attributed to humanitarian motives. Casualties, indeed, had been miraculously light: one rating killed and two wounded.

Boldero was the last man to take to the Carley floats. Before he did so, he signalled to MTB 09 and the signal was like the instructions of a dog owner to the vet, asking him to put down a trusty and well-loved friend.

'Drop depth charges,' the signal said, 'and make sure she sinks.'

But the crew of *Cicala* had not finished with the Japanese yet. Four hours later they were fighting as infantrymen in the area of Bennett's Hill. . . .

Many other counter-attacks were made and all were pressed forward with tremendous resolution and gallantry. But they were hastily organised and piecemeal affairs: the Winnipeg

Grenadiers and Royal Rifles of Canada, with companies reduced to barely platoon strength, flung themselves despairingly at strongly fortified Japanese positions and suffered fearful casualties; mixed parties of gunners, sappers, volunteers, sailors, airmen, military policemen and clerks were hastily formed into assault squads and manfully stormed positions which might have daunted crack regiments of foot guards. After Brigadier Lawson's death West Brigade had no commander because news of his gallant last stand never reached Fortress Headquarters.

The War in Japan, Volume One, makes the sweeping and condemnatory accusation that 'there was a lack of co-ordinating authority in the fighting zone during this critical period . . . which probably affected the whole course of the operations'. The men on the spot declared in terser terms that if Marlborough (or Wellington or Montgomery or Rommel) had been in command, the result would have been the same. A bitter artillery major, whose guns had long since been lost, put it even more bluntly and used a phrase which, so the pocket Oxford dictionary tells us, is not in polite use. "It was," he declared, "like farting against thunder."

These abortive counter-attacks were made without preliminary reconnaissance by troops already exhausted by ten days of hard fighting. The blame for this melancholy state of affairs cannot be placed at General Maltby's door, for he was shouldering a tactical burden which was rapidly becoming intolerable.

Some objectives were won at fearful cost, but could not be held. Even if they were briefly held, they could not be consolidated.

The Oxford dictionary defines the verb consolidate as 'to make strong by coherent organisation'. There was no coherent organisation in Hong Kong on December 20th except in Lieutenant-General Sakai's headquarters. Like a cat which has eaten all available cream, Sakai was planning an annihilating advance which, he confidently predicted to Tokyo, would put Hong Kong in Japanese hands within twenty-four hours.

There was little talk of counter-attacks in Fortress Headquarters that night. There was, indeed, little talk at all. There was only feverish preparation for holding a line which was becoming progressively weaker every minute.

One episode on this desperate day stands out in the memory

of Second-Lieutenant Iain MacGregor. Fortress Head-quarters—the White Sepulchre as it was known to the irreverent—was coming in for its fair share of Japanese hate: shells and mortar bombs were bursting in uncomfortable proximity; bullets were whistling spitefully on all sides.

MacGregor saw a lone figure walking towards Headquarters with the nonchalant air affected by stockbrokers on their way to lunch. His clerical grey suit was a masterpiece of subdued tailoring; his grey Homburg sat on his head with the suspicion of a jaunty slant. It was the Governor and Commander-in-Chief of the Colony, Sir Mark Young.

"Sir," said MacGregor, "hadn't you better get under cover?"

The Governor hardly seemed to hear him. With unhurried steps he walked into Maltby's office.

What transpired between these two men, whose responsibilities were so terrible, has never been recorded. In his despatch General Maltby laconically wrote: 'At 1130 hours I was visited by His Excellency the Governor and Commander-in-Chief who stressed the importance of fighting it out to the end however bad the military outlook might be. Every day gained was a direct help to the Empire war effort.'

The gravity of the situation even percolated into the editorial office of the *Daily Mail*. 'We cannot expect to retain the Island,' observed the *Mail* with depressing finality. 'All we can hope to do is inflict the maximum loss on the enemy.'

The *Daily Telegraph*, however, refused to be deflated. 'On the mainland opposite Hong Kong,' it announced cheerfully, 'Chinese forces were stated by the Chungking military spokesman to be only ten miles from the Kowloon border.'

It was possibly just as well that no one in Hong Kong read the *Daily Telegraph* that morning. . . .

CHAPTER TEN

THE AUTOMOBILE Association Handbook defines a five-star hotel as follows: 'De luxe hotels of the highest international class offering impeccable standards of excellence in accommodation, service and cuisine; private sitting rooms with bedrooms and bathrooms *en suite* available: full service on all floors.'

This grandiloquent description, however, barely does adequate justice to Hong Kong's Repulse Bay Hotel. It is doubtful if any hotel in the world surpasses it in luxury, service and beauty of surroundings.

Repulse Bay is a slice of heaven by the sea. It is situated on the Island's south shore and the guide books which describe it as a natural paradise aren't trying to kid anyone, for that's exactly what it is: a place of sweet rest filled with sunlight, moonlight, tranquillity and sybaritic peace. A sojourn at the Repulse Bay Hotel can induce romantic feelings in the most bile-ridden businessman; case-hardened foreign correspondents have introduced a lyrical quality into their normally corrosive prose while staying there.

The hotel is a long, white, rambling building resting at the feet of towering peaks. Below it are miles of golden sand beaches and the softly rippling blue sea. Guests to whom breakfast is a rude word swim in the early morning and attack bacon and eggs with gusto; the cocktail bar produces a feeling of figurative alcoholism in the most abstemious; the menus for lunch and dinner are eight pages long; the Filipino dance band—small, serious, olive-skinned men in faultless white tuxedos—coax married men on to the dance floor when prior threats of infidelity have failed.

That's how the Repulse Bay Hotel was before it became a battleground. . . .

A two-star hotel, so the indispensable yellow volume of the AA tells us, has 'well-kept accommodation and furnishings, offering a good standard of comfort and good lounge accommodation; hot and cold running water in most bedrooms; meals available to non-residents at all reasonable times; adequate clean modern toilet facilities'. The scribe of this handbook would have allotted no stars to the Repulse Bay Hotel on December 21st.

'The well-kept accommodation' was occupied by one hundred and eighty civilian guests and two hundred soldiers; the most important furnishing had become a sandbagged window from which there was a good field of fire. The Repulse Bay Hotel, normally a blaze of gay light, was illuminated by a few guttering candles. There was a good standard of accommodation if fourteen persons of all ages and both sexes to a suite can be termed spacious. The lounges, formerly venues of card parties, cocktail parties and the clinching of business deals, were packed with soldiers. What little water there was was used for washing dirty bandages, making tea and drinking. In peacetime if you wanted a shower in the Repulse Bay Hotel you simply manipulated a lever; on December 21st being dirty was not enough: you had to be wounded or in an extremity of thirst—and even then there probably wasn't any water.

'Meals available at all reasonable times. . . .' The smooth running of the hotel in peacetime had been the responsibility of Marjorie Matheson, a woman of unshakable poise and enormous organising ability. Hers was a big job, even in happier times; with no electric light, little water, fast dwindling stocks of food and practically no staff, it became positively herculean. People who had rung room service for a light midmorning snack of caviare and champagne found themselves queueing for soup and meagre portions of stew.

"One would have thought," said the Lady Bridge Player in tones of glacial disapproval, "that they would have made *some* sort of arrangements for an emergency."

'Adequate clean modern toilet facilities. . . .' Excrement was level with the tops of almost every seat and the sickening smell permeated every room in the hotel: constipation had ceased to become an affliction; now it was almost a boon. Hank Marsman, a millionaire Dutch engineer, had made fortunes from the constructions of all manner of buildings: now he found himself in charge of sanitary arrangements in the hotel in which it had been costing him ten pounds a day to live. Realising that the existing situation could only result in a fearful epidemic, he organised parties of British, Canadian, American and Chinese armed with pails. His prompt action in the carrying out of this distasteful task undoubtedly saved many lives.

The Repulse Bay Hotel had arrived at this deplorable state of affairs because large numbers of civilians had decided, now that the Japanese had landed on the Island, that it offered the best chance of safety. Consequently men, women and children of no fewer than twelve different nationalities had elected to take their chance within the hotel's hospitable walls. The oldest guest was eight-three; the youngest three months. Their assumption that the Repulse Bay represented safety was entirely mistaken; but, as things turned out, it was as safe as anywhere else on the Island.

There were elderly American men and Chinese babies; young French married women and old British businessmen; middle-aged Dutchmen and Englishwomen who might have been any age. There were men who needed alcohol, babies who needed a change of nappies and women who needed a touch of lipstick and a few drops of eau de Cologne. There was also the Lady Bridge Player who, according to Gwen Dew of the *Detroit News*, needed a man-sized kick in the rump.

Gwen Dew was tough and resilient as befitted a dedicated foreign correspondent; but she was a woman of infinite compassion and understanding. She was also youthful, good looking and courageous. The Lady Bridge Player was none of these things and disliked Americans in general and American newspaper women in particular. They both took it from there and the resultant clash of personalities was as inevitable as it was vitriolic.

The Lady Bridge Player was impossible from the start. She resented the fact that she could no longer lord it over the lesser strata of Hong Kong society; she resented the giving up of her spacious house on the Peak, where a dozen or more Chinese servants had done her every bidding; she resented the fact that the Japanese had taken the Power Station and therefore dislocated the Colony's supply of electricity; she resented the presence of weary and grimy soldiers in the lounge, the cocktail bar, the dining room and the card room. But most of all she resented the presence of Chinese in the Repulse Bay Hotel—and Gwen Dew.

"What," she demanded in a ringing voice, "are all these Chinese people doing here?"

Gwen Dew, who had spent two years in China with the American relief forces, was up in arms at once.

"Why shouldn't they be here?" she demanded.

The Lady Bridge Player regarded her with ineffable scorn. "This is a hotel," she said icily, "not a refugee camp."

"And you, of course," said Gwen Dew with dangerous sweetness, "are not a refugee, *are* you?"

The Lady Bridge Player searched her mind for a devastating *riposte*, failed to find one and effected a majestic exit, muttering darkly about "ill-mannered Americans". A Canadian soldier, a fascinated eavesdropper to this conversational exchange, said: "You sure won that round, ma'am."

Meanwhile, the Japanese had surrounded the hotel. . . .

Few of the soldiers in the hotel knew what they were supposed to be doing there; many, indeed, should not have been there at all. There were Canadians—remnants of the Royal Rifles and Grenadiers—who had been cut off from their units. There were naval ratings, bewildered administrative troops and a few Middlesex. Many had stopped there in the hope of a meal or a night's sleep; still more were there because no one had told them where else to go. Allegedly in command was a Canadian major who was unsuccessfully seeking military inspiration from a bottle of Scotch whisky.

All of them were tired, dirty and hungry. Some of them didn't care who won the war as long as they could get some sleep. A few, following the example of their commander, were drunk on looted liquor supplies—they took the view that they might as well drink the stuff before the Japs got at it. But there were several who were imbued with an offensive fighting spirit and desired nothing more than to get to grips with the enemy; no single man desired this more than Lance-Sergeant Robert Heath of the Royal Engineers.

Heath was a high-spirited young man and an extrovert to a marked degree. He had an insatiable zest for living and his past liaisons with the opposite sex had caused his company commander, Major Dan Grose, to shake his head sadly on several occasions.

Heath was unmarried and had every intention of remaining so. Not for him the steady 'dahnhomer', he believed in safety in numbers. But there was nothing safe about indiscriminate sexual forays in Hong Kong and Major Grose had suggested to him that he should either get married or resign himself to very serious trouble. To which Heath blandly replied: "But, sir, there's no worse trouble than being married."

But right now Sergeant Bob Heath was not thinking about sex. He was concerned with the killing of as many Japs as possible.

When the Japs began to shell and snipe the hotel, Heath seemed to be everywhere at once. He directed fire; he organised fighting patrols; he rescued a bren gun from a broken-down carrier. He encouraged the faint-hearted, comforted the wounded and heaped fearful derision on the shirkers. He ignored shells and bullets and seemed to be able to do without sleep for indefinite periods. "Watching him," said Gwen Dew, "you felt sure you were viewing a fully-charged high-voltage electric wire in action. His steel helmet was on the side of his head and he had a smile as grand as sunshine on tumbling surf."

The soldiers in the Repulse Bay Hotel were virtually leaderless. They no longer had the cheerful offensive spirit of Second-Lieutenant Peter Grounds, for he had been killed at the head of his platoon of Middlesex in an attack on the hotel garage. The Japs had occupied the garage earlier in the day and from this natural strongpoint had brought a murderous fire to bear on the hotel. Grounds had attacked with the utmost resolution and evicted the Japanese from the garage. In their hasty departure the Japs left twenty of their own dead and five prisoners—four naval ratings and a Middlesex private—who had been trussed up like chickens and were firmly convinced of their impending death.

Lance-Sergeant Heath, for all his unflagging energy and dauntless courage, could hardly exercise command over one hundred and fifty men from a dozen assorted units.

The Repulse Bay Hotel garrison was an uneasy mixture of suicidal heroism, exhaustion, sloth, fear and extreme bewilderment. There were some men, inevitably in close proximity to Heath, whose fighting spirit no threat of encirclement and annihilation could subdue. Others, who had been fighting continuously for days, were practically out on their feet and seemed incapable of grasping the simplest order. Others, again, had done no fighting so far and were in no hurry to start. There were some who bitched and griped and got in the way of everyone who was doing a worth-while job of work. There was a hard core of marked individualists who volunteered for the most dangerous and suicidal missions; there were others who desired nothing more than to keep out of the way. There were others, mercifully only a few, who were convinced that staying in the hotel could only end in disaster and said so with dogged and truculent persistence. There was even one who advocated surrender; unfortunately for him, he did so in the hearing of Lance-Sergeant Heath, who meted out swift and unofficial punishment. The Commanding Officer, with one bottle of whisky inside him and a fresh one at his elbow, was buttressing the fortress with a spirited but off-key rendering of 'The Maple Leaf Forever'.

The hotel under siege needed a leader and they needed him quickly.

They were soon to get one. General Maltby, hearing of the chaotic conditions prevailing in the hotel, despatched Major Robert Templer of the 8th Coast Artillery Regiment. Maltby's orders to Templer had been simple and unequivocal:"There's a hell of a mess in that hotel, Bob," he had said. "Go and clean it up."

Robert Templer is a big man in every way. For twenty years he had been patiently mastering all the intricacies of gunnery in anticipation of the war that he knew must some day come. The outbreak of war had found him in Hong Kong, virtually a peace station, while officers many years junior to him had taken their regiments to France and North Africa.

Now he found himself without guns, and a dedicated artillery officer without guns spells trouble for someone. Templer collected a small force of his own coast gunners and Canadians and headed for the Repulse Bay Hotel.

According to one of the less belligerent members of the garrison, Templer went through the place like a dose of salts. His effect on the defenders was correspondingly lubricant. "We knew that we'd got to fight whether we liked it or not," said a rueful Canadian, "but, hell, the spirit of that guy was such that we *wanted* to." Which is praise.

Templer wasted no time. In half an hour he had transformed an extemporaneous rabble into something like a cohesive fighting formation. Like a new headmaster appointed to an unruly seat of learning, he strode about the hotel. Militarily, the situation was far from reassuring but Templer infused a fighting spirit into the force which had long been absent, or at best uncontrolled. The outpost, isolated like a ship on a wide and unfriendly sea, became a not-unhappy ship. The spirit of the leader became the spirit of the men: tireless and ubiquitous, Templer never seemed to sleep; he reorganised defensive positions, he led fighting patrols, he did everything that energy, courage and devotion to duty could do to put the tails of the garrison up. Lance-Sergeant Bob Heath, for one, was profoundly relieved when Templer arrived: fighting and responsibility, he decided, did not go together; whereas it seemed that he could not get enough of the former, he had had more than enough of the latter.

Templer's first offensive action was to fill two trucks with Canadians and lead yet another assault on the Japanese positions in the Wongneichong Gap. But his force was too small; the Japs were securely dug-in and their fire power was overwhelmingly superior. With the meagre forces at his disposal, Templer had no choice but to report back to Maltby that a break-through to the Gap was out of the question.

Slowly, but hideously surely, the Japs closed in on the hotel. By this time the patrician rooms presented an extraordinary appearance: bullets and mortar bombs had bitten large chunks out of the ceilings; the floors were littered with spent bullets; there was dirt and dust from a hundred pairs of boots; shattered glass was scattered everywhere like confetti.

Casualties were mounting fast and the wounded soon found themselves in evil case. Ministering to them with unfailing devotion was Elizabeth Mosey, the hotel's permanent nurse. But for her attention, many wounded men would undoubtedly have died during the siege. Her trim white uniform, a symbol of security and physical well-being in the peacetime life of the hotel, was bespattered with the blood from a score of wounded men; her face was streaked with grime and dust; her grey hair was in wild disorder; her nose shone unashamedly—nay, proudly. She seemed to be motivated by an almost divine sense of mission: to succour the wounded and helpless without any thought for herself.

At about 8 pm on the evening of December 21st, Major Robert Templer sat in his makeshift headquarters thinking lovingly of a large Dry Martini followed by clear turtle soup, *suprême* of turbot and *filet mignon*, the whole washed down with a bottle of Veuve Cliquot. This gastronomic reverie was interrupted by the appearance of Bombardier Harry Guy. Between Templer and Guy existed a David and Jonathan-like partership: they had started the war together and meant to finish it together.

"Sir," said Guy, "them bloody Japs are in the West Wing."

"The devil they are," said Templer, "come on."

To this day Templer cannot remember the exact composition of the force which evicted the Japanese from the West Wing. There may have been sailors, there were probably Canadians, there was at least one cook; there was certainly Bombardier Guy and Lance-Sergeant Heath.

The West Wing houses some of the most expensive and sought after accommodation in the Repulse Bay Hotel. There is a long and richly carpeted corridor; on either side of the corridor are suites of unparalleled luxury. Each man in Templer's party took as many hand grenades as he could carry.

The Japanese, displaying either rare courage or extraordinary stupidity, had erected a light machine gun at the far end of the corridor and were industriously firing at nothing at all. At a rough guess, Templer records, there were a dozen of them.

'It was,' continues Templer's story, 'a most exhilarating experience. We rolled the grenades along the beautifully carpeted corridor, for all the world as if we'd been in a bowling alley. Yells of chagrin and the abrupt silencing of the machine gun told us that our aim was accurate.'

Templer had thrown the Japs out of the hotel, but there were still something like five hundred of them outside. . . .

There is a song, invariably unprintable, about almost every branch of the British Army: cavalry, infantry, artillery, engineers and all the miscellaneous 'odds and sods' of administrative troops who, according to front line infantrymen, live a life of sybaritic luxury miles behind the line.

One of these songs, roared with cynical tolerance in a thousand wet canteens, went like this:

If it wasn't for
The Ordnance Corps
Where would old England be?
(Chorus: '——ed if I know!')

The Royal Army Ordnance Corps supply the Army with weapons, ammunition, boots, button sticks, fly buttons, steel helmets, groundsheets, medal ribbons, blankets, water bottles, socks, targets, enamel mugs, boot laces, knives, forks and spoons. They are to be found in BODs (Base Ordnance Depots) and CODs (Command Ordnance Depots). They operate improbable sounding units such as Mobile Laundries and Mobile Bath Units. Many of their personnel in Hong Kong were elderly, undersized, astigmatic, dyspeptic or for other reasons unfit for combat duty. Their lives were bounded by stores, indents and forms in triplicate. They were rarely to be found in desperate last-ditch stands against overwhelming hordes of enemy. The RAOC were rarely called upon to die heroes' deaths, but they were in Hong Kong.

But the fighting in Hong Kong was the exception to every rule of normal warfare. On December 21st men of the RAOC, together with a few details of the RASC, a few naval ratings and a small party of Canadian stragglers, found themselves on the Ridge overlooking the Repulse Bay Hotel surrounded by a strong force of Japanese who were sniping and mortaring them with vicious intensity. Ordnance men, who normally only concerned themselves with the issuing of rifles to their less privileged brethren in the infantry, were firing as fast as they could ram fresh clips of ammunition into their magazines.

In command of this motley, bewildered and determined force was Lieutenant-Colonel Macpherson. Macpherson had served as an infantry officer in Kitchener's army and was gratified to find out that his fighting knowledge had not entirely deserted him. But one did not need to be an expert in infantry tactics to see that his present position would all too soon be untenable by a platoon of foot guards, let alone by a handful of storemen, artificers and clerks. Two probing attacks had already been beaten off with heavy loss to the enemy—a middle-aged, bespectacled and clerkly bren gunner, whose previous acquaintance with the light machine gun had only been on paper, despatched six Japanese with one burst.

The next attack, Macpherson knew, would be in force.

Macpherson and his men held out all that night. It was a night of no sleep and constant alertness by the men of the Ordnance Corps, many of whom had not spent a night out of bed for many weeks and certainly never on an isolated hillside under sustained enemy fire. But the Ordnance men held their ground and beat off a succession of enemy attacks.

As December 22nd dawned Macpherson knew that the Japs would come in for the kill. He had to make up his mind whether to attempt a withdrawal, fight it out to a finish or surrender. Macpherson's natural instinct was to hold the position to the end, but food, water and ammunition were practically finished.

A withdrawal was out of the question because the Japs covered every escape route. Twenty of his men were wounded, all more or less seriously.

Macpherson conferred briefly with Captain David Strellett of the RASC, the only other officer in the party. Strellett said: "What d'you think of our chances, sir?"

"Not a lot," said Macpherson. "I'm afraid we'll have to shove out a white flag." There was, indeed, little choice: the Japanese outnumbered his force by more than ten to one and had the Ridge effectively surrounded.

Strellett tied a white handkerchief to a stick and held it out of a window; a burst of machine gun fire promptly shot it out of his hand.

"That settles it," said Macpherson. "We'll hold 'em up for the rest of the day—if we can. When it gets dark, every man who can walk must leg it to the Repulse Bay Hotel."

"What about you, sir?" asked Strellett.

"I'm staying with the wounded," said Macpherson. "We'll have to take our chance on Japanese hospitality."

Towards evening it became increasingly evident that the Japs were resolved on the destruction of this stubborn little garrison of 'administrative details'. The term 'administrative details' is always a slightly contemptuous one because it has been said with some truth that the 'administrative tail' of British divisions is out of all proportion to the actual fighting men. General Maltby, however, found these Ordnance men anything but contemptible and neither did the Japs. In his despatch Maltby paid tribute 'to the very gallant fighting qualities displayed by the administrative details on the Ridge under Lieutenant-Colonel Macpherson.'

As darkness fell Macpherson gave the order 'make for the Repulse Bay Hotel'. The enemy were hemming in the force from every side and would certainly attack again that night. If they did, the defenders would stand no chance.

In small parties the Ordnance men slipped off the Ridge almost under the very noses of the Japs. But their troubles were very far from being over yet: in the pitch darkness it was impossible to keep in touch with one another; Japanese patrols were on the alert; few of the men knew the direction to the hotel.

The fate of the majority of these men was a grim one. Many were cut off and in attempting to fight their way out were captured and bayoneted. A few managed to get near the hotel, which by this time was surrounded by the enemy, and had to run the gauntlet of machine gun fire as they made their final dash through the glare of a searchlight. Less than a dozen men got through to swell Templer's sadly depleted force in the hotel.

Barely a quarter of an hour after the last man had left, the Japs swarmed on to the Ridge. They found only Lieutenant-Colonel Macpherson and twenty wounded. They were tied up and savagely beaten with rifle butts. Then the Japs roped them together in threes and bayoneted them. Six days later their bodies were found, contemptuously piled in a heap like carelessly swept up rubbish.

At a time when miraculous escapes from death were becoming almost commonplace, the experience of Company Sergeant-Major Hamlon must take pride of place.

Hamlon, together with three riflemen of the Royal Rifles of Canada, was captured at Eucliff. After stripping them of their arms and equipment, the Japs beat them about the head and face with rifle butts. As they disarmed the three Canadians, the Japs threw clips of ammunition in their faces. Their hands were then bound behind their backs. They were prodded forward with bayonets to the edge of a cliff and made to sit down facing the sea.

Coldly and impersonally Hamlon told his story at the War Crimes trial of Colonel Tanaka: "We knew that we were going to be shot because on top of the bank were pools of blood and at the bottom of the cliff, near the sea, were dozens of dead bodies and it was evident that they had been shot on top of the cliff and had fallen down. Then a firing squad came forward and we were all shot.

"Owing to the fact that I turned my head to the left as I was being fired at, the bullet passed through my neck above the left shoulder and came out at my right cheek. I did not lose consciousness and the force of the bullet hitting me knocked me free from the others and I rolled down the cliff."

Hamlon finished up face downwards on a concrete path and the bodies of the three Canadians rolled down on top of him. They were all dead. . . .

Later fifty-three bodies were found in this area: some had been shot; some bayoneted; some beheaded. The final damning words which helped to send Tanaka to the gallows were spoken in evidence by Lieutenant William Markey of the Royal Army Ordnance Corps who was despatched to Eucliff in charge of a burial party.

"Every man," said Markey, "had his hands tied behind his back. *Without doubt they had been taken prisoners and destroyed later.*"

Before the campaign started, Colonel Tanaka is alleged to have made the following statement regarding the treatment of prisoners-of-war: 'The Hong Kong campaign will be a historical one, carried out with the eyes of the world looking on. Most likely many prisoners-of-war will be captured. The treatment of prisoners-of-war must be carried out in accordance with International Law on the basis of humane principles and justice. The laws and customs of war must not be violated.'

To this the fifty-three victims of the Eucliff Massacre gave mute answer.

Another man with a seemingly charmed life was Company Sergeant-Major 'Trudy' Begg. He managed to evade the Japanese patrols and was heading for the Repulse Bay Hotel only to come under heavy fire from Eucliff. Several men were hit and the survivors took refuge in a cave. In the cave were a party of Canadians.

Begg at once realised that any attempt to reach Repulse Bay overland would be suicidal. There was equally little chance of getting to Stanley, for the Japanese by this time were infiltrating on all sides. Begg looked out of the cave: above him were the towering and inhospitable cliffs—at this moment, he guessed (rightly, as it happened) men were being lined up and shot. In sombre confirmation of this theory, he heard a fusillade of rifle shots followed by the bumping of bodies down the cliff.

"That settles it," said Begg decidedly. "We swim for it."

"He's right," said a Canadian, "me, I'd rather drown than get carved up by those monkeys."

"I don't swim so good," said another.

"I can't swim at all," said a third.

"Well, now's your chance to learn," said the sergeant-major. "Now then, who's for compulsory bathing?"

Just before Begg led his party into the water, CSM Hamlon appeared. He presented an extraordinary appearance, for his head, face and neck were a mass of blood. "I looked," said Hamlon afterwards, "like an underdone steak."

But this party, too, were doomed almost to a man. The phosphorescence in the water betrayed the swimmers and the Japanese on the cliffs swept Repulse Bay with machine gun fire. Some of the swimmers were hit and sank; some died later of cold and exhaustion. On Christmas Eve Sergeant-Major Begg and two others arrived at Stanley after nearly twenty-two hours in the water. Of those men who elected not to swim for it, nothing is known. But the indestructible Sergeant-Major Hamlon ("If he ran into a tank, he'd dent the —— tank," said Sergeant Dick Stone of the Middlesex) reached safety and, like many others who had felt swift and terrible death breathing down their necks, lived to testify at the War Crimes Trials.

By the afternoon of December 22nd it was woefully clear to Major Templer that the Repulse Bay Hotel was no longer tenable: it was completely surrounded and the Japanese were in occupation of all the hills overlooking it. It was only a matter of time before the Japs closed in for the kill which would inevitably mean the annihilation of the entire garrison and the civilians.

Templer's first thought was for the evacuation of all the civilians by road to Stanley and he asked General Maltby for lorries to be sent to effect their removal. Maltby, however, would not agree to this: he took the view that the chances of an evacuation of the civilians was remote; they would, he pointed out to Templer, be going straight from the frying pan into the fire for it appeared certain that Stanley would be put under siege before very long. Eventually it was decided that the civilians would have to remain in the hotel and, as things turned out, the decision proved to be a wise one: if an evacuation had been attempted, the lorries carrying the civilians would have had to run the gauntlet of Japanese patrols.

Plans were finally made for the evacuation of the garrison shortly after midnight. It was a hideous decision for Maltby to make, but every rifleman who could stand was required for the defence of Stanley. Maltby was of the opinion that if the Japanese occupied the hotel everyone, fighting men and civilians alike, would be killed; on the other hand, if they found only unarmed civilians there was a chance that the Japs would observe the decencies of warfare.

At ten o'clock that night Templer stood at the front door of the hotel looking out into the darkness. With him were Bombardier Guy and half a dozen Canadians. Every man peered into the blackness, straining their tired eyes in an endeavour to pick up the silhouette of a Jap.

Guy suddenly drew in his breath with a sharp hiss, nudged Templer and pointed. At first Templer could see nothing, but he could hear a faint rustle such as wild animals make when creeping through undergrowth.

Then Templer saw them: a party of about twenty Japs creeping round the front of the hotel. Guy said: "Shall we let 'em have it, sir?"

As a target they could hardly be better. Templer admits that the itching of his trigger finger was almost unbearable; the temptation to throw discretion to the winds and open up with everything he had was practically irresistible. But he knew that to start a battle now might be disastrous: everything depended on a silent evacuation of his force and the less noise they made the better. With a feeling of overpowering regret Templer hissed at his men: "Don't fire!"

At 1 am Templer assembled his force in the hotel's big hall: men half asleep; men cursing; men tripping over other men in the darkness. 'It was,' records Templer, 'the most terrible order that I have ever had to give—the order to abandon women and children to the Japanese. But I realised that Maltby had been right: Stanley was hardly the place for two hundred unexpected civilian guests.'

Templer's linguistic capabilities were strained to the utmost that night, for he had to repeat the orders in Hindustani for the benefit of the Indian soldiers and in French for some of the Canadians. His orders were that the evacuation of the hotel was to be made via the tunnel leading from the hotel to the Lower Beach Road and thence past the Lido up to the main Island Road; from there the withdrawal would be made either by the road or over Stanley Mound. In order to ensure absolute silence, every man removed his heavy ammunition boots.

Gwen Dew expressed the numbed feeling of all the civilians when she wrote: '. . . I knew that meant we were surrendering. Taking down the British flag . . . putting up the white flag . . . bowing to the bloody banner of the Rising Sun. . . .'

It was time to go, and some of the civilians came to see the soldiers off. "The awful shame that I felt can be imagined," said Templer. But no word of reproach was spoken and even the Lady Bridge Player was silent. Throughout the siege Andrew Shields, a prominent businessman of the Colony, had been a tower of calm strength and he spoke for all the civilians. "You've got to go," he said to Templer, "we all realise that. Only men with rifles are important in Hong Kong now."

Next to Shields stood Sister Elizabeth Mosey: calm, dignified and supremely composed. Templer knew that any words of his would be inadequate, even if he were capable of speaking. He turned abruptly on his heel and gave the order: "Ready to move."

Templer withdrew his men in the nick of time. Almost before the last man had left the Japs rushed the hotel from all sides.

Now there were only old men, women, children and wounded soldiers in the Repulse Bay Hotel. . . .

The Japanese herded the civilians into the lobby where they stood with their hands raised. An officer, ceremonial sword clanking at his side, walked up and down the line. At every door was a soldier with bayonet fixed. The officer was clearly determined that the civilians should taste to the full the bitter dregs of humiliation.

"Your soldiers have gone," he said with an outsize smirk. *"But do not worry ; Japanese soldiers will protect you."*

The wounded—some forty in number—were in the cocktail bar which had been transformed into an emergency hospital. Now, instead of the clink of glasses and the happy buzz of apéritif-time chatter, could be heard groaning, coughing and the meaningless blasphemies of men hideously hurt by war. Elizabeth Mosey sat with a young Canadian who had been shot through his right lung: he was dying fast, but was talking to her quite lucidly of his mother, father and three young sisters in Alberta. Every five minutes or so Sister Mosey wiped away his life's blood which was trickling away out of his mouth. He held her hand in a fierce and possessive grip.

A party of six Japanese, with bayonets fixed, brushed aside the white flag, on which had been hastily embroidered a red cross, and stood grinning at the entrance to the cocktail bar. One of them picked up a bottle, prized the cork free with his teeth and took a long and comprehensive swig. Elizabeth Mosey gently freed her hand from the dying Canadian boy's grip and stood up. She stood alone in front of the Japanese with her arms akimbo: five feet and two inches of grey-haired English womanhood and the only defence that stood between the Japanese bayonets and the wounded soldiers.

She said steadily: "You'll have to kill me first." She regarded them like a schoolmistress confronted with six grubby small boys who had been detected in the act of passing notes in class.

The Japs stared at her openmouthed. The one with the bottle stood speechless, the liquor trickling ridiculously on to the floor. They looked at each other, at the wounded soldiers and at Elizabeth Mosey. Then, muttering among themselves, they backed away and left the room.

"That's better," said Sister Elizabeth Mosey and went back to the Canadian.

Practically every man in Templer's party got through to Stanley. Their retirement was covered by a platoon of volunteers, most ably and gallantly led by Second-Lieutenant David Prophet who beat off successive strong enemy attacks for five hours.

Meanwhile, Lieutenant-General Sakai continued to pour men ashore and they swarmed over the Island like locusts. But somewhere along the coast line voices spoke—voices unmistakably from London's East End. They said: 'Just you wait, you yeller bastards. We ain't even *started* on you yet. . . .'

These were the voices of the 1st Battalion the Middlesex Regiment (the Diehards).

CHAPTER ELEVEN

Like CHEERFUL and ribald London policemen cordoning off a rough district, the Middlesex were in their pillboxes, guarding almost the entire length of the Island's coast line. 'A' Company (Captain J. H. S. Hudson) was manning the eleven pillboxes from Sandy Bay to Aberdeen Island; 'C' Company (Major Henry Marsh) nine pillboxes from Brick Hill to Repulse Bay; 'B' Company (Captain Martin Weedon) ten pillboxes from West Bay to Red Hill; and 'D' Company (Captain D. West) nine pillboxes from Tai Tam Bay to Lye Mun Barracks. Only the short stretch along the northern shore from Lye Mun to Causeway Bay was outside the responsibility of the Middlesex for beach defence.

Since December 8th the men of the Middlesex had led a claustrophobic existence in the concrete pillboxes. Each pillbox contained from two to four machine guns and was manned by a crew of nine. Each pillbox was a self-contained community with stores of ammunition, hand grenades, food and water and each was connected by telephone to company headquarters.

In addition, there was the heterogeneous 'Z' Company (Captain Christopher Man), which was responsible for the fourteen pillboxes in the north-western sector, covering Kennedy Town and the waterfront and stretching from Causeway Bay to Belcher Point. Lieutenant-Colonel 'Monkey' Stewart, that iron man of courage and discipline, whose perpetually twinkling pale blue eyes belied the ultra military appearance and the fierce moustache, had his headquarters on Leighton Hill.

'Monkey' Stewart loved these men with the single-minded devotion of the professional soldier who has nothing else to love: loved them, despaired of them, congratulated them, railed at them with terrible fury, thought continuously of them whether waking or sleeping. His feelings for them were like those of a stern but kindly father towards motherless children who must be watched every minute of the day. He knew every man by name; what was more, he knew the personal characteristics of all of them: he knew the malingerers, the 'fiddlers', the smart alecs, the sluggards, the alcoholics (real and potential), the rebels, the 'couldn't care less types' and the mediocrities. He knew that Private A would make a good NCO if he could keep off the beer; he knew that Corporal B's wife was being accommodated in Stepney by an exempted factory worker; he knew that Lance-Corporal D was having a clandestine liaison with Private E's 'dahnhomer'; he knew that Sergeant F had paid Sergeant G five dollars to do his guard for him last Tuesday fortnight; he knew that Lance-Corporal H had stopped his wife's allotment and was instead paying it to a cinema usherette in Cricklewood.

'Monkey' Stewart was not the type of Commanding Officer who sat in his headquarters immersed in turgid paperwork; he had an adjutant for that. The occupants of the pillboxes never knew when that questing eye and belligerent moustache would appear round the corner with a barrage of questions about gun positions, ammunition returns, the condition of boots, the length of hair, or the state of health of someone's mother.

The 'consummate conceit of the Cockney' was a favourite dictum of 'Monkey' Stewart and he found ample evidence of it in every pillbox he visited. He remembered the times without number when something had gone grievously wrong with a rehearsal for a ceremonial parade. He had castigated RSM Challis who had assured him with a beatific smile that it would be "all right on the day" before lamming into the senior NCOs who had produced the same bland assurance. The sergeants, snorting the vitriolic comments peculiar to sergeants, were told by the junior NCOs and privates: "It'll be all right on the day, sarge." This optimistic assessment of the future, peculiar to the Middlesex Regiment, covered such varied activities as camp concerts, inter-regimental football matches, King's Birthday Parades—and battle. Somehow, incredibly, it was always 'all right on the day'. In spite of the fact Lance-Corporal Poole was fifteen pounds in debt, Private Marshall had omitted to shave, Private Aldridge had no fly buttons on his shorts and Private Stutz had no detonators in his hand grenades, 'Monkey' Stewart returned to the headquarters more than ever convinced of the 'consummate conceit of the Cockney' and secure in the knowledge that it would be 'all right on the day'. The day, for the Middlesex, was not far off.

Although they had been standing-to in their pillboxes since December 6th, the Middlesex were not committed to hard action until December 19th. They had, it is true, been bombed, shelled and mortared almost continuously but as yet the itching fingers of the 'Number Ones'[1] on the machine guns had not been assuaged by a really worthwhile target.

It transpired that the motley collection of 'odds and sods' comprising Captain Christopher Man's 'Z' Company were to be the first in action, a fact which caused some annoyance to the more conventional military minds of 'A', 'B', 'C' and 'D'. Two of the first men to draw blood were Lance-Corporal 'Tookie' Poole and Private 'Witch' Aldridge (so nicknamed because of an unruly mop of spiky red hair which no brush, comb or brilliantine could subdue).

The single stripe on Lance-Corporal Poole's arm was precarious and represented the zenith of his promotion prospects. Its progress on and off his arm had started in 1938, but the inevitable proximity of pay night to Monday morning had resulted in his reduction to the ranks on no fewer than four different occasions.

Shortly before the Japanese attack the Adjutant discovered a vacancy for a lance-corporal in the battalion. With his heart in his mouth, he recommended Private Poole. 'Monkey' Stewart consulted Poole's conduct sheet and acidly asked the Adjutant if he were trying to be funny, because if so it was too hot. The Adjutant stuck to his guns and shortly afterwards a notice appeared in Battalion Orders to the effect that Private Poole, A. had been promoted to lance-corporal. The Adjutant breathed a silent prayer, 'Witch' Aldridge bet 'Ninny' Marshall five dollars that 'Tookie' would be busted within the fortnight and the Colonel said, "Horrible man that you are, Poole, I think there might be some good in you. For God's sake try to keep that stripe for a month."

Poole not only kept the stripe (thereby enriching 'Ninny' Marshall by five dollars), but on December 20th found himself elevated to section commander. A direct hit on a pillbox at Causeway Bay killed Corporal Dick Radley.

[1] Number One of a machine gun crew is the man who actually fires the gun.

"Blimey!" said 'Witch' Aldridge, "now we're bound to lose the —— war."

Between Poole and Aldridge existed a strange friendship. They enlisted together, got drunk together, occupied neighbouring beds in the barrack room and were Number One and Number Two respectively on the same machine gun. It was a friendship characterised by their inability to agree on any conceivable subject and a brisk continuous exchange of insults. Since the Japanese attack on Kai Tak, they had been telling each other that it would be for the good of the community at large if the other was killed.

Thus, if it is Poole's turn to buy the drinks he does not say to Aldridge: "What are you going to have?" He says: "I suppose I've got to buy you a drink, you carroty-headed bastard." If Poole has some cigarettes and Aldridge has not, this would be the exchange:

Aldridge: "Give us a fag, Took."

Poole: "See what I mean? Too bloody mean to buy any fags."

Aldridge: "I thought you was my mate."

Poole: "Well, you can —— well think again."

Aldridge: "Ah, come on, Tookie, give us a fag . . ."

Poole: "I only got one."

Aldridge: "Well, I only want one."

And now they were together on a gun and the Japs were advancing on them in waves which kept coming as fast as they were shot down. 'Tookie' Poole kept his thumbs on the firing lever while 'Witch' Aldridge fed the belts of ammunition into it. Poole said disgustedly: "Here I am with half the bloody Jap army coming at me, and I have to get lumbered with a —— like you. . . ."

Poole and Aldridge dealt out fearful destruction on the Japs, as did Drummer Charlie Tully and Private 'Boo-boo' Clark on a light machine gun just to the right of them. A third-class certificate of education had persistently eluded Clark during his five years of service, but he was a deadly marksman. Poole and Aldridge argue to this day about how many Japs they killed on this occasion and they both take sole credit for it. Official records credit Poole, Aldridge, Tully and Clark with the killing of seventy-five of the enemy, although 'Boo-boo' Clark swears it was three hundred. But, then, he had not got his third-class certificate and arithmetic was his worst subject of all. . . .

The Reverend Herbert Davies, Chaplain to the 1st Middlesex, had his problems—728 of them in all. The spiritual welfare of 728 Cockney hard cases was his responsibility and it was not always easy to promote the Kingdom of Heaven to some of them who, prior to their enlistment, had hardly seen the inside of a church since their christening—and not all of them then.

The large majority of recruits who joined the Middlesex Regiment between the wars were of the Church of England, although many, when asked by the recruiting sergeant what their religion was shuffled their feet uneasily and grinned sheepishly, rather as a Hottentot would if you asked him for the address of his tailor. The more cunning souls, however, had heard that church parades were only compulsory for Church of England men, and proclaimed themselves variously to be congregationalists, methodists, baptists and Plymouth Brethren. One or two men described themselves as free thinkers, but 'Monkey' Stewart was on to them. "Church of England parade for you," he said, "it's free and you'll get plenty of opportunities to think in church."

Chaplain Davies's battle post was St Albert' Hospital where the succouring of the wounded and the burial of the dead kept him busy, but whenever possible he visited his flock in their pillboxes. War, it seemed, had brought with it a spiritual awakening and the response of the men of the Middlesex to his ministrations pleased and saddened him at the same time: these men who lived in the close confines of pillboxes lived in close proximity to one another; at the same time they had come closer to God.

The language of the pillbox was the same as that of the soldier the world over, if not more so; the usual adjective made its appearance in every sentence; the subjects under discussion were limited to the usual trinity. But there was not a man in the Middlesex who did not feel better for a visit from the padre, and not only because he invariably brought generous quantities of cigarettes which were not always obtained by strictly Christian means.

Davies distributed cigarettes and took the place of mail from home by talking of home and families. Like 'Monkey' Stewart, he knew every man by name and every man's family by their photographs. Before leaving a pillbox he would say, "And now let us say a few prayers."

Men of all denominations stood bareheaded with the Chaplain outside the pillboxes: Roman Catholics and Anglicans; Methodists and Congregationalists; men with Atheist and Agnostic written defiantly on Page One of their pay books. Every man found himself strangely uplifted by the presence of this gentle priest who seemed to be a symbol of peace, dignity and sanity in a world gone mad. His soft, lilting Welsh voice magically cleared the brow and strengthened them for the morrow.

And so it came to pass that Herbert Davies spoke one day with Privates Burke and Ball, both destined to die in the desperate defence of pillbox Number 14.

Burke jerked hist humb heavenwards. "You reckon there's someone up there looking after us, sir?" he said.

"I know there is," said the Chaplain.

Ball, too, had a religious problem. "What d'you reckon God thinks about blokes who only pray when they're shi—I mean dead scared of being knocked off?" he asked.

"God loves all men, whether they're frightened or not," said the Chaplain simply. "You see, we don't only pray to be spared. We pray for strength to die, if necessary, as Our Lord died on the Cross."

Private Ball, who had not looked at it quite like that, returned comforted to his pillbox. . . .

To Corporal Charles Goddard of the 1st Middlesex the Canadians will always be an incalculable race. Goddard was not the only soldier in Hong Kong who found them so, for they were alternately demoralised and determined; cowardly and courageous; ill-disciplined and fiercely self-reliant. You never knew, said Goddard, whether a Winnipeg Grenadier or a Royal Rifleman of Canada would stage a one-man bayonet charge, save your life or run like hell.

Goddard—nicknamed 'Pop' because of premature baldness —had been in the Army for eight years. He had started his military career as a band boy, but the best efforts of the bandmaster, accompanied by the direst threats, had done nothing to make him an accomplished saxophonist. During band practice at least half of his mind had strayed to a more practical weapon of war: the Vickers medium machine gun.

After missing three whole bars of the Pomp and Circumstance march at an Officers' Mess guest night, Goddard got his wish and was transferred out of the band to a machine gun platoon.

Goddard stands six feet three inches and weighs one hundred and ninety-six pounds, not an ounce of which is superfluous. He fought in the regimental boxing team as a heavyweight and performed prodigies of valour for the rugby football team in the middle of the back row.

Goddard was pleased to hear that the Japanese had landed because for twelve days and nights he had been shelled and bombed in a pillbox without seeing a single Jap. This did not suit Goddard's temperament and he said so with dogged persistence. His determination to get into battle drew from one of the more phlegmatic members of his section the statement that "old 'Pop' wants to win this bloody war all on his own". On December 21st, however, Corporal Goddard viewed his assignment with marked displeasure.

His section had been detailed to provide support for a depleted company of Royal Rifles of Canada. It was at once apparent to Goddard that these Canadians needed all the support they could get.

They were in marked contrast to the cheerful, ribald and indomitable Cockneys of the Middlesex. These men of the Royal Rifles wanted no more part in this war: within a fortnight of their arrival in the Colony they had been bombed, shelled, sniped and thrown into costly and abortive counter-attacks. There was nothing glorious about the war they found themselves in: the men who had vociferously expressed their confidence in licking the pants off any goddam sonofabitch Jap were leaderless (their officers had all been killed), dispirited and demoralised. They lay around the foot of Stanley Mound in inert heaps, smoking apathetically.

They were not advancing because they were too tired and had been without chow for twenty-four hours; in any case, no one had told them to advance. They were not retreating either, because they did not know where to retreat to. They should have been digging in, but the ground was rock hard and in any event they had no entrenching tools. They should have been doing something about the small party of Japanese established on the top of Stanley Mound, who sniped at them with insulting impunity. With rare effrontery a Japanese machine gun sprayed them and sent them burrowing further into the inhospitable terrain.

"I'm getting out of here," declared a disgruntled private.

"That's a great idea," said his neighbour bitterly. "Where d'you figure on going?"

Goddard remembered the arrival of the Canadians: they had been confident and cheerful and had marched from the troopship with a springing quickstep. Now they were grey-faced with fatigue, dirty, demoralised and fed-up—a miserable and dispirited rabble.

Goddard put his section into position under the disinterested stare of the Canadians. "Just our luck to get lumbered with a bunch like this," said Private Milroy disgustedly.

The other members of the section expressed their dissatisfaction in uncompromising terms:

"We was supposed to leave the Japs to them."

"Yes, promised us we wouldn't never be needed."

"Look at 'em now. . . ."

"Couldn't fight their way out of a —— paper bag."

The Japanese machine gun opened up again and the bullets whined spitefully over Goddard's head.

"Get on that gun," Goddard ordered Private Jack Milroy, "and give 'em a few bursts. I'm going to find out who's in command of this lot."

"When you find him, tell him I want a posting," said Milroy.

Goddard made a quick appreciation of the situation. The Japs, he judged, were not on Stanley Mound in any great force: indeed, judging from the volume of fire coming from the top, there could not be more than twenty of them. It was, he decided, a ticklish position but not one that sixty determined and well-led men could not take care of. With two platoons of 'D' Company he'd go up that hill like a dose of salts. . . .

Goddard found a thin, sharp-featured sergeant sheltering in a small cave at the bottom of the slope. The sergeant was lighting a cigarette and regarded Goddard with open hostility.

"You in command of these blokes?" asked Goddard.

"What's that to you?" countered the sergeant insultingly.

"I asked you a question."

"Yeah, I heard you. Now blow."

Goddard tried another method. "You're not just going to sit around and let those bastards snipe you, are you?" he said.

"If you wanna be a hero, then go right ahead," said the sergeant indifferently. "Me, I like it here."

In full view of a group of astonished Canadians, Goddard took two paces forward and lifted the sergeant bodily off the ground by the front of his shirt. "You'll either fight them or me," he said ominously.

And such was the steely inflexibility of Goddard's voice and grip that the challenge went unanswered.

"Okay, you guys," said the sergeant. "Get off your tails. We're going in."

Goddard strode among the Canadians. He harangued, derided and cajoled them. He told them that they reminded him of a bunch of old whores on a picnic. But he infused in them a fighting spirit that had long been absent.

"Blimey," said Private Milroy admiringly, "old 'Pop' thinks he's a —— general or somethink."

"Take that gun to the left, Jack," said Goddard to Milroy, "and give us covering fire. Pump it into 'em as hard as you can. I'm going to take that hill."

"And the best of luck," said Milroy, who had been on a charge for insubordination more than once. "You and who else?"

"Less of your lip," said Goddard. "Get on that gun."

Soon Milroy was firing long bursts up the hill. With Goddard at their head, the Canadians swarmed up the slope. They were halted at the crest by a hail of grenades which tore ugly gaps in their ranks, but the attack was pressed home at bayonet point and the Japanese were driven off.

"Hell, *I* didn't want to go into that attack," said a Canadian private afterwards. "But the spirit of that bastard was such that we had to." Which is praise.

"It was," said Captain Henry Marsh, "like talking to men in a submarine, knowing full well that they'd never come to the surface again." He was talking of telephone conversations with his pillbox crews in the Little Hong Kong area.

In the case of pillbox 14, Marsh's reference to a submarine was apt enough, although the NCO in charge, Sergeant George Rich, never gave any indication of alarm. "Old 'enery's a bit of a worrier," confided Rich to Corporal 'Timber' Wood. "Reckon I'd better cheer him up a bit."

And cheer him up he did, for there was something about the

191

cheerful self-assurance in this young sergeant's voice that was a positive denial of defeat. On December 23rd pillbox 14 was continuously attacked by hordes of Japanese and Rich's men took a fearsome toll of their number. To Marsh's query: "How are things with you, Sarn't Rich?" came back the inevitable answer: "Mustn't grumble, sir. We're bowling 'em over like ninepins."

Five, six, seven assaults were made on '14' and soon the area round the pillbox was piled with Japanese dead. "Fahsands of 'em," reported Sergeant Rich cheerfully, "but you don't want to worry about us, sir. Blimey, we ain't started yet." 'The consummate conceit of the Cockney,' thought Marsh, echoing his Colonel's favourite dictum.

But late in the afternoon of the 23rd Marsh spoke to Rich on the telephone for the last time. Corporal 'Timber' Wood, Lance-Corporal George Bailey, Privates Reg Bosley, Don Burke, Bill Ball, Walter Bywaters, Eddie Edwards and Harry Newbury poured a hail of fire into the Japs who were just twenty yards from pillbox 14.

The telephone in the pillbox rang and Sergeant Rich answered it for the last time. He said: "There's such a bleedin' racket going on I can hardly hear you, sir. What's that, sir? Are we all right? '*Course* we are."

Then the line went dead. . . .

There were no survivors of the crew of pillbox 14. The Japanese surrounded it and threw hand grenades through the loop-holes. When they got inside Rich's men fought them with bayonets, rifle butts, boots and fists. As at Albuhera, one hundred and thirty years before, the men of the Diehards were found with their faces to the enemy and all their wounds in front. . . .

There were no survivors of Sergeant Bert Bedward's section on Bennett's Hill. Bedward—the Immortal Sergeant of the Middlesex—was in sharp contrast to George Rich: he had, in fact, enlisted when Rich was a grubby urchin aged four. Bedward was dark, lean, leathery and tough. Fifteen years spent in India, Egypt and Hong Kong had burned his face to a deep mahogany colour—a face as brown as a kipper and as devoid of expression. He was extensively tattooed: snakes and dragons writhed up his gnarled brown arms; the thick black hair on his chest all but obscured the ship in full sail put there in 1924 by a one-eyed tattoo artist in Cairo. He was unshakable and indestructible; he used appalling language, exploring the uttermost depths of obscenity in his everyday conversation; he had a swallow like a thirsty horse and gallons of beer made not an atom of difference to his speech, gait or immaculate bearing on early morning parade. Here was a Man.

Never a great conversationalist, Bedward had an intense dislike for the telephone and his replies to Henry Marsh were clipped and economical. But terse as they were, they were as reassuring as Sergeant Rich's. His last report to his company commander was a laconic: "They're all round us, sir."

Then his line, too, went dead. . . .

'Monkey' Stewart, 'Mickey' Man, Henry Marsh, Major Hedgecoe (the Black Prince), RSM Challis, Jack Milroy (the Black Mamba), the 'onourable 'orrible Marable, 'Pop' Goddard, Herbert Davies, the Welsh parson; Sergeant Bert Bedward—these are the men the Middlesex talk lyrically of at reunions nearly twenty years later, for these are the men whose conduct in the battle was consistently brave and in the finest traditions of Diehards.

But there is always another name that will come up—that of Private Walter Stutz. Prior to December 23rd, 1941, mention of 'Stutto' was accompanied by gales of mirth because Stutz was a soldier who, if he remembered to do a thing at all, invariably did it wrong.

If a man dropped his rifle on the King's Birthday Parade, it was inevitably Stutz; if a sergeant-major was seen to clench his fists and raise his eyes beseechingly to heaven, it was more than likely as a result of a clash with Stutz; if, on the range, orders were given "don't fire on first exposure of target", a round from Stutz's rifle winged unerringly into the middle distance, yards wide of the target; if someone told Stutz that metal polish was good for shining boots, then Stutz would try it; if it was ordered that the spare pair of boots should be displayed for inspection, Stutz, wearing a beatific smile, produced his gym shoes. Whatever he did, it was always good for a laugh.

But no man in the Middlesex laughed at Private Stutz after December 23rd, 1941.

It was, of course, entirely his own fault that he was wounded. While every other man of his section was safely under cover, Stutz was unconcernedly lighting a cigarette on the skyline. A Japanese machine gun swept the crest of the hill and Private Stutz received three bullets in the stomach. "Not enough sense to get out of the bloody rain," said his platoon sergeant bitterly.

On the march back to the final line at Stanley, Stutz marched with the rest, but his slow and painful pace became the pace of the rest of the platoon. "You'll have to leave me," said Private Stutz.

"We ought to," said the platoon sergeant, "but we ain't going to. Give him a lift along, a couple of you."

But progress was painfully slow. That night the platoon rested in the darkness. The men, practically asleep on their feet, dropped where they stood. From Private Stutz, with terrible cavernous wounds in his stomach, came no sound because Private Stutz was no longer there. Like Captain Oates, another gallant English gentleman, he had crawled away in the darkness to die alone.

Second-Lieutenant Charles Cheesewright was the archetype of all courageous young infantry officers—the colonel's and private's dream subaltern. In the First World War the average life of these young men in the front line was fairly accurately assessed at fifteen days; in both world wars they swelled the names on their public schools' war memorials. These were the boys who, frequently still in the virgin state, died before they had even begun to live. Today, senior officers of the Middlesex Regiment quote Charles Cheesewright as an example to flighty young newly-joined officers whose thoughts tend to stray away from their platoons to cocktail bars, night clubs, race meetings and accommodating young women.

Cheesewright was like a genial young Napoleon: his whole life evolved around Number Eleven Platoon: he boxed with it, ran cross country with it and played rugby football with it. He not only knew every man in it as an old married man knows his wife; he knew every man's size in boots, leadership potentialities, religious denomination (thereby making the Chaplain's life easier) and domestic problems.

On December 22nd Cheesewright's platoon were manning their pillboxes along the eastern shore of Repulse Bay. They were in grave danger of being cut off by the relentless Japanese pressure in that area, and that night Cheesewright was ordered to evacuate the pillboxes in Repulse Bay and join up with the Stanley Peninsula party. Cheesewright was reluctant to comply with this order: his men, in fine fettle as always, had inflicted tremendous slaughter on the enemy hordes, who advanced with apparent disregard for casualties; he was well supplied with food, ammunition and water. Cheesewright, in fact, was fully prepared to hold on as long as there was breath in his body and blood in his veins. But orders were orders, and Cheesewright prepared to move his platoon shortly after midnight. As the enemy were all round him, he gave orders that the move should be made in stockinged feet so that there should be no sound during the march.

Shortly before midnight the Japanese attacked Cheesewright's position with rifle fire and a hail of hand grenades. They were driven off, but reorganised for a second attack. It was not slow in coming and was launched just as the pillbox crew was due to start on its march to Stanley Peninsula. Cheesewright ordered his men to pick up every available weapon and, with Private 'Jessie' Matthews in close attendance, opened the door of the pillbox.

The Japanese, expecting a near walk-over, walked straight into a shower of grenades, thrown with unerring accuracy by Cheesewright and Matthews. This had the effect of throwing the Japs in wild confusion and Cheesewright bawled: "Everyone out!" Before the bewildered Japs had a chance to re-orientate themselves, the platoon had slipped away into the night.

The march to Stanley took five hours and Cheesewright brought his platoon in without suffering a single casualty. The whole march was made without boots; the roads had been freshly covered with granite chips and every man's feet were cruelly lacerated. Yet they arrived at their destination still cheerful and ready to fight on, and brought with them all their guns and ammunition. On arrival, Cheesewright said: "Everyone all right?"

"Yes, sir," said Sergeant Arthur Manning, indomitable and facetious as always. "What about a boot inspection?"

Sergeant Manning was yet another Immortal Sergeant of the Middlesex. A product of the East End of London, the 1st Battalion the Middlesex Regiment was the only real home he had known for twelve years. He was the sort of man who, finding himself on an exposed hillside in teeming rain, says: "Wish I was a bleedin' duck." When it is freezing cold he makes remarks about brass monkeys. He invariably sang 'Trees' at Sergeants' Mess socials and encouraged recalcitrant machine gunners with comparative references to sexual prowess.

During this frightful march, a disgruntled soldier said morosely:

"All we do is —— well retreat."

Manning said: "Who's retreating? We're just going the other —— way."

Cheesewright died of malnutrition in a Japanese prison camp. Manning, his spirit totally unimpaired by four years of poverty and brutality, received the Distinguished Conduct Medal from His Majesty King George VI at Buckingham Palace. Afterwards he said to Sergeant Dick Stone: "Nice place he's got there, hasn't he?"

Throughout December 23rd and 24th Christopher Man's 'Z' Company continued to hold Leighton Hill against practically continuous Japanese attacks. The whole surrounding area had been shelled until it was reminiscent of Flanders in 1918; the slopes of the hill, covered with Japanese corpses, was a stinking shambles of death.

For two days and two nights the hill was lit with flame that flickered from above and below. There was no need for the defenders to pick their targets because they could hardly miss them; bursts of twenty, thirty, forty rounds were fired from the machine guns and around each position were little mounds of spent cartridges.

Occasionally there was a brief lull for the men of 'Z' Company because so great were the Japanese losses that the attackers had to draw off for reinforcements. But as the night of December 23rd waned, fresh hundreds of Japs were hurled against the hill and the exhausted defenders, by now reduced to forty men, had to face still more assaults. "It didn't seem to make any difference how fast we mowed them down," said Man, "they just kept coming." For every casualty, there were six more Japs to take his place.

"The bastards must be breeding down there," said 'Witch' Aldridge to 'Tookie' Poole.

"Them stiffs don't half ponk," said Poole.

"You don't smell so bloody nice yourself," retorted Aldridge.

Christmas Eve dawned and 'Z' Company were still on Leighton Hill. Filthy with sweat and dust, unshaven, weary nigh unto death, they peered towards their enemies with red eyes. Captain Man felt a surge of pride as he walked round the positions; this was 'Z' Company: the 'odds and sods', the bandsmen, the men whom the other four companies had gleefully disposed of when a circular was sent round from Battalion Headquarters that a new company was to be formed: Cooke, Price, Pacey and French, whose combined conduct sheets must have added up to twenty pages; 'Tookie' Poole and 'Witch' Aldridge insulting one another with undiminished fervour; Bandsman Johnny Hymus, the finest euphonium player in the Regiment and the most accomplished liar; Bandsman Charlie Dickens, who had got drunk on his wedding day . . . that had been on October 2nd, 1940—Man wondered where Topsy was now. Possibly she was——

"*Watch your front!*" shouted Man suddenly, "they're coming again. . . ."

"Bastards don't want to live," said 'Tookie' Poole sourly. "Shove along another belt of ammo, 'Witch'."

"You may be the section commander," said 'Witch' Aldridge, "but you don't have to tell me how to do *my* job."

At a quarter to five on the afternoon of Christmas Eve, Colonel Stewart ordered Man to withdraw from Leighton Hill if he possibly could. Despite the fact that the Japs had infiltrated past both flanks, thirty-two men managed to get away with their guns. Eight of the garrison, who were holding the further end of Leighton Hill, found their retreat cut off and stayed to fight it out to the end.

'Z' Company had made a contribution to the battle which was priceless: time after time the Japs had stormed the position, only to be halted and hurled back.

'Z' Company took up new positions in the Wanchai area, together with the remnants of a Royal Scots company, and a motley assortment of gunners, naval ratings, airmen and marines. Wanchai, however, suited 'Z' Company, for in this area were the homes of many of the 'dahnhomers'. Bandsman Dickens claims a practically unique distinction: while waiting for the next Japanese attacks on their new position, he disappeared for long enough to achieve the pinnacle of amatory endeavour in an upstairs room of the house which accommodated his section.

"Only Dickens," pronounced 'Tookie' Poole, "could have done it at a time like that."

Soon there was street fighting in the Wanchai area. A mixed party of Royal Scots and Volunteers fought for four hours to hold a four-storey building with huge plate glass doors and windows on the ground floor. A furious battle raged round 'Jimmy's Beer Kitchen', a famous peacetime rendezvous of British soldiers. A section of Royal Scots were badly burned when the top floors of one building collapsed; choked by smoke, they fought on.

Corporal Harry Tarrant of the Volunteers remembers the street fighting; he also remembers Lance-Corporal 'Tookie' Poole and Private 'Witch' Aldridge, who carried him to safety after he had been wounded.

"Pity there wasn't no one watching us," said Aldridge afterwards, "we might 've got the VC."

"What you?" said Poole, "you orter get ten bloody years. . . ."

They are but a small army now: the men who are to be seen at Waterloo Station's buffet, drinking a quick pint of bitter before commuting back to Berkshire, Surrey and Sussex; earlier in the day they have lunched, with a faint feeling of guilt and nostalgia, in the Army and Navy Club.

They are forty-sevenish, dark-suited, bowler-hatted, serious of mien, faintly worried by a world which is neither straightforward nor uncomplicated, as it was when they left Sandhurst for their regiments in the early 1930s. They are the ex-officers who were put 'in the bag' by the Japs: the regular infantry officers—former company commanders of the Royal Scots, Middlesex, Loyals, Manchesters, East Surreys, Leicesters, Sherwood Foresters, Norfolks, Suffolks, Gordons, Argylls—the doomed battalions of Singapore and Hong Kong. They are the men who found that four years of beatings, humiliation and a diet of coolie rice had put them far behind in the British Army's promotion race; the higher posts in the Regular Army demanded fit, ambitious and decorated men—many of these men were decorated, many more were ambitious but none, after Siam, Kobe and Argyle Street were fit. Consequently, after the war, they could do little else but swell the ranks of the 'deadbeat majors'. (This was not inevitable: Captain Christopher Man, who commanded the indomitable 'Z' Company, is now a brigadier and is busily instilling the Leighton Hill spirit into Liverpudlian territorials.)

They are a little worried in 1960, these lost warriors, for few of them have attained the higher ranks of commerce. They have, it is true, been generously pensioned off, but the majority of them have sons whom they are determined will follow them to public schools, if not into 'The Regiment'. Few of them have extensive private means and life is something of a struggle—some evidence of this struggle is to be seen in the faces of these commuters as they drink their bitter at Waterloo.

One of this band, who even in 1960 displays a certain specialised brand of heroism, is Major Martin Weedon, MC. But in December, 1941, the only thing that seriously worried him was the fact that the best company of the 1st Middlesex (every company commander worth a row of beans was convinced that his company was the best) had not been in action against the enemy. 'A' Company had been continuously bombed and shelled; 'C' were isolated and cut off, but had inflicted tremendous casualties on the enemy; 'D' Company had been in fierce actions in the Stanley Mound area and had been virtually decimated in the Mary Knoll position; 'Z' Company had been materially responsible for the slowing down of the Japanese advance all along the front. But Weedon's 'B' Company had been standing-to since December 5th without seeing a single Jap. It was a situation which was causing Martin Weedon considerable annoyance. This unsatisfactory state of affairs was to come to an abrupt conclusion on Christmas morning.

By this time the situation on the Island was extremely critical, for the Japanese held more than half of it and were steadily increasing their pressure everywhere. Suddenly Martin Weedon found himself transformed from a conventional company commander with reasonably clear-cut orders into the commander of a mixed force committed to a desperate last ditch stand.

In addition to his own 'B' Company, Weedon found himself responsible for the remnants of 'A', 'C' and 'D'; mixed elements of volunteers, driven back from their precarious positions near Stanley village, attached themselves to him; stragglers from the Royal Rifles of Canada, who had performed without any sort of distinction so far, found in this imperturbable young captain all the qualities of leadership that made them want to resist to the end. Of the Royal Rifles Weedon said: "They were bewildered and didn't know whether they were coming or going. But if they found an officer who appeared to be in control of the situation—and apparently I filled the bill in that respect—they glued themselves to him and fought with quite extraordinary tenacity."

There was, indeed, no talk of defeat in Weedon's mixed force of Middlesex, volunteers, Canadians, gunners, sappers and prison warders: they had a leader, something that many of them had been lacking for three days or more, and with Weedon to command them they felt capable of brave and wonderful deeds.

There were brave deeds in plenty and Weedon was directly concerned in almost all of them: Japanese frontal attacks ran into withering and skilfully controlled fire; an enemy party, who had ensconced themselves in a temple, were evicted by a band of desperate men (with Martin Weedon, inevitably, at their head) who climbed on to the roof and hurled hand grenades down the chimneys; the Japs found that this stubborn force, which appeared to be under inspired leadership, bitterly contested every inch of ground.

Fighting as hard and as effectively as anyone was ex-Captain Chattey of the Middlesex. The 'ex' requires a little explanation: Chattey, a regular officer with a promising military career seemingly assured, had fallen from grace shortly before the Japanese attack on Hong Kong. December 8th, 1941, found him in Stanley gaol, undergoing an eighteen month sentence. No one knew what had caused a man of Chattey's calibre to ruin his life and be broken on the wheel of the most damning evidence. The precise nature of his offence would have given reporters of English Sunday newspapers, had there been any in Hong Kong, the finest full-page spread of 1941. But on December 8th the Governor, realising the need for the presence of every available trained solder in Hong Kong, sanctioned Chattey's release from prison and he took his place in the fighting line.

It was a situation that could only have arisen in Hong Kong: men who had discussed his case with fearful fascination now found themselves under Chattey's command. They found that this man, broken and disgraced as he was, still knew his job as a soldier: men who had speculated morbidly on the precise nature of his misdeeds found themselves listening to a voice which still had the rasp of authority and command.

"When I got pushed into the line at Stanley," said Corporal Harold Middleton, an RASC clerk, "I didn't know whether I was coming or going, but I soon did when Captain Chattey took over command of a bunch of us."

Chattey, a marksman of some repute, used his revolver with devastating effect in the closing stages of the battle. Prison warders, who had been watching over him for the past twelve months, found themselves doing exactly what he told them. The official hangman, who also found himself under Chattey's command, proved himself an able executioner with a rifle.

But in spite of all this gallantry, the end was tragically near. . . .

In his preface to *The Middlesex Regiment*, Lieutenant-Commander P. Kemp wrote: '. . . in the final analysis it is the junior officers and the rank and file who bear the main brunt of battle, and I could have wished for more space in which to record their invaluable contribution, in sheer courage and endurance, to the prowess of the "Diehards" throughout this last war. . . .'

That goes double for the writer of this story.

CHAPTER TWELVE

By DECEMBER 24th the pattern of the battle had resolved itself into furious struggles by isolated and mixed detachments to stem the Japanese sweep towards Stanley. The composition of one gallant and stubborn force—and there were many others like it—illustrates the straits to which the defence had been reduced: it comprised 34 Canadians (all that was left of a company of Winnipeg Grenadiers), 14 airmen, 10 sailors and 43 men of the Dockyard Defence Corps.

Prominent in all these last ditch stands were the Volunteers: the importers and exporters; the clerks and the insurance brokers; the civil servants and the accountants. Of these men General Maltby wrote in his despatch: 'I wish to pay a special tribute to the Hong Kong Volunteer Defence Corps. They proved themselves to be a valuable portion of the garrison. In peace they had surrendered a great deal of their leisure to training, their mobilisation was completed smoothly and quickly, and in action they proved themselves stubborn and gallant soldiers. To quote examples seems almost invidious but I should like to place on record the superb gallantry of No. 3 (Eurasian) Company . . .'

Half-caste . . . half-breed . . . 'a touch of the tarbrush' . . . chilli-cracker . . . *café au lait* . . . blacky-whites—these were the contemptuous expressions used about Eurasians in India under British rule. Like the Welsh, they spoke English in singsong, lilting voices and went to extraordinary lengths to deny any Asiatic origin: they talked nostalgically of 'home', although few of them had ever seen the skies over England; they blamed their dark complexions on the sun; they referred to the Indians as 'wogs'. They had the suffocating inferiority complexes that afflict only the socially insecure; they never really got anywhere; they were, in short, neither one thing nor the other.

But the offspring of European-Chinese marriages in Hong Kong were Eurasians and proud of it. They were, it is true, largely a self-contained community with their own club, but this was of their own choice: they did not regard themselves as inferior in any way to their counterparts of pure European blood. In business they contributed largely to the prosperity of the Colony; in academic pursuits at the University of Hong Kong they more than held their own.

So did they in the fight for Jardine's Lookout.

The Eurasian Company were fortunate in their officers: Major Evan Stewart (subsequently to be awarded the Distinguished Service Order) was headmaster of St Paul's College; Lieutenant Bevan Field, a director of the Hong Kong Land Investment Company; Captain Larry Holmes and Lieutenant Donald Anderson were also schoolmasters.

The defence of Jardine's Lookout by the Eurasian Company was unanimously acknowledged to be one of the finest actions of the entire campaign. Attacked by overwhelmingly superior numbers of Colonel Shoji's regiment, they held out for two days without the smallest hope of relief. Repeated calls to surrender were greeted by catcalls, jeers and a hail of machine gun fire. In an endeavour to intimidate the Eurasians, the Japs hoisted flags—derisively known as poached eggs—at strategic points round Jardine's Lookout. The response of 3 Company was to shoot them down as fast as they were put up.

The Eurasian Company was finally overwhelmed by sheer weight of numbers. When all machine gun posts had been knocked out, the Eurasians fought in the open with rifles, hand grenades and bayonets. Bevan Field, wounded no fewer than four times, led the defence until he collapsed from loss of blood, after Major Stewart had been disabled and Holmes and Anderson killed.

Colonel Shoji had good cause to remember the Eurasian Company. In his war diary he recorded that Jardine's Lookout was only taken after sixteen hours of ferocious fighting which had cost him eight hundred casualties.

Equally fine was the defence of Barton's Bungalow by 1st Battery, HKVDC and a platoon of Middlesex. Here, as at Jardine's Lookout, suicidal Japanese attacks were beaten back over and over again. Eventually, in near desperation, the Japs brought up a flame-thrower but even this ghastly weapon of war failed to dislodge the defenders. Burned, blasted by mortar fire and completely beleaguered they fought on: they had heard what had happened to some units which had surrendered and were resolved to go down fighting.

The battle of Barton's Bungalow was a fight to the finish; no quarter was given or asked for and the battle-crazed Japs bayoneted every recumbent body, dead or alive. But they counted their own casualties by the hundred, piled along the ridge and around the bungalow, for the men of 1st Battery, like their comrades of the Middlesex, 'died hard'.

Number 2 (Scottish) Company, too, were all but decimated in the later stages of the fighting. War historians have always had a special place in their hearts for the Highland Regiments —the Ladies from Hell, as the Germans styled them in the Kaiser War: the regimental colours of the Black Watch, the Gordons, the Argylls and the Seaforths are smothered in battle honours. Number 2 Company never had any colours, but if they had then 'Stanley Village, 1941' would be fiercely emblazoned upon them.

The Scottish Company, so said Lieutenant Eric Bryden with affectionate cynicism, had in their ranks 'Scotsmen of every nationality'. For all that, they were *plus écossais que les écossais*: they wore the kilt and the glengarry with an air of conscious pride.

The wild wail of the bagpipes figures large in the stories of every Scottish formation and Number 2 Company even had their own piper: Alexander Mackie, a wicked and ribald old man, had been pipe-major of the Argyll and Sutherland Highlanders when they had been stationed in Hong Kong before the war. On the expiration of his army service, he had remained in Hong Kong in some ill-defined capacity in the dockyard. When the Japanese attack came, he hurried, like a superannuated homing pigeon, to the Scottish Company of the Volunteers. His equipment for war was simple and consisted of his bagpipes and a case of Scotch whisky—'for medicinal purposes', as he explained to the company commander.

The company commander was Major Henry (Rusty) Forsyth, World War One gunner officer and peacetime chartered accountant in the Colony. According to eye-witnesses, he was deserving of the Victoria Cross if anyone was. His conduct in battle may have been equalled by regular officers, but it can hardly have been surpassed.

The Scottish Company were bloodily engaged throughout December 23rd and Christmas Eve in Stanley Village against Japanese infantry and tanks who intended to force their way through the defences with the minimum of delay and total disregard for casualties. The fighting performance of No 2 Company compared favourably with the Seaforths at Atbara, the Gordons in the Tirah, the Black Watch at Tobruk and the Argylls in Malaya. Despite all Japanese attacks, the Scots continued to hold their ground.

They were continually led and inspired by 'Rusty' Forsyth, who, in spite of being wounded early in the action, refused to be evacuated. An anti-tank gun knocked out two enemy tanks: the crews scrambled out, only to be cut down like chaff by the Scots' machine guns. Forsyth was wounded again but continued to lead and direct the defence, although now unable to stand. From time to time fearful oaths and snatches of music from the bagpipes proclaimed that Pipe-Major Alexander Mackie was in the forefront of battle.

Slowly and relentlessly the Scots were forced back, although corpses littered the area in front of them. Forsyth, his voice by now reduced to a whisper, ordered a withdrawal to Stanley Fort. "Get 'em back," he said to Company Sergeant-Major Tom Swan, "get 'em back and leave me here."

"I'll no do that, sir," said Swan.

"You'll do what you're told, Sergeant-Major"—Forsyth's mind was wandering now and his voice was scarcely audible—"I'm giving you a direct order."

"I heard you, sir. I'm staying here."

"Then you'll consider yourself under arrest, Sar-major."

"Verra good, sir."

The remnants of the Scottish Company had slipped away in the darkness. Forsyth and Swan sat together, alone. Swan knew that his company commander was dying fast.

Just behind them they heard the drones of the bagpipes as Alexander Mackie filled them with air. Then 'Hielan' Laddie' broke on the still night air, followed by 'Hey, Johnnie Cope, are ye wakin' yet?'

The Japs closed in on them: Forsyth, by now in a coma; Mackie, playing 'Cock o' the North' with Caledonian impertinence; Swan with a new magazine on his tommy gun.

"Surrender, Englishmen!" they shouted.

Mackie increased the tempo of his piping. Swan shouted:

"Englishmen be ——ed!" and loosed off a burst of fire into the darkness.

The Japs charged forward and Mackie's pipes gave a final wail, like a soul in torment.

Then there was silence.

There was, believe it or not, a Portuguese company in the Hong Kong Volunteer Defence Corps. There had, of course, always been a Portuguese community in Hong Kong for this tiny and opportunist nation had opened the Orient for trade and there had been Portuguese merchants in China since 1541. Four centuries later they were still there and their principal stock in trade, as always, was wine—ever an essential commodity in Hong Kong.

As a race, the Portuguese have never been famed for their warlike qualities and in the First World War their army was distinguished mainly for its reluctance to go into battle. The Portuguese love easy living, luxury, food and wine: they like to laugh, sing, dance, make money, throw parties and breed: in Hong Kong facilities for these distractions were practically unique.

Portugal was regarded as something of a joke in the Second World War; bathed in perpetual sunshine, it became an international playground. It was about the only place in the world where English, Americans, Germans and Italians could meet at cocktail time without thoughts of killing one another. In the Aviz, Lisbon's ritziest hotel, Nazi spies rubbed shoulders with international socialites while the Portuguese beamed upon the scene with benevolent neutrality.

But there were no thoughts of neutrality among the Portuguese community in Hong Kong when the Japanese came, for Hong Kong was their home and therefore something to be fought for. On December 8th, 1941, prominent businessmen, all with the dark and mobile features of the Latin and surnames like De Silva, Da Costa, Gomez and Henriques, hastily swallowed their glasses of madeira in the *Club de Recreio* and hurried to take up arms against the yellow invader.

The men of Number 6 Company were officered by Major Bothelo (now Senior Crown Council in Hong Kong), Captain d'Almada Castro (now Registrar of the Supreme Court), and Captain Rodriques. The legend of the unmartial Portuguese dies hard, but they have a tradition of heroic endurance which

Number 6 Company tenaciously upheld. In 1813 a half starved army of British and Portuguese defeated Napoleon's soldiers; if the Portuguese did not defeat the Japanese in 1941, they certainly gave them plenty to think about. 'One of the most heartening memories I have of the Hong Kong campaign,' records Lieutenant-Colonel Eric Mitchell, second-in-command of the HKVDC, 'is the sight of these Portuguese volunteers manning front-line positions. No one thought they'd ever get into the front line, let alone stay in it.' But they did and remained there until the end. . . .

The Royal Rifles of Canada had become a spent force. They had suffered fearful casualties—18 officers and 359 rank and file killed, wounded and missing—and had lost all heart for further fighting. They had been ceaselessly shelled, bombed and pushed in to strengthen the line in a dozen different places. They had been flung into counter-attacks which had achieved nothing except further crippling casualties. They were bone weary; drained and exhausted; fed and used up.

By Christmas Eve the Rifles were so tired that they fell asleep where they stood. They slept by the side of roads, in ditches, behind bushes; they were oblivious to the air bombing, shelling and mortaring which was increasing every minute. They were issued with entrenching tools with which to construct new defensive positions but were too exhausted to dig.

The Royal Rifles had bought their knowledge of warfare at a frightful price and the hardships that they suffered were all the greater because of their lack of battle experience. They also lacked the sturdy independence of spirit which enabled the Middlesex and Royal Scots to 'live hard' off the country when rations failed to put in an appearance; indeed, on more than one occasion, the Royal Rifles abandoned positions because they had run out of food (in similar circumstances Sergeant Dick Stone of the Middlesex purchased six ducks from a Chinese farmer, decapitated them with a razor blade and roasted them over an open fire for Christmas dinner). But Stone and his men were luckier than the majority of the defenders, many of whom were to go without Christmas dinner on this most terrible of Christmases. . . .

The real trouble with the Royal Rifles of Canada was that one of their most experienced senior officers made no secret of the fact that he considered further resistance to be useless and, in the full hearing of his men, said so to anyone who would listen to him. At one stage he even went so far as to suggest a separate peace between Canadians and Japanese. It was hardly likely, having regard for the unmartial utterances of their commander, that the men of the Rifles viewed any further fighting with enthusiasm. Eventually, Brigadier Wallis had no choice but to send them back into reserve in Stanley Fort, replacing them with men of the Middlesex whose views on the subject of possible surrender were not for print.

The Royal Scots, with companies reduced barely to the strength of platoons, clung to positions in the Mount Nicholson and Mount Cameron areas; Lieutenant Norman Brownlow, in command of 'A' Company—by now reduced to Company Sergeant-Major Alec Whippey and ten men—held Mount Cameron under ceaseless mortar fire until the afternoon of December 25th. Other Royal Scots, hastily discharged from hospital and in many cases still bandaged, redeemed the name of the First of Foot.

The Deputy Assistant Adjutant General is normally a desk-bound staff officer whose duties embrace such diverse and prosaic subjects as Courts Martial, Courts of Inquiry, Dress Regulations and Recommendations for Honours and Awards. Courts Martial and Courts of Inquiry had become things of the past; Dress Regulations were limited to the wearing of a steel helmet when waking or sleeping; Recommendations for Honours and Awards were not to reach the War Office for four years. Major Moody collected a mountain of files, minutes, briefs and inter-departmental memos and watched the labour of two years disintegrate into ashes. Then, arming himself with a tommy gun, he collected a party of clerks, signallers, orderlies and military policemen (Red Caps) to reinforce a hard-pressed detachment of Middlesex holding Morrison Hill.

"When I saw them —— Red Caps going to war," observed Signalman 'Snickie' Allen (who had fallen foul of the military police on more than one occasion), "I knew there must be something wrong."

Major 'Monkey' Giles and his sailors (the bespectacled writer's rifle was justifiably filthy by now); Captain George

208

Farrindon's Marines; Major Kumpta Prasad's company of Punjabis—all eight of them; Petty Officer Peter Paul with his shipmates from HMS *Thracian*; Lieutenant Walter Davis and the gallant *Cicala*'s crew; Captain Keith Valentine with his company of Chinese clerks; Major Dan Grose and his sappers; Lieutenant-Commander William Fogg (who as a barefooted Boy 2nd Class had served in sailing ships in the nineties) and the crew of his boom defence vessel; Commander Francis Crowther of the Dockyard with seven stokers, two telegraphists and a Chinese messboy—these were the men who took up positions and prepared to obey the order 'the position will be held to the last man and the last round'. . . .

Such was Christmas Eve in Hong Kong.

CHAPTER THIRTEEN

THE DAWN of Christmas Day brought with it nothing but bad news. Half the Island was already in Japanese hands and they had driven a wedge between East and West Brigade which appeared to have put an end to any further prolonged resistance.

Isolated mixed detachments were either by-passed, surrounded and annihilated or forced to surrender; a few managed to stagger into Stanley. Although remnants of Middlesex, Royal Scots, Rajputs and Punjabis continued to fight with dogged fury—in particular, the survivors of Major Henry Marsh's 'C' Company at Little Hong Kong inflicted astronomical casualties on the enemy, as did a party of sailors under the command of an Australian supply officer, Major Arthur Dewar—the defenders were in a bad way: they had few mortars and no mortar bombs; all heavy machine guns had been knocked out; for weapons they were reduced to a few light machine-guns, rifles, hand grenades and bayonets; they had been on short rations of food and water for several days; they were exhausted after so many sleepless days and nights.

There were barely enough men left to hold the line; clearly now the intensive artillery and air bombardment, to which they could make no reply, was only the prelude to a full-scale attack. There was no sign of the relieving Chinese 7th Army and there was a growing feeling in the garrison that there never would be.

The last wireless set had been knocked out by shell-fire and all communications with the United Kingdom and Singapore had ceased. The last message from England, in fact, had been a message from the Prime Minister to Sir Mark Young, directing that 'the enemy should be compelled to expend the utmost life and equipment'. This message ended with the words: 'Every day that you are able to maintain your resistance you help the Allied cause all over the world, and by a prolonged resistance you and your men can win the lasting honour which we are sure will be your due.'

This was heartening indeed; the message that General Maltby received early on Christmas morning was scarcely consistent with Mr Winston Churchill's exhortations.

Two civilians—Major Charles Manners, manager of the Kowloon Dockyard and Mr Andrew Shields, a member of the Hong Kong Executive Council—had been captured at the Repulse Bay Hotel. They were then sent to Maltby under a flag of truce with instructions from the Japanese 'that they could talk freely'. The story they told, in Maltby's opinion, merited an immediate audience with the Governor.

Manners and Shields told of the terrible march of old men, women and children from Repulse Bay Hotel, via Wong Nei Chong Gap to North Point—a march along roads littered with blackened and stinking corpses, both British and Japanese. They told, accurately as it turned out, of the incredible number of enemy guns and troops seen during the latter part of their march. They expressed the opinion that it would be useless to continue the struggle.

Sir Mark Young, apparently influenced more by the Prime Minister in London than by two men on the spot, immediately called a special defence meeting, where it was decided that there could be no talk of surrender. He then sent out a Christmas message which read as follows: 'In pride and admiration I send my greetings this Christmas Day to all who are fighting and to all who are working so nobly and so well to sustain Hong Kong against the assault of the enemy. Fight on!'

And so, the men who were still able to stand, fought on. . . .

The *South China Morning Post* were determined to allay any feeling of despondency in the Colony. 'Hong Kong,' it declared festively, 'is observing the strangest and most sober Christmas in its century-old history. Such celebrations as are arranged for today will be subdued, with an eye to Japanese opportunism, but they will be none the less high-hearted on that account.'

The *Daily Express* were in the mood for heroics: 'The battle for Hong Kong,' it said, 'surpasses the sieges of Lucknow and Mafeking.'

Tokyo Radio was overpoweringly nonchalant: 'The fall of Hong Kong has not yet been announced because the Japanese, with victory assured, have taken things easy.'

The Japanese *Domei Agency*, however, was in no mood for

double-talk. 'The last British resistance,' it said unequivocally, 'is being crushed.'

Not every soldier managed to get home for Christmas, but at home or abroad Christmas Day in the British Army was traditionally given over to light-hearted rejoicing, so far as the exigencies of the service permitted. The sergeants took early morning tea to the men in bed and the officers waited on them at table. It was a day of riotous over-indulgence, comic football matches, unbridled intemperance and uninhibited fraternisation between all ranks. The Commanding Officer became fatherly, the RSM avuncular and the Adjutant positively brotherly. If a soldier could not be at home for Christmas, his regiment did the best it could for him.

Even in 1941—the most perilous and fateful year in Britain's history—a large proportion of the British Army managed to celebrate Christmas in traditional style.

But in Hong Kong Christmas was a day of misery, despair, anguish, and unspeakable bestiality.

St Stephen's College, for thirty years a distinguished seat of learning, had been hastily converted into a makeshift hospital. Now the only evidence of culture were the desks in the classrooms, hurriedly pushed to one side to make room for the flood of wounded. In all, there were ninety-five patients in the College: Canadians, Royal Scots, Middlesex, gunners, engineers, volunteers.

During his five years in the Royal Army Medical Corps Captain John Whitney had seen military illness in its every real and imagined façade: he knew the men who seemed to be permanently 'excused boots' but nevertheless performed prodigies of valour on the football field; he knew the men who achieved fortuitous coughs at the mere mention of night manoeuvres in the rain; he knew the men who unaccountably vomited when their names appeared on the company detail board for guard duty; he knew the men with inexplicable pains in the back (a mysterious pain in the back was nearly always good for an X-ray); he knew the men who swallowed quantities of boiling tea just before sick parade in order to raise their temperatures; he knew the men whose all-consuming ambition was an appointment with a specialist.

But there were no malingerers in St Stephen's College on

that Christmas morning: there were only men with their lower jaws shot away; with gaping wounds in the stomach and chest; with fingers missing, faces blown in and feet a soggy red mess. There were men who had died when the medical orderlies were not looking, men who would assuredly die before evening and men shot through intestines and lungs who wished they could die now.

A British nursing sister from the Military Hospital, six British VADs, four Chinese nurses and three medical orderlies did all that devotion to duty could for the wounded, but it was little enough: due to the degree of unpreparedness in the Colony, which affected the medical branch as grievously as any other, there was a shortage of morphia, first aid equipment and no blood for transfusions. All units had been sent seasonal greetings from the Governor and from Fortress Headquarters, but seasonal greetings did little to alleviate the smell of sweat, blood, urine and incipient gangrene which enveloped St Stephen's College on the nineteen hundred and forty-first birthday of the Prince of Peace.

There were many British doctors in Hong Kong before the war, but the *doyen* of them all was Doctor George Black. While he was credited with well over sixty-five years, many a *taipan* aged fifty or more swore that Doctor Black had brought him into the world. Black had long since lost count of the years he had spent in the Colony; he was as much a part of it as the Peak or the Peninsula Hotel.

Doctor Black epitomised the staunch and reliable old country General Practitioner of fiction; his was the ideal broad shoulder for hypochondriacs of both sexes to weep upon. For nearly half a century he had soothed away high blood pressure, embryo duodenal ulcers and migraines with the practised touch of a man who knew that soft living, over indulgence and business worries were at the root of them. He went to all the best parties and saw his flock with their over-tuned nervous systems, their jaded palates and their erratic bloodstreams: he knew all their ill-defined symptoms by heart and was their ever present help in trouble.

At the outbreak of war Black had joined the Volunteers as a medical officer and turned his very considerable medical knowledge to blisters, cuts and all the multifarious afflictions that beset soldiers on field training. On his breast were the ribbons of the First World War, for Doctor Black had patched up wounded men in Flanders and (according to the more graceless of his younger patients) in the Crimea. A revolver which he had never fired, hung menacingly from his hip.

In December, 1941, the men whom Black had told to go easy on the Martinis and steaks were manning front line posts on a diet of bully beef and tooth breaking biscuits. Doctor Black felt a surge of pride as he saw them, for he had brought many of them into the world.

Just before the Jap landings, Doctor Black was appointed to the command of the emergency hospital in St Stephen's College. It was tactfully explained to Captain Whitney that Black was in command, although to this day no one really knows how the old man got there in the first place. Whitney, a regular RAMC officer, got the gist of the thing at once and treated the gallant old man with the proper deference while doing most of the work himself. But Doctor Black was proud of his command—his first in war and, as it happened, his last.

At about 5.30 am on Christmas morning the patients stirred to painful wakefulness. Nurses and orderlies, eking out precious supplies, saw to it that every wounded man had a cup of tea. In Colonel Black's office was a crate of liquor, provided by himself; he had made up his mind that, Japs or no Japs, every patient should have a tot on Christmas Day.

A party of six Winnipeg Grenadiers, cut off from their company, came into the hospital at 6 am. They were met by Colonel Black, kindly and genial as ever. He could see that these men, although unwounded, were far gone in exhaustion. "Merry Christmas, boys," he said. "Anything I can do for you?"

"Some Christmas," said one of the Canadians. "You'd better evacuate the hospital, sir. The Japs are heading this way."

Black shook his head. "We can't do that," he said. "These men are too badly hurt to be moved." He pointed to the Red Cross flag fluttering from its mast on the roof. "That's our protection and we'll be all right. But you won't if the Japs find you here. You'd better move on. But just before you go, come in here a minute."

Six double whiskies vanished down six parched throats. Outside, the sounds of battle were coming ever closer. "And now you'd better get along," said Doctor Black. "The best of luck to you, boys."

"And to you, sir," said the Canadians. "An' thanks a whole lot for the drink."

"I wish you could stay," said Black. "We're having a little party in here at twelve o'clock."

As the Canadians staggered on towards Stanley, one said to another: "That old guy's got a lot of guts."

"He's gonna need 'em," said another.

Barely a quarter of an hour after the Canadians had left, Black looked out of the front door. About two hundred Japs were advancing towards the hospital. They were a disgusting and terrifying sight: many of them were palpably drunk and walked unsteadily; others were singing and shouting; some paused to vomit on their way. Black sighed gently and looked backwards towards his patients. Then, squaring his shoulders, he strode forward to meet them.

Black placed an arm across the front door, barring the way. The Japs stopped and looked at him through eyes glazed with alcohol.

"This is a hospital," said Black with dignity. "You can't come in here."

The two leading Japs nudged one another and laughed. Then one of them, with his bayonet fixed, advanced grinning on the doctor. Black stood his ground unflinchingly, his arm still stretched across the open door. The Jap took deliberate aim and shot him through the head.

A single Jap voice called out *"Banzai!"*

Then there were no more voices, only the jostling movement of urgent and heated bodies as the Japs surged forward. Colonel Black's body was bayoneted a dozen times as he lay on the floor, blood welling from the wound in his head. Captain Whitney started bravely forward and brought down a Jap with his revolver before he received six bullets in the stomach. As he fell, a press of bodies bore down upon him: the bayonets rose and fell again. . . .

The nurses could only stand helplessly and watch the slaughter of the defenceless wounded men. The Japs ripped bandages from torn bodies and from the stumps of recently amputated arms and legs. They plunged their bayonets into the men in the beds. One nurse, flinging her body across a patient, was bayoneted with the man in the bed; it took the Jap quite a long time to get his bayonet out of their bodies. In the space of thirty minutes fifty-six wounded men had been hacked to death. A few patients managed to hide under beds and in dark corners while the orgy continued.

Temporarily sated, the Japs paused in their bloody work and started to talk and laugh among themselves. The nurses, numb with shock and terror, moved to the men who had been done to death with such wanton carelessness and did what they could for them; it was little enough. Then into the ward came the wounded Canadian.

His arm was in a sling and he dragged his left foot painfully behind him. His eyes stared out of his head with a look of mad hate.

Drawing on some incredible reserve of strength, the Canadian staggered towards the young Japanese lieutenant who stood in the centre of the room. The nurses paused in their work of mercy, hardly daring to look. A terribly wounded man croaked: "Get back, Joe!" But Joe ignored everyone; everyone that is, except the Jap lieutenant.

During his terrible progress he stumbled and fell; then he dragged himself upright again. He spoke jerkily through clenched teeth: "You lousy, stinking, yellow bastards." He enunciated every word with deadly clarity, like a judge passing sentence of death.

The Jap lieutenant yawned and lit a cigarette. His revolver hung loosely in his right hand.

The soldiers stood expectantly around him. One or two moved nearer to the lieutenant, but he waved them back with an imperious gesture. They stood, slack mouthed and expectant; their bayonets dripped blood on to the floor.

The Canadian was now a bare ten feet from the lieutenant. He was nerving himself for his final, despairing charge. He said again: "Stinking, yellow bastards. I'm going to kill you, you rotten cow's son."

The lieutenant yawned again. Then, very deliberately, he shot the Canadian through the heart. . . .

But there was still worse to come. . . .

It seemed that the Japs had tired of the comparatively hum-drum entertainment of hacking wounded men to death and were in need of more subtle diversions.

The nurses, their white uniforms bespattered with blood, were roughly shoved into line. The Japs leered at them, their liquor-laden breath reeking in the morning sunshine. Then, at an order from the lieutenant, the nurses were taken away. . . .

The few survivors of the massacre were forced to carry the dead bodies and blood-soaked mattresses outside. Men, scarcely able to walk, staggered under the weight of corpses and bedding. They were urged on by the staple Japanese instruments of persuasion: rifle butts, pricking bayonets, open-handed slaps and kicks.

The desks in the college had been broken up for firewood and soon a huge fire had been lit. The Japs stood near the crackling flames, discussing the day's sport. This had been a day to remember.

It was an obscene and monstrous funeral pyre; an authentic picture of hell. In the acrid, choking black smoke disappeared any Japanese claims to be regarded as a civilised race.

A scene of almost identical bestiality was enacted at the Jockey Club in Happy Valley which had been turned into a hospital. The Japs charged in among the wounded, just as they had done at St Stephen's College. But one Jap—a diminutive officer carrying a sword almost as large as himself—met his match on this occasion.

Among the patients in the Happy Valley Hospital was a giant artilleryman—a 'Geordie' from Britain's northernmost frontier. 'Geordie' had been a miner before the depressed thirties sent him into the Army in search of the three square meals a day that his huge frame craved. A giant of a man, he stood six feet five inches in his ammunition boots. He handled heavy artillery pieces as if they were children's toys. When this undersized monster of a Jap lieutenant tangled with 'Geordie' he found that he had bitten off considerably more than he could chew.

'Geordie's' face was practically entirely covered with bandages, for it had been peppered with fragments of shrapnel. But his giant strength was unimpaired and he could see his comrades being bayoneted on all sides.

The Jap lieutenant drew his sword and took a swipe at 'Geordie's' head. The gunner ducked with an agility remarkable for a man of his bulk and stood waiting for the next onslaught. His giant arms hung by his side, the fingers large as a baby's arms, were slightly curved. A few Jap soldiers gathered round to watch the fun.

"Do tha' agen," said 'Geordie' very distinctly, "an' I'll break your —— back."

The Jap swung the sword again. As his arm came down, 'Geordie' seized him by the wrist and the sword clattered to the floor. He held the kicking and screaming Jap for a moment before transferring his other hand to one of the lieutenant's ankles. Then, in the manner of a man breaking sticks for firewood, he bent the struggling Jap across his knee.

Five or six Japs rushed to their officer's aid in response to his frenzied cries, but the officer was as clay in 'Geordie's' giant clutches. Clubbed by rifle butts, pierced by bayonets, the gunner did not surrender his hold of the Jap until a crack like a muted pistol shot announced that he had carried out his threat. Then, and only then, did he sink to the floor in a pool of his own blood.

Lance-Corporal Harry Harding of the Middlesex witnessed the raping of nurses from the shelter of a large linen basket. Badly wounded in both legs, he had been thrust there by the nurses just before the arrival of the Japs. Through the wicker Harding watched the defilation of these nurses and listened to their screams of anguish.

Two women escaped this outrage. Tania Tckencho, daughter of Kowloon's premier *restaurateur*, jumped into bed with a dead man and escaped detection. Olive Grenham fainted and was assumed to be dead: one Jap, indeed, seized her by the hair but by some incredible manipulation of her facial muscles she stared back at him, her mouth open and her eyes fixed in a lifeless stare.

Gwen Dew later interviewed one of the survivors of this horror. Gwen Dew is tough and resilient, as only an American newspaper woman can be; in her career as a journalist she has interviewed monarchs, presidents, police chiefs, racing motorists, international playboys, film stars, murderers and assorted hoodlums. She has interviewed in joy, sadness, hope, despair and anguish; but never, up to that day, had she interviewed in bitter, scalding tears.

'I hesitated a long time to ask her to live through the hours again with me,' wrote Gwen Dew in her book *Prisoner of the Japs*, 'but I felt that I must have the story direct from one who knew every damnable second of it. No woman on earth is going to tell of being gang-raped by enemy soldiers unless it is imperative, and only the bravest would be willing to tell her story to the world. I marvelled at the inner strength which made her able to answer my most searching questions, and yet I sensed all through it the perspective which she had taken of the blackening experience: she was a soldier at her post; she had suffered grievous wounds which would leave scars on her soul for ever. . . .'

'She told her ghastly story undramatically and methodically, but there were black circles under her eyes, and her thin nervous hands which kept knitting the air, gave hints of the inner turmoil that retelling it occasioned. . . .

' "They kept us in a small room," the nurse said, "and whenever a Jap wanted us he came and took us away. All Christmas Day. All Christmas night. I lost track of the times they used each one of us. Twenty-four hours of it—can I ever, ever forget it?"

'She couldn't say more. I couldn't ask more. . . .'

Mabel Everett, sister at the Queen Mary Hospital at Repulse Bay, saw some of these women afterwards. They came to the hospital: the young and the not so young; dazed, bruised and with black eyes. Although they were numbed with shock and misery, every one of them requested to be sent back to work. Only in the wards, where broken men awaited their ministering care, could they forget the torment that they had been through.

Yet another military hospital had been opened in the Hong Kong University, but here the patients and nurses fared better. No excuses are being offered for Japanese barbarity, but it should be said here that the atrocities at St Stephen's College and the Jockey Club had been perpetrated by drunken and undisciplined soldiers with only junior officers to command them. By comparison, the occupation of Hong Kong University was an orderly affair.

News of the atrocities had filtered through to the medical officer in charge, Doctor Gordon King, and he had given orders that all liquor listed under 'medical comforts' in the hospital precincts should be destroyed. Sisters Beryl Skipwith and Marjorie Simpson had other ideas: there were some two hundred wounded men in the University and these ladies were determined, by honest means or otherwise, to provide every man with a drink on Christmas Day. By the exercise of a marked degree of feminine cunning they managed to bring this about.

Conditions were scarcely conducive to high morale, but it improved considerably with the appearance of medicine tumblers of brandy. Afterwards the two architects of this alcoholic scheme were observed by Doctor King carrying a crate of empty bottles outside.

"I understood," said the doctor coldly, "that I gave orders for all liquor to be destroyed. What is the meaning of this?"

"These are empty bottles," said Beryl Skipwith with disarming innocence.

"What happened to the liquor?"

"Well, it wasn't exactly *destroyed*," prevaricated Beryl. And as she spoke, sounds of singing could be heard from one of the wards.

"I was never a great expert on medicines," said Beryl Skipwith, "but this particular tincture seems to have done some good."

Best of all, Beryl Skipwith remembers Gunner Fred Gilmore. A high explosive shell had whipped a dozen jagged splinters into him, from the buttocks to the shoulder blades. Consequently, he was only able to lie on his stomach. In this position he kept up an unending stream of what are politely known as 'smoking stories', illustrating every possible aspect of marital betrayal, athletic love and lavatorial mischance. None of the stories were fit for mixed company; but on Christmas Day in Hong Kong nothing was. . . .

The Japanese takeover of the St Albert's Hospital was not accompanied by the type of incident that was later listed under the heading of 'atrocities', but the credit for this must go to Matron Mary Currie.

The Japs, drunk with victory, vociferous and truculent, swept into the hospital and at first ugly incidents seemed inevitable. Mary Currie was the first to suffer and received a vicious kick across the shins from a leering monstrosity armed with a rifle and bayonet almost as large as himself. Mary Currie is a tall woman and topped her tormentor by a good four inches.

The pain was excruciating and a sick, weak feeling flooded through her. But Matron Currie favoured the Jap with the look that she specially reserved for British soldiers who had sprinkled their bedding with cigarette ash, and turned to a nearby Japanese officer.

"This man is a barbarian," she said icily. "I was under the impression that the Japanese were civilised. It seems that I was wrong."

"For God's sake, Sister," said a British doctor in an agonised whisper, "be careful what you say; you'll get us all shot!"

"I'd rather be shot than pushed around by monkeys like this," snapped Mary Currie. She regarded the soldier who had kicked her in the manner of someone who contemplates a bad egg at close range. Probationer nurses, idle medical orderlies and unruly patients had all encountered that look and, incredible to relate, the effect on the Japs was much the same.

The English-speaking Jap officer barked something at the soldier and said in an affronted voice: "Japanese soldiers are civilised."

The Matron sniffed and regarded him with extreme disfavour. Her shins still hurt vilely but she did not propose to bandy words with undersized vandals without the remotest notion of how to behave. "It certainly doesn't look like it," she said.

The mood of the Japanese was ugly enough and for a moment the thought occurred to Mary Currie that she might have overplayed her hand. She had no concern for her own safety, but there were young nurses in the hospital and the Japs were already eyeing them with predatory appreciation. She had heard of what had happened at St Stephen's College and the hospital at Happy Valley.

She turned to the officer and said: "If you want to see how *civilised*"—she put a wealth of meaning into the word civilised —"people treat their wounded, then come with me."

That morning a Japanese officer had been brought into St Albert's. He had been terribly wounded in the stomach by a burst of machine gun fire and it was at once obvious to both doctors, nurses and medical orderlies that he could not live for more than one agonising hour. Nevertheless, the same care and attention was lavished on him as was given to British, Canadian and Indian soldiers. He died shortly before the arrival of the Japs.

The Jap officer lay on the bed between snowy white sheets. In life he had been a snarling, murderous nightmare; death, in some extraordinary way, seemed to have ironed away some of his brutish expression and he looked oddly small and pathetic. A Japanese flag had been wrapped round his middle.

"We couldn't save him," said Mary Currie simply. "But he was a soldier and wounded and we did the best we could for him." In this simple statement she spoke for every nurse in the QAIMNS.

There was no more brutality in St Albert's Hospital after that.

For Christmas dinner in Hong Kong there was no liberally stuffed roast turkey with bread sauce and sizzling sausages; there was no Christmas pudding with brandy butter; there were no oranges, nuts, mince pies and port.

Major-General Maltby and Second-Lieutenant Mac-Gregor, seated on upturned ammunition boxes, shared a small tin of asparagus and a half bottle of luke-warm Liebfraumilch; Captain Charles Pope of the Royal Engineers toasted Captain Bill Price of the Royal Rifles of Canada in tinned beer, before joining him in bully beef and biscuits; Lance-Corporal 'Tookie' Poole and Private 'Witch' Aldridge lunched *al fresco* with Bandsmen Johnny Hymus and Charlie Dickens on pickled onions and cognac; a shell burst scattered the bully beef pies which were being cooked for Captain Keith Valentine and Second-Lieutenants Robert Geer and Stanley Cooke; a bomb showered pieces of ceiling into the approximate stew which had been placed in front of Petty Officer Peter Paul; one of Sergeant Dick Stone's ducks, its moment of execution at hand, rushed quacking into the middle distance and eluded all attempts at recapture.

Sergeant the 'onourable 'orrible Marable's Christmas dinner was in a unique category of misfortune. From his machine gun, from which he had fired something like 10,000 rounds in three days, Marable could smell chickens roasting. The Japs in front of him and the roast chickens behind him induced in him a feeling of fearful rage, for his last meal had been biscuits and bully beef at five o'clock the previous evening and the smell of the roasting chickens nearly drove him crazy. He inflicted terrible slaughter on the advancing Japs before Private Milroy, grinning and replete, relieved him on the gun.

"Plenty left for you, Sarge," said Milroy.

"Wot, after you've been at it?" retorted Marable.

Marable, his mouth watering in anticipation, was barely twenty yards from the improvised cookhouse when it received a direct hit from a shell. . . .

It was plain to General Maltby that the end was near. The Japanese were now on the Island with overwhelmingly superior forces of infantry and their artillery could shell his positions at will. His men had fought for seventeen days without relief of any kind; the Island was vulnerable to unlimited air attack; a serious water famine was imminent; fires were raging everywhere; ammunition was in short supply. Maltby, a man to whom the word 'surrender' was abhorrent, knew full well that further fighting must mean the slaughter of the remainder of the garrison, would risk a form of retaliation on the civilian population which was too hideous to contemplate, and could not possibly affect the final outcome. The 7th Chinese Army, if they were coming at all, would have to attack the Japanese in the rear during the next three hours. There was no sign of them: there were only more and more shells; more and more men being vilely mutilated; the threat of more and more senseless destruction every minute.

Very soon Maltby knew that he would have to make a decision—a decision which boiled down to two perfectly clear cut alternatives: to save life or wantonly to expend it.

Lieutenant-Colonel 'Monkey' Stewart was wearing his habitually fierce expression when he toured his company positions on that Christmas midday, but it covered a feeling of pride which was almost akin to love. To Stewart the casualty returns—94 killed and died of wounds, 25 missing, 110 wounded—were more than melancholy statistics of battle: each one represented a deep personal loss, a separate bereavement. Soon, Stewart knew, there would be more.

Here and there the Colonel saw a strange face, for volunteers, Rajputs, Punjabis, Royal Scots, Canadians, gunners and administrative details had become intermingled with his battalion.

He heard a few snatches of conversation which told him conclusively that there was nothing wrong with the morale of the Middlesex:

"Them Chinks ought to be coming soon."

"Taking their time, ain't they?"

"There's only one Chink I want to see . . ."

"Who's that?"

"My dahnhomer."

"Don't you never think of nothing else?"

"They ain't 'alf made a mess of Jimmy's Beer Kitchen."

"Them chickens was a bit tough."

"They wasn't chickens, they was —— seagulls."

"If 'e's a cook, I'm a bleedin' bishop."

". . . that fat bit we met in the Nathan. . . ."

"Face like a bloody car smash. . . ."

"Wot abaht a nice bit of Jap?"

They were magnificent, thought Stewart: indestructible, invincible and undaunted. But there were so few of them. . . .

At 2 pm General Maltby telephoned Stewart at his battalion headquarters. The General said: "I have to make a grave and important decision. What's the position on your front?"

"Damned sticky, sir," said Stewart.

"What are your men like?"

"Good as ever—what's left of 'em. But they're almost asleep on their feet."

"How long d'you think you can hold out?"

Stewart's natural inclination was to say: 'As long as there's one man still on his feet,' but he knew that this was not the answer Maltby wanted. He wanted to tell the General that the 1st Middlesex would stand fast until the Jap bayonets finished them; he wanted to say: 'These men are the Middlesex —they'll hold on as long as I tell them to.' This was the true answer, the only possible answer for a Diehard. But Stewart knew that it was the wrong answer.

"An hour at the outside," said Stewart at length.

Maltby spoke slowly and with a kind of desperate finality. "The decision I have to make," he said, "may mean"—he faltered over the hateful word—"surrender. But the decision is mine, and mine alone. You understand?"

"I understand, sir," said Stewart. He knew what Maltby must be going through, but he wanted to spare his feelings as much as possible.

But there was one question that Stewart had to ask, although he knew the answer in advance. "Have you any reserves at all?"

"None," said Maltby. "You'll hear from me again."

Stewart replaced the receiver. As he did so, he heard one signaller say to another: "Tell you what: if anyone packs up, it ain't going to be Monkey."

"Cut 'is —— froat first," agreed the other signaller.

There were no communications with the isolated force at Stanley. Brigadier Cedric Wallis—austere, self-sufficient, immaculate and monocled—had been told by Maltby to defend the position 'to the last man and the last round'. This was the last order that Wallis had received.

Militarily, the situation was far from reassuring: Stanley was under continuous air and artillery bombardment; the water supply was damaged beyond repair; Wallis had no artillery or mortars fit for action and very few hand grenades. Wallis, however, had his orders and was resolved to carry them out.

At Wallis's headquarters the Brigade Major, Major Hector Harland and the Staff Captain, Captain Peter Belton, were busily filling bren and tommy gun magazines. "All we could do," said Belton wryly, "was prepare to die as bravely as possible."

At 3 pm Maltby went to Government House. He told Sir Mark Young that, in his considered opinion, no further useful military resistance was possible.

At 3.15 pm Maltby issued orders to all commanding officers to break off the fighting and to capitulate to the nearest Japanese Commander, as and when the enemy advanced and opportunity offered.

Early that evening at the Peninsula Hotel, Kowloon, Sir Mark Young, Governor and Commander-in-Chief, Hong Kong, formally surrendered the Crown Colony without conditions to Lieutenant-General Sakai, Commander of the Japanese 23rd Army.

This, then, was almost the end—but not quite. . . .

There were men on Hong Kong Island who refused to surrender and fought on: these were the men whose very nature rebelled against any thought of capitulation while there was still breath in their bodies and ammunition in their pouches. One of these was Major E. W. F. de Vere (Ted) Hunt of the Hong Kong and Singapore Regiment of Artillery, formerly of the Royal Horse Artillery—the Horse Gunners.

If you have been to the Military Meeting at Sandown Park, then you will have seen replicas of Ted Hunt. They wear well cut tweeds, bowler hats tilted slightly to the front of their heads, stiff collars, and Royal Artillery ties. Their speech, like their moustaches, is clipped. They seem vaguely sorry for anyone who is not a horse gunner: they grudgingly acknowledge the Household Brigade and refer to the infantry of the line as 'The Feet'; hussars, lancers and dragoons are lumped together under the heading of cavalry, invariably pronounced 'kevelry'.

Apart from the ceremonial King's Troop of the Royal Horse Artillery, they have no acquantance with the horse in the nineteen-sixties except at race meetings and point-to-points. At Larkhill and Sandown they hurl their mounts into the fences in the same manner as their forefathers galloped the guns into action in bygone campaigns. Today, in place of horses and limbers, they have new and terrifying weapons of destruction. Let us sleep sounder in our beds in the knowledge that we have such men.

Major Ted Hunt was a horse gunner *par excellence*. In appearance he was a veritable Beau Brummel: tall, blond and devastatingly good looking; he was the embodiment of military perfection from his immaculate service dress cap with its glittering chinstrap to the toes of his field boots which shone like polished chestnuts. He was a brilliant performer at all sports: an Irish hockey international and a positive joy to watch on the polo field. He rode as if he were part of the horse. On field exercises in pre-war days he inevitably took with him a picnic basket from Aspreys in Bond Street.

Most important of all, Hunt was a brilliant artilleryman. During the mainland fighting, while commanding a Sikh mountain battery, his guns gave deadly and unfailing support to the hard-pressed infantry. In the evacuation from the mainland he led his battery over difficult and precipitous country without the loss of a single man or gun. When he lost his guns, he brought his qualities of leadership and boundless confidence to bear in infantry fighting and was in the forefront of battle to the end.

On hearing of the surrender, he acted with characteristic promptitude. He armed himself with two tommy guns, one under each arm, and went along towards the Japanese positions in the Wongneichong Gap area. He was never seen again.

To be trapped in a tight corner was no new experience for Private Jack Milroy of the 1st Middlesex. He was nicknamed the Black Mamba because, when representing the battalion at boxing, his sliding and menacing shuffle into the centre of the ring was strongly reminiscent of that deadly reptile.

Milroy's civilian occupation must have caused a certain amount of head-scratching at the recruiting office, for he had been an escapologist. Prior to enlisting in the Army he had spent a considerable portion of his young life encased in a sack, secured from end to end by chains. Milroy, by the very nature of his civilian training, was immune to any form of claustrophobia.

Immersed from head to foot in his sack, Milroy and the senior partner in the 'chain and whip' act entertained the theatre queues until the police moved them on. The senior partner, or 'spieler' as he was known in the busking trade, kept up a harrowing running commentary as Milroy strove to extricate himself from the suffocating confines of his sack. Milroy, said the 'spieler' with tears in his eyes, was his own son and "there he is, ladies an' gents, dying a slow death of asphyxia in front of your very mince pies." When Milroy, sweating and triumphant, had emerged into the open air the 'spieler' took the hat round and they split the proceeds.

When the news of the surrender came, Milroy was still firing his machine gun in the area of Stanley Village. His Number Two, a timid young man lacking in militant fire, sighed with relief. "We're surrendering," he said.

"Who's surrendering?" demanded Milroy.

"We all are. Order's just come through."

"Well, I —— well ain't," said Milroy and fired a long burst at a concentration of Japs.

"About time, if you ask me," said the young soldier.

"No one didn't ask you," retorted Milroy and struck his Number Two on the nose. . . .

Four Royal Marines, finding themselves cut off from any cohesive unit, armed themselves with a light machine gun and set up a defiant and alcoholic strongpoint in the Garrison Sergeants' Mess. This particular mess, with its exceptionally well-stocked bar, had always been the focal point of non-commissioned social activity and its Saturday night parties were a talking point for weeks afterwards.

The four marines regarded the well-stocked bar as their

legitimate prey, and while one manned the gun the other three made merry on gin, whisky, beer, brandy and liqueurs. For over three hours they fired defiant bursts at any Japanese approach: a truck load of Japs received a direct hit and the kill was duly celebrated in Benedictine.

Taking the view that it was only a matter of time before they were called upon to surrender and endure captivity—things abhorrent to any Royal Marine—they drank with renewed enthusiasm and continued to engage the enemy. It finally took the combined efforts of a platoon of Jap infantry and a light tank firing at point-blank range to liquidate this gallant quartet. The Garrison Sergeants' Mess was reduced to a pile of smoking rubble; the biggest and best party ever to be held within its walls was over. . . .

Shortly after the surrender, Second-Lieutenant Michael Holloway of the Royal Engineers heard that his fiancée, a nurse at the hospital at Happy Valley, had been killed by the Japanese. He took a tommy gun, as many hand grenades as he could carry and, alone, walked away from his lines.

Like Major Ted Hunt, Michael Holloway was never seen again. . . .

At Stanley, Brigadier Cedric Wallis received the order to surrender and flatly refused to believe it: in his view, surrender was unwarranted by the local situation. Colonel Ronald Lamb of the Fortress Engineers reported to Wallis with verbal orders to surrender. In the absence of written orders, Wallis declared that the Stanley garrison would continue to hold out until he received orders to capitulate in writing, and sent Major Hector Harland to get the necessary authority. It was after midnight on Boxing morning when Wallis sent the following signal to units under his command:

'By order of His Excellency the Governor and General Officer Commanding His Majesty's forces in Hong Kong have surrendered. Stop. On no account will firing or destruction of equipment take place as otherwise all lives of British hostages will be endangered. Stop. Units will organise themselves centrally forthwith. Stop. (Signed) C. Wallis, Brigadier, 0045 hrs. 26.12.41.'

This, then, was the end. Gradually an exhausted silence descended on the Colony. . . .

After the First World War—the war to end all wars—Great Britain promptly forgot about the men who had made victory possible at Mons, Loos, Cambrai, Passchendaele, Suvla Bay and Kut: victory did not bring easy living any nearer and ex-majors counted themselves lucky to land jobs as clerks at five pounds a week. What was left of the old Regular Army counted themselves lucky too, for they still ate three times a day. They continued to serve abroad (if they were lucky) and if not, the General Strike of 1926 produced a semblance of active service. When this tragic debacle came to an end, few British soldiers knew what it had been all about, although a certain section of British society insisted on celebrating it as a victory. The British soldier continued to curse, copulate and carouse as opportunity offered.

During the mean spirited and slothful thirties Great Britain gave little thought to her Regular Army. There were, of course, the Foot Guards who looked after the Royal Family and looked reassuringly superb in scarlet tunics and bearskins; the Household Cavalry, in their gleaming breastplates and mounted on magnificent horses, were a source of never ending delight to American tourists. Apart from them, one very rarely saw a soldier except in out of the way places like Aldershot and Salisbury Plain. Admittedly, Miss Cicely Courtneidge sang a song about them: undoubtedly there *was* something about a soldier, but no one knew or really cared what it was.

Everyone knew that we had soldiers in India, Egypt, Singapore and Hong Kong (which was in China or somewhere). They were funny men with bare knees and weird and wonderful tattoo marks. They got drunk and sang rude songs. They went abroad for years on end and came back with strange coffee-coloured wives and, according to Lady Astor, terrible diseases. Their government paid them two shillings a day and then promptly forgot about them. The only authoritative information available about the British Army abroad in the period between the wars was provided at three shillings and sixpence per copy by Rudyard Kipling.

In Hong Kong on Christmas afternoon 1941, British soldiers were being herded together like animals by undersized monsters who beat them, spat at them, humiliated them and kicked them.

In the Wanchai area wounded men lay in the streets: these funny men with bare knees which were now cut, calloused and filthy. They were not getting drunk because the majority of them had not even got any water left in their bottles. Not a few of them, however, were singing rude songs. From a Middlesex private, both legs broken by machine gun fire, came the death-less stanzas of the Cockney soldier:

> I painted 'er!
> I painted 'er!
> Up 'er belly a' dahn 'er back,
> Ev-ery 'ole an' every crack
> I painted 'er
> Dahn in Drury Lane
> Painted 'er old termahter
> Over an' over again!

The legend of the Angels who appeared before the Tom-mies at Mons may or may not be true; the Angels of Wanchai wore, not white robes and wings, but gaily-coloured cheong-sams, slit to the thigh. These were the 'dahnhomers' who came to the battered soldiers of Hong Kong with water, looted cigarettes, beer, bandages and food: Mabel Hoong, Betsy Hong, Lulu Sen, Winnie Chong and Suzie Wong (a hot property in 1941 as well as 1960). At a time when English ladies in Singapore were finding that service in the ARP and Auxiliary Nursing Service interfered with tennis tournaments and amateur dramatic societies, the 'dahnhomers' came to the wounded men of Hong Kong and succoured them. Later, many of these Angels of Wanchai—loose women, amoral women and even diseased women—risked brutal beatings by the Japanese to take parcels to the men behind the wire who had no one else to cherish and comfort them.

In Oxford Street today stands a commissionaire: upright, impeccably shaved, beribboned, meticulous in his dressing as only an old soldier can be—this is 'Tookie' Poole, late Lance-Corporal of the 1st Middlesex. In the breast pocket of his smartly pressed serge uniform, sandwiched between his foot-ball pools coupon and a National Health Medical card, is a coloured photograph of a Chinese girl—a slant-eyed Chinese maiden by the name of Who Flung Dung, he calls her. But she came to him when he was weak and helpless in Wanchai and he remembers her.

St Mark has it thus, and the circumstances were not so very different:

'And when the Sabbath was past, Mary Magdalene, and Mary the mother of James, and Salome, had brought sweet spices, that they might come and anoint Him.'

POST MORTEM

By the end of 1941 Great Britain, conditioned by air raids, defeats on land, crippling losses at sea and Pearl Harbour, was used to disaster: the loss of Hong Kong was like an additional twinge of pain following acute and agonising appendicitis.

In 1921 the Committee of Imperial Defence had come to the conclusion that there was no possibility of making the Colony sufficiently secure against enemy attack: nothing was done about it then and little more had been done about it twenty years later.

In 1928 it was decided by the Government that no war was likely for ten years. In the unlikely event of war, they declared, Great Britain would get ten years' notice. A succession of 'incidents' in China during the 1930s seemed to indicate that ten days was a more likely period of grace; the Japs, in fact, did not even give ten minutes.

In 1937 the Chiefs of Staff came to some weighty conclusions on the subject of Hong Kong. They accepted that the period before relief could not be less than ninety days, and agreed that, although it was not possible to assess the time that the garrison of four battalions could hold out, 'its powers of resistance would be materially increased if it were reinforced'. It is hardly possible to argue against such inspired reasoning.

The Chiefs of Staff (who had all been prefects at school) went on to say that there could be no question of evacuating or reducing the garrison on the eve of the outbreak of a war with Germany, for such an evacuation would entail a loss of prestige, and only by remaining in Hong Kong could Great Britain hope to encourage resistance to Japan. Hong Kong, therefore, was to be regarded as an important though not vital outpost to be defended for as long as possible.

Of Gunga Din, Rudyard Kipling wrote:

> For I'll meet 'im later on,
> In the place where 'e 'as gone. . . .

In that same place, Sergeant George Rich turns to Sergeant Bert Bedward and says: "Hear that, Bert? We're important, but we ain't vital. . . ."

In May, 1938, Japan extended her aggression to South China; in February, 1939, Japanese troops landed on Hainan Island, some 300 miles south of Hong Kong. The isolation of the Colony was almost complete and a first-class new Japanese gents' hairdresser had just been installed in the Hong Kong Hotel.

In 1939 it was agreed that, in the event of war with Japan, Hong Kong was bound to fall. With this cheering assessment to guide him, Air Chief Marshal Sir Robert Brooke-Popham proposed that the Colony should be reinforced by two more battalions of infantry, making six in all. This plan was vetoed in strenuous terms by Mr Winston Churchill who wrote on a minute:

'This is all wrong. If Japan goes to war with us, there is not the slightest chance of holding Hong Kong or relieving it. It is most unwise to increase the loss we shall suffer there. Instead of increasing the garrison it ought to be reduced to a symbolical scale. Any trouble arising there must be dealt with at the Peace Conference after the war. We must avoid frittering away our resources on untenable positions.'

("We was frittered away, George," observed Sergeant Bedward to Sergeant Rich.

"Lucky we wasn't down to symbolical scale," observed Rich.)

'Japan will think long before declaring war on the British Empire,' continued the Prime Minister's minute, 'and whether there are two or six battalions at Hong Kong will make no difference to her choice. I wish we had fewer troops there, but to move any would be noticeable and dangerous.'

After the surrender of the Colony, experts of both the professional and amateur variety went to work on the subject. General Maltby, needless to say, came in for his share of the recriminations. *The War Against Japan* says severely: 'News of the loss of Hong Kong after only eighteen days' fighting came as a shock . . . it may be asked whether resistance could not have been prolonged.'

Lord Moyne said: "It is probable that no Imperial Garrison

since the epic defence of Gordon at Khartoum has ever fought against greater odds."

A *Daily Mirror* headline said: '6000 BRITONS STACK ARMS.'

A correspondent to *The Times* burst into explosive print almost before the ink was dry on the surrender document:

'Sorrow at the fall of Hong Kong must be mingled with misgivings as to the advisability of attempting to hold it, thereby scattering instead of concentrating the limited forces we had available in the Far East.

'The reflection arises in the lay mind that the Navy, Army and Air Force personnel locked up in Hong Kong should have been utilised instead in the defence of the Malay Peninsula.

'Prestige and sentiment are powerful factors and must always be given full weight, but they should not be allowed to override or obscure essential military priorities.'

The War Against Japan says discouragingly: '. . . The Colony had no strategical importance, and the few extra days of resistance which were gained by the presence of the two reinforcing battalions sent at the eleventh hour could not, and did not, have any effect on the course of events. The despatch of these reinforcements proved to be a lamentable waste of valuable manpower.'

("Jesus!" said the spirits of the 500 Canadians who died, "who are they trying to kid?")

Someone must have the last word, and who better qualified than Cassandra of the *Daily Mirror*?

'The defenders of Hong Kong put up a brave show and the Governor takes his place in history.

'I suppose this loss of life was unavoidable.

'The British Government advised Sir Mark Young to hold on and then, after a week of desperate fighting, they told him to let go. It seems a pity that we could not have made up our minds some time ago as to whether Hong Kong was a reasonable defensive position. The Japanese provided a sharp and cruel answer.

'The swift and ominous fate of Hong Kong suggests that our arrangements for the defence of the British Empire in the Far East have been more ramshackle than resourceful. Our administrators, who control these distant lands, have not raised hell's delight because they have felt their grip weakening around the South China Sea.'

'They have said nothing.
'They have been content.'
'No one has resigned.
'No one has sounded the alarm.'

There, so far as the British Press is concerned, the matter rests.

It is easy to be wise after the event: to talk of 'major tactical blunders', 'lamentable waste of manpower', 'the possibility of more prolonged resistance', 'strategical importance': such things are not within the scope of this book, for this is a story of a gallant fight against overwhelming odds; the battle for Hong Kong was just that.

General Maltby's more severe critics are invited to take note of the figures of Japanese casualties, the best and most practical tribute to our fighting men in Hong Kong. Although they were never published in strictly reliable form, Maltby's estimate of 4000 killed and 9000 wounded can be taken as a fair one and, if anything, an understatement.

Our own casualties were grievous: killed and died of wounds 1045; missing 1068; wounded 2300. Thousands more died, in varying circumstances of horror, in prisoner-of-war camps.

Perhaps the whole tragic affair is best summed up by two men of the 1st Middlesex. On several occasions General Maltby referred to Hong Kong as 'a hostage to fortune'. The phrase filtered down to the other ranks.

Private Fred Corrigan was particularly fond of this phrase and, indeed, it could hardly be bettered. Just before the final Japanese attack overwhelmed the Middlesex men on Brick Hill, Corrigan said morosely: "'ostages of bleedin' fortune, that's what we are"—the phrase, he considered, would bear repeating: "'ostages——"

"I'll 'ostage you," said Sergeant Bert Bedward, that Immortal Sergeant of the Middlesex, "if you don't get a move on with that —— ammo . . ."

The Fall of Japan 40p
William Craig

The spellbinding story of six incredible weeks in 1945 which changed the course of history. An agonizing, blood-stained mosaic of conflicting human emotions.

The ruthless ferocity of Okinawa . . . the maddening horror of the Kamikaze . . . the torture of American prisoners . . . Hirohito delivers his people to the enemy . . . the day of retribution.

'The most violent, shock-filled chapter in human history' NEW YORK TIMES BOOK REVIEW

Arnhem 35p
Major-General R. E. Urquhart

'Two days,' said Monty. 'Hold the bridge two days . . . They'll be up with you by then.'

Lieutenant-General F. A. M. (Boy) Browning was not so sure . . . 'We can hold it for four,' he replied. 'But I think we might be going a bridge too far.'

But the battle of Arnhem lasted for nine terrible days – to end in tragic retreat. What went wrong? In this exciting story Major-General Urquhart, the genial giant who led the 1st Airborne Division, gives the answers – and tells a tale of unparalleled heroism.

'A thundering good book' SUNDAY TIMES

The Bruneval Raid 75p
George Millar

27 February 1942 . . . A daring do-or-die raid to seize the secrets of a German radar station involves the first successful use of British paratroops and sends a shockwave of alarm through Hitler's headquarters.

It was an aggressive reminder of the unseen war which top defence scientists of both nations had been waging since the 1930s.

The mission was to help Britain achieve that radar supremacy on which air supremacy and so ultimate victory depended.

'Fascinating . . . gives a dramatic account of the contribution of French Resistance leaders and of the sea- and air-borne participants' SUNDAY TELEGRAPH

'Vivid, well-documented . . . much interesting material on the development of radar in Britain and elsewhere . . . a taut, exciting narrative' NEW YORK TIMES

'Excellent blow-by-blow account . . . he lifts the lid so effectively on such an interesting story' OBSERVER

73 North 60p
Dudley Pope

The Russian Run . . . fearful cold, freezing spray, mountainous seas, dense fog, increasing submarine and air attacks, a fifty-fifty chance of death . . .

Fourteen merchantmen of convoy JW 51B sailed through this desolate hell escorted by Captain St Vincent Sherbrooke with four small destroyers.

A German pocket-battleship, a heavy cruiser and six destroyers were ordered to intercept and attack.

On New Year's Eve, 1942, the urgent ringing of Action Stations aboard HMS *Onslow* began the Battle of the Barents Sea — one of the most heroic and far-reaching naval actions in either of two world wars.

Alamein 40p
C. E. Lucas Phillips

There was a tingling silence over all the desert as the moon and stars looked down on an army waiting to spring forward along a thirty-eight-mile front. At forty seconds before zero, when the first shells were due to burst on their targets, came the order: 'Fire!' The battle of Alamein had begun . . .

Magnificently illustrated with action photographs and extremely clear maps and diagrams, fully documented from personal and official sources, here is a definitive history of the battle which will appeal to the student of war and to all who admire heroic deeds.

'Quite the best detailed story of that battle I have ever read . . . a superb book'
FIELD MARSHAL MONTGOMERY

Selected bestsellers

- [ ] **Jaws** Peter Benchley 70p
- [ ] **Let Sleeping Vets Lie** James Herriot 60p
- [ ] **If Only They Could Talk** James Herriot 60p
- [ ] **It Shouldn't Happen to a Vet** James Herriot 60p
- [ ] **Vet In Harness** James Herriot 60p
- [ ] **Tinker Tailor Soldier Spy** John le Carré 60p
- [ ] **Alive: The Story of the Andes Survivors** (illus) Piers Paul Read 75p
- [ ] **Gone with the Wind** Margaret Mitchell £1.50
- [ ] **Mandingo** Kyle Onstott 75p
- [ ] **Shout at the Devil** Wilbur Smith 70p
- [ ] **Cashelmara** Susan Howatch £1.25
- [ ] **Hotel** Arthur Hailey 80p
- [ ] **The Tower** Richard Martin Stern 70p (filmed as *The Towering Inferno*)
- [ ] **Bonecrack** Dick Francis 60p
- [ ] **Jonathan Livingston Seagull** Richard Bach 80p
- [ ] **The Fifth Estate** Robin Moore 75p
- [ ] **Royal Flash** George MacDonald Fraser 60p
- [ ] **The Nonesuch** Georgette Heyer 60p
- [ ] **Murder Most Royal** Jean Plaidy 80p
- [ ] **The Grapes of Wrath** John Steinbeck 95p

All these books are available at your bookshop or newsagent:
or can be obtained direct from the publisher
Just tick the titles you want and fill in the form below
Prices quoted are applicable in UK

Pan Books, Cavaye Place, London SW10 9PG
Send purchase price plus 15p for the first book and 5p for each
additional book, to allow for postage and packing

Name (block letters) _____

Address _____

_____

While every effort is made to keep prices low, it is sometimes
necessary to increase prices at short notice. Pan Books reserve the
right to show on covers new retail prices which may differ from
those advertised in the text or elsewhere